# Aiming for the Pinnacle

## Living and Coaching for Meaningful Results

Séamus Scanlan

# Aiming for the Pinnacle

## Living and Coaching for Meaningful Results

Séamus Scanlan

**LOGOSE® Publishing**
Seattle USA.  Dublin Ireland.
e-mail: info@logose.com


© Copyright 2007 Séamus Scanlan.

All rights reserved. No part of this publication may be reproduced or distributed in any form or by any means or stored in a database or retrieval system, without the written prior permission of the publisher.


ISBN: 978-0-6151-6103-7
1st Edition USA - Paperback
August 2007

To Niamh...

A person may be able to articulate the concepts in this book.

This does not necessarily mean that they know how, when and where to apply them in the way that was intended in its writing.

When we know *how*...
we may do a job.

When we know *why*....
we may know what job to do...and when.

## Contents

| | | |
|---|---|---:|
| Overture | | 1 |
| Chapter 1 | Coaching or Living. *Chicken or Egg?* | 5 |
| Chapter 2 | Personal Growth. *The Heart of the Matter.* | 13 |
| Chapter 3 | Effectiveness. *Metrics & Measurements.* | 32 |
| Chapter 4 | Coaching Revisited. *Generic or Otherwise.* | 69 |
| Chapter 5 | Dialogue. *Seen and Unseen.* | 118 |
| Chapter 6 | Self-Worth. *Crucial Milestone.* | 172 |
| Chapter 7 | Emotional Ownership. *The World is Round.* | 193 |
| Chapter 8 | Ethics. *Growth on a Plate.* | 230 |
| Chapter 9 | Organizations & Leadership. *Managers, Visionaries & Prophets.* | 252 |

# Overture.

Human knowledge could be defined as all of that which is consciously known - by humans. In doing so, one could surmise that there has never been a time before today, in the history of humankind, where so much was known by so many. If wisdom, on the other hand, is defined as knowledge of a type that is important, I am not so sure we are at such a peak – in the history of wisdom, in the hands of humanity.

Every human being goes through stages of development – at least will those who live long enough to do so. In very simple terms, these could be summarized in birth, childhood, adulthood and death. There are, of course, many other ways of noting developmental stages, these being suggested by disciplines such as psychology, philosophy, and spiritology.

Whatever simple or complex model you use to describe the process, I suggest that human development has elements that are unpredictable and elements that are, at least somewhat and sometimes very, predictable. For example, it is reasonable and realistic to expect that an adolescent will change in certain ways during puberty. It is reasonable to predict that, on the law of averages, a child who grows up under an 'authoritarian' parenting style will develop in different ways to one who grows up under an 'authoritative' parenting style. It is reasonable to predict that a person subjected to bullying will be weaker during the bullying and a person surrounded by integrity over an extended period of time will likely find it easier to trust.

This book aims to help a reader better predict the requirements of genuine personal growth – that they would better understand the conditions necessary for optimal expression of the highest elements of our humanity – the pinnacle of our humanity. Furthermore, I suggest that the reader, if they get this far, will also realize that that understanding had been within them all along. It just needed to be accessed.

The term 'coaching' has attracted steadily increasing attention and use particularly since the 1980s. Every year, more and more books on the subject of coaching appear on the shelves of book shops. They stand proud alongside the bustling ranks of popular psychology books or they act as moderating carbon rods in the nuclear reactor of the business excellence and management section. But while there are common themes amongst many coaching and personal development books, there are also differences. Sometimes these differences are overt and sometimes they are revealed in the nuances. The challenge for the seeker is one of discernment...and even time!

As if this were not complex enough, when we factor in the possible variations of developmental stages of readers, at the time of reading, and the unique perceptions of even just those sharing one stage of development, we discover a complex system of expression and interpretation amongst millions of participants. In effect, we see the outer surface of a gradual cultural revolution where belief systems are massaged and temporarily, or sustainably, replaced. In turn, those new belief systems are exposed to further marination as the self-development marketplace evolves to its next stage and we tag along for the ride, or try to keep up.

Once we work out what life is all about of course we simply pass it on to the next generation. Could it be as easy as that? Alas, it seems not. If it were so, each nugget of wisdom mined in the early chapters of man would have been welded into place for all who follow. We would now be living in a gem-studded palace of insight with a valance of virtue around the veranda. We would be confidently aware of how to consistently activate the fountains of fulfillment and steer clear of the insults of iniquity.

No, it seems that, to a large degree, each new generation needs to take a spade and uncover, or recover, nuggets for themselves – including those pertaining to leaving a legacy.

It does seem however, that each one of us, for better or for worse, has a different level of interest in this mining process and varying faculties with which to craft the resultant product into something of value. We cut the diamonds of discernment from the coal of consciousness. We mold the gold bars of grace with the ore of enlightenment – all in our own way.

As I navigate the next stage of my life, I reflect that I have spent my time, so far, in two broad modes. One mode is where I was staying more or less the same. The other mode was when I was changing. In earlier years the changing was as a last resort when it no longer worked to cling on for dear life to who I was – or thought I was. More recently, I find myself honoring who I am as if it is simply rented accommodation. I make myself comfortable but don't get too attached and keep open to new possibilities.

Such is the path of personal growth – at least for me – and, I believe, for all of us. I hope this book will invite you to open new doors to your consciousness and to new understandings of your potential as a human being. I hope you will consider renting 'new rooms.' I hope you will move that little bit closer to offering the world the gift of who you really are – aiming for the pinnacle of your humanity.


Séamus Scanlan
Kildare, Ireland.
2007

# Chapter 1
# Coaching or Living.
*Chicken or Egg?*

Coaching, in the context of this book, is a word describing a way of being with people that invites them to make better use of what is available to them.

My years spent delivering professional coach training have taught me to expect certain predictables. Perhaps the most reliable is when new recruits seek the urgent imbuement of 'skills'. Hot on the heals of such expectations, I know to anticipate requests for a coaching 'toolbox' – or at least the beginnings of one. However, from the word go, the trainers make it clear to all that the nature of training in the LOGOSE® model of coaching is to elicit accelerated personal growth amongst all involved (including the trainers). The principle at work is that skills and tools, without understanding and insight, are of very limited value. The same principle applies in the material presented in this book. What growth means in this context will be covered in the next chapter.

If you only want to collect checklists and tools as a portfolio to be wheeled out with each 'client' you would like to coach (I use client in the broadest possible way – we could be talking about your 8 year-old-child or my 80-year-old neighbor) – if this is your priority – you may find this book doesn't fully meet your desires.

On the other hand, is your desire to plunge yourself into potentially new depths of understanding of the human psyche and their implications for how we can better live our lives? Would you like to be able to respond in the most growthful way in the broadest range of scenarios? If so, this book may be one worth adding to that bundle of nominated self-help books lying on your bedside cabinet and, if you are like me, which scream mutely at you every time you go to bed overtired and clutching a handful of the tattered pages of intention.

So, simply stated, when considering effective coaching, it is not a selected bundle of 'interventions' that matter. It is the sum total of what you do, inside of yourself and outside of yourself and the timing of all these responses which make the difference. If this is true, then developing yourself as a coach will be more about raising your awareness of certain events than any other variable. High value coaching is about helping clients to raise their awareness of themselves and their surroundings so that they can make more constructive decisions more frequently. As the book progresses, I will be exploring a range of issues with relevance to coaching. Suffice it to say, at this point, that measuring the clients current happiness is not, in my opinion, enough alone to identify the effectiveness or otherwise of coaching. Awareness of the systems nature of a coaching relationship will allow the coach to respond in a more precise way – just as clients' understanding of the systems operating in their lives will allow them to respond in a more precise and effective way to challenges in their lives.

So – how do we raise our awareness? We could read a lot of books – like this one perhaps. We could commit ourselves to daily meditation with a view to moving to higher levels of enlightenment. We could attend ongoing workshops, seminars and courses designed to help us realize our full potential. We could join groups, associations, movements to help us along the way. We could go into therapy. We could employ a coach! All this could be noted in our record of CPD – 'continuous professional or personal development.' Having done all of the above over many years, I have come to the conclusion that these activities can re-enforce or replace our blind spots as well as raise our awareness. In fact, they may do both at the same time. The lost soul who gets swept up in the wave of 'positivity', with a group of thousands at a workshop, can walk away with new insights manhandled by old mental constructs. Or, they can shed a piece of destructive thinking in favor of something more hygienic. Or, more simply, they can just have been persuaded to see things another way – but, whilst this new way feels like an insight, it is simply another chunk of indoctrination dressed in promised enlightenment and with a blank space for credit card details.

In effect, I am saying something that probably most coaches, at least experienced coaches, will have heard before. In coaching, it is not what you do that matters but *who you are*. Who you are will determine the cumulative effect of your overt, and not so overt, actions.

One way of organizing this concept is to put it in the form of a playful mathematical formula. I call this the 'PEAK' formula.

## The 'PEAK' Formula:

$$E = A \times P \times K$$

Where:
P = the Power of the coach.
E = the Effect of Coaching.
A = the Awareness of the coach.
K = the coach's Knowledge (relevant to personal growth).

If you are like me you may be tempted to add in other variables but please bear with the simplicity of the formula. What this is saying is that 'A', the awareness of the coach in combination with 'P', the power the coach has in the situation and 'K' the knowledge the coach has (relevant to personal growth) will determine the potential effect of the coaching. 'E' can be positive or negative. In other words, the effect of the coaching can be either growthful or destructive (or presumably neutral – although some would say that there is no such thing as a neutral inter-personal transaction). Let's look at some examples. Please remember that this is conceptual – as soon as we start to dismiss the concept because we have not yet agreed on how to measure the variables, we run the risk of missing the point.

John found Mary, a coach, and decided to avail of her services. He had been told by a friend of his that he, the friend, had availed of coaching (not with Mary) and had found it to be very valuable. John had looked at Mary's website, which she had had designed by an experienced website design firm, and he decided to give it a go. Mary has twenty years experience of HR management in a large corporation. Over those years she was valued within the organization for her articulate and assertive communication style and her loyalty to the company's goals. John was aware of Mary's HR background. Last year, Mary had received a large redundancy package from her long-time employer and used it to train in coaching and set up a city-centre practice.

Let's look at some of the possible elements of power in this scenario.

1. Mary is an articulate and assertive communicator. John likes that in a person.

2. Mary has a history in HR. John has a managerial background and assumes, rightly or wrongly, that Mary's background augers well for her competency as a coach.

3. John has heard good reports about the value of coaching and assumes that Mary will be able to deliver such value to him.

4. John has enough experience of business to know that fancy websites are easy to publish if you have deep enough pockets. However, without realizing it, his perception of the website is adding to his positive perception of Mary's credibility.

5. Mary is in her mid-forties, has a nice figure and a pretty face. John is influenced by this although he would deny this if it was suggested to him.

6. Mary's practice has all the usual tangibles of professionalism – rooms in the 'right' location, expensive furniture, nice brass plate outside lined up with those of the medical consultant and accountant also renting rooms in the same building.

Just including the above list, Mary has, potentially, an amount of power to start with. All these elements give her the opportunity to begin a relationship with John with a fair degree of credibility – which, you will notice, I am including as a type of power.

Let's say that we give Mary, in relationship with John, a power value of 8 out of a total of 10. Lets also give her an arbitrary K value of 1.

With these values, the PEAK formula would look like this:

### Mary with John 'PEAK' Formula (first meeting):

$$E = A \times 8 \times 1$$

So if we knew what 'A' was we could contemplate 'E' – the effect of the coaching.

Let's just say that Mary has a positive 'A' value and give her 5. This then gives the following formula:

**Mary-John 'PEAK' Formula:**

**E = 5 x 8 x 1**

**therefore...**

**E = 40**

So what this is saying is that, at the starting line, Mary has the potential to deliver '40 units' of growth when coaching John! No doubt the veil of cynicism is slowly lowering itself across your field of view at this point. How could you possibly determine what 40 units of growth would be? Experienced coaches who are with me so far might be able to snatch themselves from such distractions. No-one is asking you to understand what 40 units of growth is. Remember, you are only being asked to understand the concept - even if you do not accept it.

Let's take it to the next stage. What if we gave Mary a negative awareness value? What if we gave her an awareness value of -3 ? Then the formula would look like this:

**Mary-John 'PEAK' Formula:**

**E = -3 x 8 x 1**

**therefore...**

**E = -24**

This means that the coaching that Mary will do with John, unless one of the variables changes, will be 'negative'. You may want to resist the idea that coaching could have an ungrowthful effect or have the effect of re-enforcing ungrowthful thinking. But can we have the benefits of claiming that coaching produces positive results and simply reject the notion of coaching ever having the opposite effect? I believe that if we did, we would be doing so at our peril and the peril of others.

So how could Mary have a negative awareness value? Well in her years of loyalty to the company she had worked for, she had simply repeated a blind loyalty she had had to her parents and to her teachers. Over twenty years she never once resisted the dictates of the company and, to this day, has not yet outgrown her loyalty – even though she is out of employment of the company. As John begins revealing himself to Mary their 'psychological contract' kicks in. Without realizing it, she is unconsciously (to her) communicating a message along the following lines: 'I know we have both been reaping the rewards of unquestioning loyalty to some commercial entity in order to achieve past goals and that it would be growthful to face any irresponsibility within this loyalty and move on from it - but I am not ready.' It is important to realize that this 'psychological contract' can be the case even if both parties have PhDs in psychology and can dialogue lyrically about the awfulness of some people's loyalty to a 'system'. More on psychological contracts later.

Incidentally, if Mary is operating on a negative coaching value, increasing her knowledge of personal growth will help her also raise her awareness. If it doesn't, more knowledge will just amplify the negative effect of her coaching. You can look at knowledge in different ways here of course. Someone with a PhD in psychology but who is unaware of the destructive effect of their relationship 'games' could be looked at as needing some more awareness not knowledge!

If you accept the concept of 'negative coaching' or 'negative growth' you will most likely see that coach training needs to embrace work around the awareness of the trainee into the equation. In doing so, we encounter what I call 'the watermark'. This is the point below which a coach tends to be out of awareness of issues that invite 'negative coaching' without understanding and willingly applying the protocols needed to protect the coaching from any such negative effects. Once coaching is above the watermark, the potency and opportunity will vary depending on the maturity of the coach, the match with the client and the degree to which either one, or both, are having a 'bad hair day'.

The good news is that by chipping away at their own subjective perceptions and out-growing them, a coach can free themselves to be able to give ever increasing value in their coaching – to work above the watermark and move towards their pinnacle.

Of course, this approach to coaching is based on the presumption of the existence of 'growth' - whatever that is. I will be looking at the concept of growth later but, in the meantime, I would like to name something which you may have already spotted. If I claim that there is a direct relationship between the level of awareness of a coach and the positive results of coaching (growth of client), am I not implying that raised awareness brings with it raised benevolence, or some other positive quality or 'goodness' in a coach (or any human being)? The answer is yes. I suggest that 'awareness', as I use it in this book, implies, by definition, an ability to see underlying universal principles at work. Perhaps most importantly, it will be about the coach seeing the degree to which they themselves are in alignment, or out of alignment, with these principles. I am not at this point, going to claim that *I* know what these principles are – just to posit that they exist and, in concert, they express a natural order that invites us to live optimally. In other words, to use a common selling term in coaching, for people to reach their '*full potential*', I am suggesting that they need to be in alignment with this natural order.

A final hypothesis, by way of a health warning: Coaching in alignment with the universal principles of growth cannot be sustainably delivered without also *living* in alignment with the universal principles of growth. As to which comes first the chicken or the egg? I have my theories but I really don't think it matters – I think it is worth it just to jump on for the ride wherever you can and let both do their magic in parallel!

**Chapter bullets:**

- The LOGOSE® approach to coaching stresses the importance of a coach's awareness of themselves, and their environment, and their growth.

- There is a relationship between the effect of coaching and both the awareness of the coach and the power of the coach in relation to a particular client.

- Positive coaching does not necessarily mean immediate happiness for the client. Growth frequently occurs at the edge of one's comfort zone.

- Two people appearing to dialogue knowledgably about an aspect of awareness does not mean that they are aware of the true implications of that aspect for them.

- Activities such as workshops, seminars, courses etc. can re-enforce or replace our blind spots as well as raise our awareness.

- Raised awareness, in this context, implies a benevolent natural order within which we are invited to reach our full potential.

- Coaching in alignment with the universal principles of growth cannot be sustainably delivered without the coach also *living* in alignment with those principles.

# Chapter 2
# Personal Growth.
*The Heart of the Matter.*

Why would someone employ the services of a coach? Is a coach not just another human being? Can I not just go to the local bar and have a chat with the barman (another human being) as he rinses and dries his glasses. Should I not be able to walk away with new insights and a spring in my step having laid my life out on a collection of beer mats? The theory is that an effective coach is specializing in something. Naming that something can be an interesting challenge.

On occasion, when I am asked what I do for a living, I answer with one word – 'sales'. I sometimes throw in a free smile depending on the situation. 'Oh. What do you sell?' is the usual follow-on question, to which I reply 'Clarity'. At this point, I can usual tell to what degree the conversation will be fun – or even if it will last for another minute!

Many years ago, when I was studying business in college, one of my lecturers asked what was then, to me, a novel question: "What are the three most important features of retailing?" I was not that interested in retailing, other than as a conspicuous consumer, (and, to be honest, had limited interest in the course I was attending), but I always remember his answer and have encountered it many times since. His answer was 'Number three is *location*. Number two is *location* and at the top of the list of the most important things to consider in retailing is – yes, *location*! When I am now asked what are the three most important features of coaching I suggest *clarity, clarity, clarity*.

I believe that there is now strong evidence to suggest that, in the last few years, large numbers of people have reported getting some value from employing services described under the general heading of professional coaching. If this is true, what explanations could be at play?

1. Clients are getting added clarity, relinquishing redundant self-limiting beliefs, and as a result, are more intrinsically motivated to live life in fuller, more meaningful, socially intelligent and healthy ways. They have come to realize that they had been

climbing the rungs of a ladder only to find that it was leaning against the wrong wall and now, as a result of their new found clarity, they are starting up a new ladder and they are confident that this new ladder is against the right wall for them. Or...

2. Clients have replaced their existing stale and over-familiar mindsets with new (to them) ways of seeing themselves and their surroundings. At time of reporting, during or shortly after coaching, they report positive results from coaching but, one or two years down the road, they discover that much of this was simply a mixture of novelty and wishful thinking and they are no happier than they ever were. Or...

3. Clients have been subtley re-conditioned by a slowly seeping cult delivered under the banner of 'coaching.' They have bought into convincing new perspectives and are happier. However, they are leaving a trail of destruction around them in terms of dysfunctional inter-dependencies the nature of which has not yet been confronted and the victims of which have not yet gotten to understand or escape. They are clients that have become part of an insidious emotional pyramid selling scheme and will posthumously provide material for research psychologists and sociologists a century from now. Meanwhile, they sing the praises of their coaches and tell their stressed-out family and soon-to-be estranged friends where they are all going wrong!

I would suggest that, under the name of 'coaching', it is very possible that each of the above has been occurring, in tandem, in various locations. It may even be possible that individual coaches can deliver a little of each depending on their own unique profile of insights and blind spots. In general, I have found that coaches are happy to operate on the basis that clients have blind-spots. However, I have found that coaches often either do not believe that they themselves have blind-spots or they give lip-service to the notion that they might.

If you want to be a 'good' coach – which one of the above three outcomes will you want to aim for and which ones will you want to avoid delivering? In other words, what is 'good' for you? In my experience with coaches and aspiring coaches, number one above is the one aimed for – without question. If you want to develop your coaching along the lines of number two, I think you will be selling yourself short in large measure. If your goal is to be the type of coach implied in number three, it will be of great relief to me if you find this book profoundly disappointing. The LOGOSE® model of coaching is about growth and number three is the antithesis of growth.

> *A 'blind-spot' is an area of awareness that a person seems not to have, that if they did, would allow them to live more in alignment with the natural order of personal growth.*
> *When we see a blind-spot in another,*
> *we may be seeing it through a blind-spot of our own.*

Before you go any further, I would like you to consider what 'growth', in the context of coaching, means to you. Try putting together a personal definition of growth (without looking it up in a dictionary or on the web). Jot it down in this box – I suggest one sentence with twenty words or less:

---

Definition of personal growth is....




---

One way of looking at growth is to look at it in terms of responsibility. What am I responsible for and what am I not responsible for? Perhaps growth is about moving a step forward into more responsibility. I wonder is there any reference to this in your definition? I would suggest that by acting irresponsibly, we are working out of harmony with the natural order I mentioned earlier, and that by acting responsibly, we are working *in alignment* with that order. If this is true, then, if I only knew what responsible and irresponsible was, I would be on my way to new and wonderful horizons – I would be becoming 'all that I could be!'

Have you ever tried to get a group of people to all agree on what constitutes 'responsible'? I have – and, generally, I have found that *full* agreement is quite elusive – especially when you start bringing in examples. Intelligent people can get quite 'emotional' as the discussion progresses (which I believe is more a good sign than a bad one). However, the group also tends to find that rationality takes on a type of aquatic form – slippery, hard to hold and with a tendency to plunge through an opening into obscurity just when you thought you had it positioned under the bludgeon! 'An ethics professor, an ethics professor, my kingdom for an ethics professor!' becomes the cry for help. Even then, someone in the group will know of an ethics professor who ran away with the dean's boyfriend, is rumored to have had 'discussions' with the inland revenue people, has a gruff manner, or just plain *looks* unfriendly! The unsaid implication is that the ethics professor is in some way irresponsible.

**A Common Theme in Worldly Matters.**

I regularly monitor current affairs discussions in the media. Many of them I actually enjoy and I think I even learn something from some of them. Others I listen to for the greater good. I persevere even at the expense of more important priorities such as attending meetings at the local chapter of the 'Politically Correct Straight-jacketed Debating Society.' Perhaps this is just a projection on my part, but the vast majority of current affairs debates sound to me like people trying to persuade the audience that they have a better understanding of responsibility than the other side. To be honest, I would probably be the same if I was involved in the debate. Whether it is witnessing a debate between United States Republicans vs. Democrats, or Irish Republicans vs. Ulster Unionists, the same theme flows freely through the bulging veins of the debate. If ever, by the way, there comes a day when United States Republicans and Irish Republicans enter into a heated debate, it will be time for me to kick off my shoes, turn my cell-phone to silent, turn down the lights and grab a large bag of popcorn. Labels can be such promiscuous bed-fellows. Like Guinness – they often don't travel well – even when we think they have a good head on them!

I actually believe that there is a common theme running through a large proportion of conversations. Understanding this common theme is crucial to understanding personal growth. Unless a coach has a robust understanding of personal growth, their coaching is more likely to inhibit growth than to facilitate it. Coaches generally use the terms 'good' and 'bad' coaching - even when they cannot clearly articulate what the two terms constitute. Without a robust understanding of personal growth, I believe that a coach can deliver 'bad' coaching and runs the risk of exploiting the vulnerabilities of the client. Remember the PEAK Formula.

> *Without a robust understanding of personal growth, a coach can unknowingly deliver 'bad' coaching and runs the risk of exploiting the vulnerabilities of the client.*

To elucidate that common theme I am referring to, I would like to present what I call 'The Prime Hypothesis of Responsibility - PHOR'.

Star Trek Fans may be reminded of 'The Prime Directive' – which I shall paraphrase as 'thou shalt not interfere with an alien civilization that is not ready for you.' Was Star Trek's creator, Gene Roddenberry, a personal growth coach I wonder?

**The Prime Hypothesis of Responsibility.**
**– The 'PHOR' Hypothesis.**

- Part 1. All human beings have an infinite capacity to deceive themselves, including to deceive themselves about how they are deceiving themselves.

- Part 2. People deceive themselves in order to avoid taking responsibility.

- Part 3. People avoid taking responsibility by, amongst other means, operating from a subjective interpretation of what responsibility means and colluding with others who share that subjective interpretation.

Some readers may nod cautiously as they consider the above propositions.

Others will suspend judgment pending further 'evidence'.

Still others will agree enthusiastically and begin writing a mental list of all the people who will be lined up against the wall when their bespoke 'PHOR revolution' takes hold of the world. Alas, that longed-for day of judgment now seems more certain than ever – when '*they* will realize that *I* was right all along – and will see just how much I have been wronged.' The theme strikes again!

A fourth group will surmise that I need professional help. They might be right – but they may not yet see PHOR at work.

If the Prime Hypothesis is true, then there could be people reading this page who will distort the statement, and/or its surrounding arguments, and their reason for this will be they are not able to take full responsibility for what the material implies for them.

But we are back to the problem of identifying what 'responsible' is! I am deliberately avoiding, at this stage, pinning my colors to the mast on the subject of responsibility – at least until later. I would, however, like to look at examples of the type that will be relatively unlikely to provoke too much emotional/cognitive dissonance amongst readers. I believe that these examples can lay some groundwork. No real names are used in any examples presented and most examples are composites of several real stories.

Consider the case of Ger and Carol.

**Case study - Ger and Carol**

Ger is 33. He is ambitious and has recently gotten one of several closely spaced promotions in his sales-management job. Over the last year, Ger

## Aiming for the Pinnacle

has been working progressively longer hours and, as a result, is spending less time with his family. Increasingly, he is only socializing with people who he sees as having potential to help him in his business development aims. Some of his friends see this – some don't. Ger has read a number of 'self-help' books. He sets goals, has what he calls 'a personal vision' and stays focused. He has little patience for those who do not do similarly.

Ger decided to employ a coach last year and is reaping the rewards already. His income has almost doubled in the last twelve months. In seeking a coach, Ger interviewed six candidates. He chose John because John seemed to 'speak his language'. John is focused and emphasizes results. In fact, when Ger begins to waver, and is vulnerable to being effected by distractions, John intervenes 'skillfully' and Ger re-doubles his efforts to go the extra mile. John wears classy suits and drives an expensive car. Everything about him says 'success' - to Ger. John's coaching is expensive but Ger knows you have to pay if you want the best – he sees it as a wise investment.

Ger considers most people around him to be irresponsible and, increasingly, he finds himself irritated by anything unfocused or immeasurable.

Carol, Ger's wife is a stay-at-home-mom and looks after their three young children. She feels somewhat lonely and isolated but puts it down to her personality – *'I was always like that'* she says to herself. She has three good friends who she meets several times a week in one of several shopping mall coffee-shops. Carol loves clothes and has an enviable and ever-broadening wardrobe. She is attractive and comes across as confident. She spends a lot on her appearance and takes pride in her modern independent womanhood. She sees herself as 'worth it'.

Ger recently noticed that he had developed a series of inconvenient physical symptoms included occasionally disturbed sleep, slight forgetfulness at times and indigestion after most meals. He was grateful that he lived in an era when he can readily obtain remedies in one of a range of convenient drug-stores. With the ongoing help of a number of such remedies, Ger has been able to maintain his customary level of focus in work.

Ger and Carol are a couple whose lifestyle is not-sustainable. On further investigation, some of the practices of Ger's firm are un-ethical. Still further exploration reveals that Carol, whilst being quite outspoken about women's rights, spends a significant amount of her money on products supplied by companies that lobby government to prioritize policies that favor industry growth over minority and women's rights. By Carol's own stated values, these corporations' practices are socially unacceptable.

Until something changes, Ger and Carol's three children are highly likely to grow up to an adulthood characterized by their dependences on unsustainable, unethical or unproductive practices. Depending on the temperament of each child, and other factors, these dependences could include, as examples, unbridled consumer spending, addictive use of drugs, alcohol, sex, pornography, a pathological need to control others, a pathological need to be controlled by others. Inherent in these dependency conditions is the inability to see them for what they are – PHOR will reign until something changes.

For all concerned, growth, if it happens, will be about finding alternatives to these dependences. If Ger's coach has the same dependences, it is unlikely that his coaching will provide any revelation in this arena and the coach will probably collude significantly with Ger. This will make it even harder for Ger to see through the mist as he tries to come to terms, in five year's time, with his own hidden affair or his wife's alcoholism.


Even though Ger is availing of coaching, there is no growth. At least the coaching is not providing accelerated growth. When Ger is older he will look back and see this chapter of his life with more mature eyes. That maturity will come as a result of growth. He will look over his shoulder and see his life for what it was and not for what he wanted to see it as when he was younger. He will wish he had been working with a competent personal growth coach or in some other arena that would have opened his eyes. He will wish he hadn't been so focused or had been focused on other things. He will grieve for what might have been for his family and be painfully grateful for the fact that, albeit later than he would has wished, in hindsight, the rug had been pulled out from under his illusionary world. He will wish every day that he had the means to better communicate to others what he now sees, including to his now adult children. He will go to his grave humbled by his experiences and, whilst there will others who will share his insights, their voices, in the main, will be faint whispers amidst the din of the global shopping mall.

**PAUSE**

Bearing Ger in mind, I would like to present what I have found to be a reliable, tried and tested understanding, and definition, of personal growth. It is *a process by which we replace an unsustainable, unproductive or unethical dependence with a more sustainable, productive or ethical dependence.*

> *'Personal growth is a process by which we replace an unsustainable, unproductive or unethical dependence with a more sustainable, productive or ethical dependence.'*

For the acronym lovers amongst us, personal growth is a...

**P**rocess by which we replace
**A**n unsustainable, unproductive or
**U**nethical dependence with a more
**S**ustainable, productive or
**E**thical dependence

Of course to clarify the concept of PAUSE, it can be useful to take a look at the notion of a dependence.

**Needs and Dependences.**

A study of psychology will usually involve some contact with the area of 'needs.' I have found over the years that, similar to what prevails in the study of personal responsibility, a group analyzing the meaning of 'needs' rarely produces complete unanimity in its deliberations. Needs, such as 'survival', tend to rest on the easy end of the continuum. Whilst 'love' is a popular contender, agreeing on what love is usually leads to some head-scratching and even some aggressive or passive inter-group dismissal or cynicism. There may even be jaw-clenching acceptance to 'agree-to-differ.' Abraham Maslow and his 'Hierarchy of Needs' are frequently rolled out and are noted as part of the staple diet of consumer behaviour and organizational psychology curricula across the world – within the English speaking West at least. I am not sure if business studies in Tehran or Beijing draw from the same pot.

I often suspect that, if he could witness the use to which his writings are applied within the world of marketing and human resources, Maslow might seek a more comfortable position in his grave or, having outgrown some of his more basic needs, he might wish to posthumously re-publish new material around the journey to self-actualization – this time with some health warnings for the public. More on Maslow later.

I like to look at areas such as needs first from as simple an approach as possible and then work up. I suggest that a need is simply something we require in order to achieve a certain desire. If I desire to live a little longer, my need might be water and the outcome life. If I desire to take a stand against an unjust regime, my need might be to speak out and the outcome death. If I desire to feel good about myself, my need might be positive feedback from others or meditation or nice clothes. If I desire to avoid feeling depressed, I might need to avail of one or more of a variety of solutions ranging from spiritual elevation to pharmaceutical sedatives to 'retail therapy' to a fantasy-based personal 'reality'.

Sometimes I believe that people have a 'need' to believe that a 'need' is in fact a need. The preceding sentence might show just how language can mean different things to different people! Another example might help.

**Case Study - Patricia and Her New Boss.**

*Patricia's boss, Andy, recently resigned to go to greener career pastures. His replacement, Maria, has a very different management style. For several years, Andy had been giving Patricia copious amounts of positive feedback on a daily basis. Whilst there was a lot about working in the company that Patricia did not like, the attention and affirmation she received from Andy tended to make the job bearable – 'at least for one more day' she would joke with her colleagues in the bar after work. Maria, whilst very reasonable and quite amiable, comes no-where near*

## Aiming for the Pinnacle

to Andy when it comes to affirming individuals within the office. In fact, had Maria been around to observe the daily interactions between Andy and Patricia, she would have seen it is 'over-the-top' and even unhealthy.

Patricia is now toying with the idea of moving job and has tentatively employed the services of Heather – an experienced professional coach. Heather works very much from intuition and, in her interaction with Patricia, despite her normal tendency to compliment and champion her clients, she is finding that 'every bone in her body' is telling her to resist the temptation to do so with Patricia.

From the first session of coaching, Patricia talked about her 'need' for affirmation. In addition, there appeared a slightly 'slippery' resentment with regard to Maria. A lot of ground was covered very quickly with Heather and a significant point was when Heather asked, crucially at a carefully awaited and chosen moment,

'What would you do, Patricia, if it looked like you would never get that type of affirmation again?'

Heather knew intuitively to leave wide open the space following the question.

Patricia sat still and said nothing – verbally. Her face however spoke volumes. Heather waited – peacefully, with a quiet satisfaction deep within her being. She felt that Patricia was moving from a 'gap' to an 'opening' (more on gaps and openings later). She knew that before her eyes, Patricia was negotiating with the nature of affirmations as needs and, more particularly, the nature of her dependence on them.

As Patricia and Heather sat together at that poignant moment, time seemed to slow down almost to a stop. It was as if everything around Patricia was on a video that was being played at super slow speed. Internally however, she felt like someone had rewound a large chunk of her life and had started playing it back to her, speeded up, with new scenes unlocked.
Heather looked on – noticing her own presence and the effortlessness of her current state – she felt 'in the zone'. When the question first made its approach, Patricia's face looked blank – as if she hadn't heard the question. It was almost as if she was somewhat out of the room or an

absent spectator to an uneventful event. Then the question landed. The lead up, the rapport between herself and Heather, and the precise timing all conspired to give that question landing clearance within Patricia's consciousness – the gap had become an opening and was receiving visitors. At the point of landing & connection, Patricia's face adopted a look of shock quickly accompanied by puzzlement. Her breathing quickened. Her eyes widened. Momentarily, she looked towards the floor to the right, no doubt out of focus, and then stared into Heather's eyes. It was as if the two women were dialoging rapidly with each other without saying a word.

Heather watched as cogs fell into place and a large stone disc rolled to one side, as if an Indiana Jones movie was playing itself out in Patricia's mind. Patricia's understanding of the affirmations she had been getting from Andy suddenly looked so different. The suggestions of resentment towards Maria, her new boss, fell limp and were swept aside by a tangible anger towards Andy. She couldn't explain it, and try as she might, certainly couldn't 'justify' it, but she suddenly wanted to 'wring his neck.' Words wanted to be set free from within her chest but, like birds who found their way down a chimney and into a house, the words seemed to collide within the walls of Patricia's inner world until, red faced and scowling, with pursed lips, Patricia uttered the word 'BASTARD'.

Patricia had assumed that Andy's affirmations answered a need of hers. In fact, she subsequently saw this 'need' as an imagined need – a perceived need. On further reflection, she saw it as a need she required to avoid seeing another need. That other need was about moving a step forward in her growth towards her own maturity. Andy's charisma had colluded effortlessly with Patricia's avoidance of that growth and the decision making that might have happened if the free supply of creative and charming affirmations had not been available. She suddenly felt like she had been manipulated for years, had forgone life opportunities and had been led by the nose into thinking that she was special to the company. All the emergency late night overtime, without notice, now seemed like nothing short of abuse and exploitation. Andy, hitherto Patricia's champion and authority figure, became a demon in her eyes – Andy was the used car-salesman in sheep's clothing. Her undying loyalty to Andy now plummeted to the depths of odium. In fact, it was the very intensity of the loyalty that demanded the intensity of the hatred. Patricia had had a breakthrough.

Patricia was replacing a dependence on Andy's affirmations with something new. Leaving aside what that new dependence might be, had Heather not been in tune with the dynamics of the relationship she could have become the replacement. That may or may not have been a move in the right direction. I have worked with coaches who, when trying to understand why they couldn't 'get anywhere' with a certain client, have realized that they fell 'hook line and sinker' into the role of replacement dependence and never spotted it at the time. They subsequently see it as a lost opportunity for powerful coaching and, like the rest of us, put it down to experience.

So, given her new insights, what are Patricia's new dependence options? Here are some possibles:

1. She can put it down to experience and move on – learning to live comfortably with the reduced supply of affirmations. She shifts her dependence 'towards the center' a little. In other words, she becomes somewhat more dependent on her own self-acceptance than on what she had been unwittingly interpreting as someone else's acceptance of her. This should free her up to look at a broader range of career options, either within her existing company or elsewhere. In doing this, she is likely to have to come to terms with a feeling of starting from scratch – 'how could I have been so blind all these years?' she might ask herself.

2. Another option is that Patricia will 'forget' what she had suddenly seen as an important insight. Within days, she will find herself again resenting Maria and yearning for the good old days of Andy. Like with a stone in a shoe that is left so long the foot no longer feels the discomfort, she finds a new equilibrium and learns to live with it. She learns to grin and bear it. Maria may even grow into the habit of providing daily affirmations. Maria may decide to do 'anything for a quiet life' and get on with the job – but at the expense of Patricia's development. Maria just doesn't have the resources or patience to take it further. Rightly or wrongly, Maria sees Patricia as too far gone and looks over Patricia's shoulder in search of young talent that can be nurtured towards promotion.

3. Patricia could of course change job. That may or may not be easy for her. Perhaps word gets out that she might be interested in moving and some Andy-type out there has just the job for her!

## Making the Distinction.

So getting back to needs, dependences and growth. I like to use the word 'need' when describing what a person says they need. I use the word 'dependence' to describe what they actually seem to need in order to achieve what they are achieving or would like to achieve. A need is easy to establish – just ask! A dependence is a little trickier. A need might be 'I need affirmations'. A dependence might be 'She is dependent on believing that affirmations are a need!'


## And PAUSE....

Let's look at Patricia's situation in terms of PAUSE – *'a process by which we replace an unsustainable, unproductive or unethical dependence with a more sustainable, productive or ethical dependence.'*

Let's say that scenario one above prevails in Patricia's case. She replaced an unproductive, and very possibly, unsustainable dependence – the belief that she needed so much affirmation. She began to dance with the notion that she could provide herself with acceptance and she found it was increasingly easy to do so albeit with the odd set-back. You could take this a stage further and argue that feeding her need for affirmations left her wide open to blindness to other issues – ethical issues for example.

Perhaps Maria has a high degree of ethical intelligence. But if Andy, or an Andy substitute, was less ethically mature than Maria and, as a result, engaged in practices of questionable ethics, what would it take for Patricia to see this and question it?

This is introducing the notion of a relationship between ethics and growth, a concept to which I will return later.


## Relieving vs. Resolving.

One last concept that is useful to consider when looking at Patricia's growth... those feelings she experienced as the cogs of her consciousness turned – the feelings of anger, betrayal, resentment – all grouped together with images of Andy? These are not feelings Patricia would actively seek out to experience. They were by-products of an insight. She didn't particularly like them but the discomfort was superseded by something else – growth. Patricia did not need 'deep' long term psycho-therapy in order to gain this insight. (I am not suggesting that 'deep' long term psycho-therapy would or would not produce something similar). By all means, her experience to date, and whatever growth she had accumulated up to that point, will have gone some way to preparing the ground. For all we know, Patricia was going to gain this insight spontaneously in a few days with or without coaching. However, I do believe that the coaching did provide an environment conducive to bringing it on – or optimizing the chances of a fresh perspective coming into Patricia's radar.

Andy's affirmations provided the opportunity to '*relieve*' certain feelings within Patricia. Effective coaching provided an opportunity to '*resolve*' the feelings – at least to some degree with more to follow later. That distinction between *relieving and resolving* the emotions, that tend to cling to existing constellations of beliefs, is a vital element in effective personal growth coaching.

An effective coach will engage with a client in a way that will maximize the opportunity for surfacing and resolving such feelings in an elegant way. This may include using a degree of relieving without taking their eye off the ball of growth. In my opinion, many conversations, including a great number conducted under the banner of 'coaching', are in fact more about avoiding or relieving such feelings, in the coach and/or the client, at the expense of the growth opportunities for both.

> *In my opinion, many conversations, including a great number conducted under the banner of 'coaching', are in fact more about avoiding or relieving such feelings, in the coach and/or the client, at the expense of the growth opportunities for both.*

In addition, a coaching conversation can do this with a veneer of 'challenge' that makes it all the harder to spot the lost opportunities.

## Growth vs. Development

As I mentioned before, effective coaching is about 'clarity, clarity, clarity.' This suggestion, in turn, is based on a hypothesis that with clarity comes automatic motivation to move, albeit after an initial adjustment period, to a new perspective. An example might be that someone 'realizes' that the reason why they have been so unhappy, and very possibly why they have been struggling with an ulcer, is that the culture of the organization in which they work is exploitative and unethical and therefore in conflict with what is important to them. Once they have adjusted to this insight (and let's imagine that, in this case, their newly established analysis is more or less accurate/grounded) they make decisions to move out and go elsewhere. No carrot and stick external motivators have been applied. No fancy inspirational speeches from the current guru of the month have sparked a new-age Damascus experience. They just got clarity and it was time to move.

An important feature of establishing this type of clarity is the idea of 'conceptual organization.' This in turn involves a use of language in a certain way. Conceptual organization (whether grounded in reality or not) allows us to organize our beliefs in ways which, hopefully, will allow us to store and retrieve them when needed and also in a way that allows us to predict cause and effect relationships or at least *imagine* that we can. This in turn allows us to move into a position of cognitive equilibrium – the matter is 'processed' – 'now I understand – what's next?' Again this conceptual organization, and the resultant cognitive equilibrium, may be grounded on reality or on delusion. 'All men are bastards' or 'All women are bitches' are examples of conceptual organization that might be open to unpacking and testing in terms of groundedness in reality. 'If you jump out any tenth floor window, you are likely to hurt yourself' might be a little more grounded – if you will excuse the pun! Both give the organizer a degree of conceptual equilibrium until a new piece of evidence presents itself in a way that might challenge that equilibrium.

In the interest of conceptual organization, I suggest that it is of value to differentiate between the terms 'personal development' and 'personal growth.' I have presented growth as a process around dependences and how we change them. I suggest that development is the accumulation of knowledge and skills. The knowledge and skills may or may not help us to grow. They may even be used by us to avoid growing. One of the most common themes in coaching is the 'wrong wall' syndrome. This is where a person reflects on their life and concludes that they have been climbing the rungs of the ladder pretty successfully but the closer they got to the top, the more they realized that the ladder was leaning 'against the wrong wall.'

Frequently in such reflections, they see significant efforts to 'develop' themselves whilst at the same time avoiding their own growth. The lost manager who thought that the MBA would be the final cherry on the cake and, once achieved, would make sense of the journey and offer some level of equilibrium and peace, might be an example - 'No more rushing and cramming.' The mother who read every book available on parenting and just cannot understand why *her* children are not model children, might be another. Worse still, because she has read every book available on parenting and the problems encountered 'must therefore be the teenagers' fault', the teenagers absorb the message and hide their real self from their mother and from the world – a recipe for trouble down the line.

In the case of the manager, he was dependent on 'success' in order to keep going. Replacing that dependence with a dependence on genuine self-worth (versus self-esteem – more on that later) would be growthful for him even if it meant he decides to give up getting more letters after his name – to ease up on 'self-development.' The mother may be emotionally dependent on seeing herself as a 'good mother' or even a 'great mother' with all the implications for approval of her parents, peers and progeny. All the child psychology courses in the world won't compensate for this need if they don't help her to see it and outgrow it.

Just as the business world has its Abraham Maslows and William Glassers to selectively interpret in order to further its marketing goals, the world of parenting has its Dr. Spocks and Maria Montessoris to rely on when we want to avoid ourselves!

**Chapter bullets:**

- An effective coach is specializing in something – and knows what that is.

- The effects of coaching can vary depending on, amongst other things, what is defined as 'good' coaching.

- There is a difference between a 'gap' and an 'opening'.

- Clarity, clarity, clarity.

- There is a theme running through many conversations – 'PHOR'.

- It is possible that a reader will interpret the material in this book in a way other than was intended in its writing.

- Ger and Carol are a couple whose lifestyle is not-sustainable.

- If Ger's coach has the same dependences (as Ger), it is unlikely that his coaching will provide any revelation in this arena and the coach will probably collude significantly with Ger.

- Even though Ger is availing of coaching, there is no growth.

- Ger will eventually go to his grave humbled by his experiences.

- PAUSE is a definition of growth.

- There is often disagreement as to what are and are not 'needs'.

- Needs and dependences are not the same.

- Patricia's understanding of affirmations as a 'need' suddenly looked very different.

- Temporarily uncomfortable feelings are often a by-product of growthful insight.

- Uncomfortable feelings can be relieved or resolved.

## Aiming for the Pinnacle

- Continually relieving these feelings usually defers growth.
- Resolving these feelings is usually a sign of growth.
- There is a difference between 'personal growth' and 'personal development.'

# Chapter 3
# **Effectiveness.**
*Metrics and Measurement.*

Coaching is often presented as a service that will help clients improve their performance. It can also be sold as something that can help one get the most out of life. In addition, there is an overt, or unsaid, claim or implication that the coaching will be effective.

In my experience the terms 'performance', 'most' and 'effective' are used by many coaches without robust clarity as to their meaning. Very often there is subjectively selective interpretation of the terms on the part of the coach and client but neither can see it. Have a look at the following case study.

**Case Study – Don & Promotion.**

Don (36) has done a two year stint as HR manager and has decided to 'up his game'. He met with a coach, Sam (38). Don has a vocabulary that, whilst not uncommon within certain corporate settings, is peppered with terms not normally found outside of that environment. Don's first meeting with Sam was quick and focused. He talked about 'upping the ante', about 'key metrics' and everything needing to be 'deadline oriented.' Don considers himself to be 'highly effective' and 'out in front'. The promotion he is looking for is 'his for the taking' but he is not taking any chances – he wants to be prepared and has decided that coaching may help.

Don wanted to look at the area of leadership skills. He felt he was strong in this area but would benefit with some work. He estimated that he had read about five books on leadership over the last two years and his own line manager, a partner in the firm, had suggested that *'leadership'* was what *'singled out the performers from the rest.'* On several occasions, Don mentioned that he considered himself to be 'highly effective.' Sam was relatively new to coaching and found herself wondering if she was able for Don – was she the right coach for him? Her main objective during the first meeting was to figure out if working with Don was right for her – and him.

Let's take a break from the case at this stage and return later after a little look at the area of 'effectiveness.'

**Joe and Bart are Carpenters.**
(And, of course, are fictitious characters created to present a point).

Joe

Bart

They both work for the same company making rocking chairs.
Joe produces 5 chairs per day.
Bart produces 4 chairs per day.
Who is the more effective?
Are you temped to say Joe?
You might suggest that the chairs are of different quality.
Let's say that they are consistently of the same high standard.
Now who is more effective?
Would you suggest that say Joe, for example, might work longer hours?
Let's say they work the very same hours.
Not only does Joe produce more but he is also a tidier dresser – he has a smart appearance.
Can you be brave enough to mark Joe as the performer in the duo?
Sometimes we feel guilty when we pin our medals onto the performers.

Imagine a coach, Susan, was contracted by a representative of the furniture company to coach Bart – let's say it was the line manager of the chairs section of the factory who contracted her – let's call him Tom. The company has decided that it will invest in coaching for its staff as a means to increase profitability. Bart was one of a number of staff in the factory who Tom had decided were in need of coaching. Tom had his eye on his own career and saw this as an opportunity to increase his value to the company. Tom reckoned that Bart was a bit slow and if he could speed him up a bit, say to Joe's speed, it would be a move in the right direction.

Susan spent quite a bit of time trying to get the contract from Acme Wooden Products Inc. This included several face-to-face and telephone conversations with Tom and two other section managers, Richard and Harold, as well as a human resources manager. She, Susan, was determined to 'produce results' – after all, that is what drew her to coaching in the first place – she liked results. Tom detected this and was impressed.

Susan began working with Bart as his coach. I do not propose going into the contracting at this stage. I would instead like to cut to an important aspect of the coaching. Susan (and Tom, Richard and Harold - others in Acme) all made at least two assumptions. The first was that Bart was 'underperforming.' The Second was that 'coaching' would do its magic and the 'problem' would be sorted. At this point, imagine that there was an objective over-viewer that could see everything and that the overviewer threw down another card onto the table. The card was the fact that Bart was actually the more effective and, as a result of in-effectiveness of Tom and other managers in Acme, proper measurement procedures were never implemented that would pin-point the amount of wood that Bart and Joe, and all the other carpenters respectively, were consuming in constructing the number of pieces of furniture they made. The key issue here is that Susan, the coach, responded to Tom et.al. as if *their* perception of the situation was accurate.

Whilst the Bart & Joe example might seem to present an obvious cul-de-sac for a coach wishing to be an independent agent in the matter, I believe that this is a feature of many 'interventions' under the name of coaching – more particularly 'corporate coaching'. Although it seems obvious in the way it is presented above, until that extra card is revealed, the issue is not 'twigged'.

In my experience of working with coaches new to a genuinely personal-growth oriented approach to coaching, this issue is surfaced often after the opportunity to do something with it has passed. Either the relationship has already finished, and the issue has surfaced during retrospective reflection, or the relationship is ongoing but the coach is already so enmeshed in the collective illusion, the *co-llusion*, that they just cannot extricate themselves – what I call 'terminal enmeshment.' In the latter case, the most skillful coach will have difficulty in pulling out to healthy detachment without a fatal compromise to whatever level of rapport has been built up in the relationship.

## DOVE.

The simple way to understand the issue of effectiveness is to see it in terms of *output* versus effectiveness. Output is what is produced. Effectiveness, on the other hand, is what is produced *with reference to what is consumed*. A manager's job is to measure both output and resources consumed. They may or may not do that effectively. *Their* manager may or may not be measuring *their* effectiveness accurately. A major part of a coach's job is to help a client to get clarity about what outputs and resources they want to measure and how. The coach may or may not do that effectively. In a nutshell, a coach needs to be able to differentiate output versus effectiveness or...

**D**ifferentiate
**O**utput
**V**ersus
**E**ffectiveness.

### Coaching Tip...
Anytime a coach finds himself or herself struggling with, or dwelling on, their own, or their client's, 'performance', it is worth remembering 'DOVE.' To further remind ourselves of this issue, it can also be useful to remember that it rhymes with love!

### Case-study revisited – Don and Promotion.

*Let's go back to Don (36) and his targeted promotion – we introduced him at the beginning of this chapter. He had started working with Sam (38) – an external coach selected by Don (as distinct to working with a coach presented to him by his employer). Don was looking at the area of leadership. At the end of the initial meeting, Sam felt that she could work with Don and said so. She also asked Don how he now felt about working with her. Both agreed to take the relationship on a meeting by meeting basis and assume nothing about a longer term relationship.*

*Whilst Sam was relatively new to professional coaching, she had done a lot of challenging personal growth work over many years. Her confidence was not as resilient as it might be in years to come. However, her humility was alive and well and would serve her well in the work. The years of 'peeling off the layers' had also given her relatively reliable access to her intuition. This was something she was increasingly embracing and valuing.*

*The first significant sense Sam noticed in her interaction with Don was that he was very convincing – intellectually. She could see how, in certain circumstances, he could 'sell' an idea to people. However, every bone in her body was telling her to keep her distance from him psychologically. After a brief period in the beginning of feeling 'sucked into his world' (her words), she pulled herself back to her own 'centeredness' and engaged with Don from a position of healthy separateness. This was a new experience for Don. In the past, Don had steered clear of people he could not easily 'lead' into his way of thinking. He was a clear and energetic communicator. Over the first three sessions with Sam, Don had come close to experiencing Sam as another human being in a new way but had broken the moment with a joke or an 'explanation'. At one point he made reference to an occasion when, at the company Christmas party, one of the staff, Josh, had called him a 'blind arrogant bastard' and had accompanied this with a few other pieces of colorful opinion. Don mentioned it in passing to Sam and seemed to quickly dismiss the comments as the 'rantings of a potential has-been.' Josh, in Don's mind, had done his own career no good in 'letting himself down' in this way.*

*Sam asked a question before she had even decided to formulate it and immediately sensed that it was her intuition at work.*
*'Were Josh's comments any use to you Don?' Sam asked – giving herself a brief internal slap on the wrist for asking a closed question and a second slap on the other wrist for being so silly as to be giving herself the first slap on the wrist! (She actually laughed heartily when she shared this later in a supervision session).*

## Aiming for the Pinnacle

*Sam thought she sensed a momentary, potentially pregnant pause before Don replied.*
*'They sure were.' He replied with conviction.*
*'It's very important to know your people's limitations – I'd be wary of Josh's capacity for leakage – could be a bad influence. It's a leader's responsibility to spot these things.'*

*Sam's sense was that there was a gap in Don's certainty that the way he saw things was the way things were. She felt that this had been one of several momentary suggestions of openings for growth within the coaching. Rightly or wrongly, she felt that Don was blind to something in himself or his environment – in fact, a coach can generally take this as a given – otherwise the value of coaching is in question. However, it is one thing to accept something cognitively and another thing to get a sense of being close to a specific, albeit unnamed, gap or opening.*

*She resisted the temptation to decide on what that gap might be but listened further to her intuition to guide her. Don's responses to Sam's engagement seemed to suggest that Don was strong enough to wrestle with some of his beliefs and perceptions. If Sam could provide the right presence and engagement, Don might just get value out of this coaching.*

*A key feature of Sam's approach to her work with Don was that she assumed that Don, like us all, was being selective in his assessment of his effectiveness, the effectiveness of others, and the resources and outputs he evaluated in his calculations. She had little temptation to assume that his assessment of the situation was objective. Any residual temptation she did have, left-over from her own conditioning, she simply looked out for and parked as required. This helped her to respond more objectively and 'centeredly' - to use one of her favorite terms.*

*As the work went on, Don began noticing more frequent instances of discomfort during his work with Sam - Don's discomfort that is. Sam seemed to remain fairly consistently comfortable – all the more challenging for Don. Whilst he found himself trying to box Sam in as having 'questionable relationship skills', he paradoxically found her presence, and her way of relating to him, quite compelling. One minute he was about to fire her, the next minute he could not wait for their next session. Added to this, he found himself hearing his own words as previously spoken at a number of staff pep-talks – 'Don't forget folks –*

*life begins at the edge of your comfort zone!'* He laughed nervously to himself as he realized that he hadn't really factored in his own comfort zone boundaries!

## DOVE continued.

I use the term DOVE as a reminder of the danger of confusing effectiveness with output. A trainee coach I once worked with suggested a great example to the class. He described a man who suffered from schizophrenia and who, despite enormous obstacles, managed to carve out a basic but fairly reliable daily life for himself. He had a strict regime of exercise, diet and interaction with other people and, through this, he managed to minimize the instances where he would need professional help - usually of a medical kind. He climbed no mountains, he created no empires, he wrote no symphonies, he crafted no works of classical art. However, given his circumstances, he was highly effective in his daily life. He was applying himself in everyway he knew to survive and to experience some level of quality of life. In fact, part of his journey towards his version of normality included a commitment to fostering gratitude within himself – something that, in latter years, he saw as a choice and could be the difference, for him, between walking or crawling through his psychological day – his mental health tightrope.

## A Continuum...

I would like to take this aspect of effectiveness a little stage further.

A common scenario in coach training is that a number, (and sometimes all!) of the members of a cohort believe that others within the class are not equipped to engage in professional coaching. Sometimes their assessment of the situation is in line with my own (subjective) assessment. However, I also often perceive that everyone in the class, including the trainers (and that includes me), is ill-equipped to present themselves as a professional coach despite whatever number of years of experience they might have. How could we be so arrogant as to think that our perception of coaching/growth/maturity/reality is more precise than the perceptions we think others have? Over the years, I have had many a conversation with a passionate trainee coach who is keen to point out the limitations of others in their class, more often in their training Peer Consulting Group (PCG), and to express their frustration in their dealings with one or more individuals. They might also point out to me that this training peer group 'just isn't working' and that they need to change to another group. Added to all that, they might express anything from collegial concern to agitated indignation that we would have allowed someone like this person onto a professional coaching course of such distinction!

In responding to these situations I see one passionate human being, say Ian, encountering what they see as the limitations of another human being, say Nancy. The way in which Ian is responding to Nancy, in turn, is expressing Ian's limitations! But he can't see this. Just as Nancy can't see the limitations that Ian thinks he sees in her (correctly or incorrectly), Ian can't see the limitations that I think I see in him.

When Ian encounters Nancy he is also encountering aspects of himself. He can assess her by certain criteria and his assessment may or may not be grounded in reality. However, his emotional responses to what he sees as her limitations are also a feature of the relationship. Nancy may well be blind to some aspect of her own thinking – there may well be a 'gap'. Ian's irritated and disdainful response to Nancy is most likely to keep that gap as a gap and postpone the opportunity to bring it forward to the foyer of coachable openings.

Let's say that Ian has seen a blind spot in Nancy that he knows to be a dysfunctional or unhealthy feature of the way she deals with the challenges of working with other people. It is an 'unproductive, unjust or unsustainable dependence' – remember PAUSE?

Furthermore, let's say that his assessment is spot-on – i.e. as grounded in reality as any such assessment can be. Let's also say that one of the reasons that Ian can see this dynamic so clearly is that, several years ago, he faced a similar dependence in himself and he knows just how subtle and unhealthy it can be. Finally, let's add an assumption – let's say that Ian does not have any other equivalent unhealthy dependence that Nancy does not also have. In this scenario, you could argue that Ian is more effective that Nancy – *in the use of the PCG resources*. It is important to emphasize this last point. Nancy and Ian come into the situation with a different set of resources – their family history, their genetic disposition, the financial support they might have available to them and a whole range of other variables. But, in joining a PCG, they get to use the time and opportunities presented in order to work on tasks and issues related to the coach training course in which they are engaged.

Let's say that Nancy's blind spot is described by Ian as a 'neediness' in Nancy. That, frequently, she will refuse to examine an issue because it might threaten her childish way of putting someone, say one of the course trainers, on a pedestal. Perhaps Ian has huge respect and admiration for the same trainer but his perception of them is realistic whereas Nancy's is not – her's is more based on a need to see the trainer as an authority figure who embodies Nancy's selective version of perfection.

In this sculpted scenario we could say that Ian is further up 'the line' than Nancy. So what might this line look like?

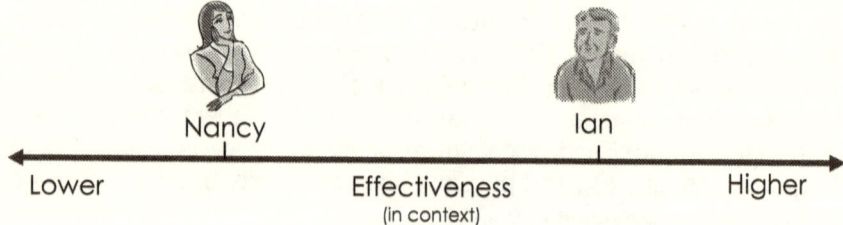

In plotting Nancy and Ian along the line, or continuum, let's say that Nancy's position is characterized by her 'need dominance.' At the time of examination, Nancy has a need to cling to a perception which, with further growth on her part, will later appear to her to have been holding her back in some way. Ian appears further up on the continuum. He has needs but they are not dominant in his dealings with the PCG. Let's say that Ian is independent of any selective perceptions that might get in the way of the normal workings of the group.

Let's say further that, whilst he is not taking anything from the group, Ian is not really adding anything. He shows up and engages but is not prepared to 'go the extra mile' for this group – or, if he does, he is expecting something in return and, to him, it doesn't look like there is much chance of that happening.

## Aiming for the Pinnacle

But Ian and Nancy are not the only ones in the group. There is also Cathy.

Cathy observes Nancy and sees the same dependence that Ian sees in her. She sees that Nancy, in holding on to this mindset, is limiting her own capacity to engage optimally with others. However, Cathy also observes Ian's responses to Nancy and believes that, whilst Ian does not seem to display any relevant limiting dependence, similar to Nancy's, his way of dealing with Nancy is none-the-less limited. He appears to be trying to 'protect' himself from Nancy's neediness and so is holding himself back. Cathy engages with both Ian and Nancy and somehow there is a 'shift'. Both Ian and Nancy begin to see more – they begin to change their mindset. I will later be offering other less fictitious examples of the dynamics of how mindsets, or dependence dominant clusters of beliefs, can soften. However, for the moment, I would just like to continue with the concept of a continuum. Let's plot Cathy alongside Nancy and Ian.

Cathy appears to the right of Ian. The model proposes that Cathy is effective in a different way to the way in which Ian is effective. I am suggesting that Cathy brings something into the equation that Ian does not. She engages with Nancy in a way that does not expect anything in return. She is still mindful of how she might be manipulated by Nancy's limiting dependence, and sometimes it takes energy and patience to deal with Nancy. But Cathy is happy, for the time being anyway, to contribute what she can for the sake of the growth of all.

The key here is that Cathy is in a position to contribute, unconditionally – she is not expecting anything in return, consciously or unconsciously, that the others have not already agreed to or accepted. For example, she is expecting, and the others have overtly accepted, that everyone will be on time for their meetings. However she is not expecting either of the others to support any un-grounded belief. Cathy is open to discovering more truth – not particularly attached to any specific truth.

Notice in the second continuum above that we had to 'zoom out' to fit Cathy in. The implication here is that in looking at effectiveness we tend to establish parameters – a particular horizon if you like. As we expand our understanding of a situation, we often have to expand the parameters also. This is an important feature of the continuum.

**The NICE Line.**

Nancy's engagement within the PCG is characterized by her 'neediness' – it is **Need-dominant**. Ian's engagement is characterized by his **Independence** of such needs. Cathy's engagement is characterized by her unconditional **Contribution**. They are all plotted by reference to their **Effectiveness**. These three ways of engagement and levels of effectiveness I suggest are stages of growth along what I call the '*NICE line*' or the '*NICE continuum*.' I have found that acknowledging such a continuum to be very useful in coaching and personal growth work. In addition, I have seen continuous evidence that it represents a process that is real and, within a patient understanding of it, predictable in a constructive way. Everyone that I have seen embracing the concept finds themselves drawn to exploring what it is to be at the contribution end of the line and what it would take to get there. People's motivation for getting up the line may differ, depending on where they are in the first place but, by the nature of the model, it will, if worked with correctly, challenge anyone to further growth.

**NICE Curves.**

The fictitious example above presented three people along the NICE line. What if we were to look at a larger group? Let's say that Acme Wooden Products Incorporated went through a period of highly successful expansion and they now had one thousand carpenters working for them in factories around the country. Imagine that an enterprising manager, Harold, decided to do an analysis of the effectiveness of all these carpenters. Out of empathy for readers with no training, or indeed

## Aiming for the Pinnacle

previous interest, in statistical presentation, I would like to build a graphical representation of Harold's findings one step at a time.

Let's imagine, for argument's sake, that the results of the analysis suggested there are only a few, say ten, carpenters at the very low end of the NICE line - at level 1.

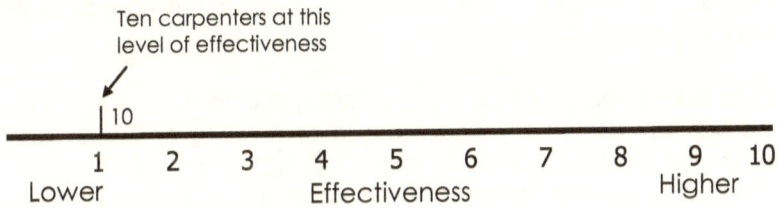

Let's say then that, similar to the low end of the NICE continuum for Acme carpenters, there are also only ten carpenters at the high end – say at a rating of nine out of ten.

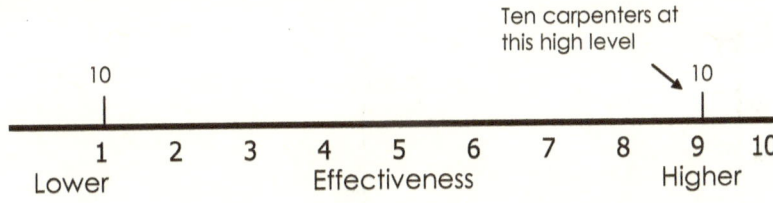

Whilst this is a fictitious example, I am sure many readers will find the notion reasonable that there would be a small number of members of a group at the low end of effectiveness, however measured, and an equally small number appearing on the high end. In almost any area of human activity you will find the same – be it in a football club based on individual members' skill level or a nation and its citizens' parenting ability. In fact, there is even a principle claiming to depict the idea – 'the Pareto principle' - named after the Italian economist Vilfredo Pareto. Also known as the 80/20 rule, in general terms, the Pareto principle suggests that 20% of a group tend to account for around 80% of a certain activity. Examples might be that 20% of a sales team produce about 80% of the team's sales. Another might be that 20% of a population commit 80% of the crimes within that population. A common one is 20% of a business' clients represent 80% of its profit.

Harold, as he collated the findings of his analysis, was not surprised to find shades of the Pareto principle at work. Having studied statistics years earlier in his management degree, he was expecting to see certain patterns emerge. In addition, as he had used average total figures over the last five years in order to determine a suitable scale and methodology, he had a hunch about where most of the work-force would feature in his findings.

Now let's take the graphical representation a little further and say that there are fifty carpenters who come in at a rating of five in Harold's analysis. Let's also add a scale to the left side of the line showing the number of carpenters at any given level of effectiveness. In statistical parlance this is normally labeled the 'population' or 'pop.' for short. In the mathematical world this vertical line would be called the 'Y-axis' and the original horizontal line would be the 'X-axis'.

Harold's findings now take on the following shape:

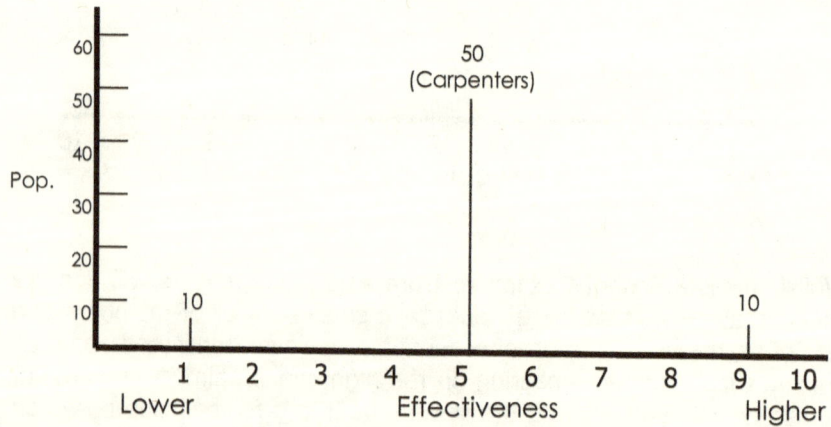

Harold (Harry to his friends and colleagues), continued his number crunching although he did notice, with some familiarity, that this type of work was not his favorite aspect of management. His motivation to continue with the analysis was finite but his interest in the resultant findings spurred him on. He was a 'people-oriented' manager and liked to 'walk-about.' However, over the last two years, the company had

# Aiming for the Pinnacle

tidied up its management information systems - after a number of expensive constructive dismissal cases and an urgent review of both the company's performance measurement systems and its coach recruitment policy. It was now possible to measure both an individual carpenter's output and their consumption of materials. With this facility, Harry was keen to establish patterns of effectiveness across the whole company in the hope of generating some management inspiration for himself. For a moment, he found himself thinking of that nice guy, what was his name?, yes Bart who used to work in Tom's section – *'Great salt-of-the-earth type of guy,'* Harry thought to himself – *'Pity he left Acme – was a good influence on the younger staff!'* Harry wondered briefly if there was a way to measure such an 'influence.' He parked the idea for another day. Back to number crunching. Harry noticed that there were forty-five carpenters coming in at both the 4 rating and the 6 rating and he established the figures for the 2, 3, 7 and 8 ratings. Finally, he carefully drew a curved line all the way from the left to the right taking in the figures for each rating. 'Nice curve' Harry thought to himself. His graphical representation now looked like this:

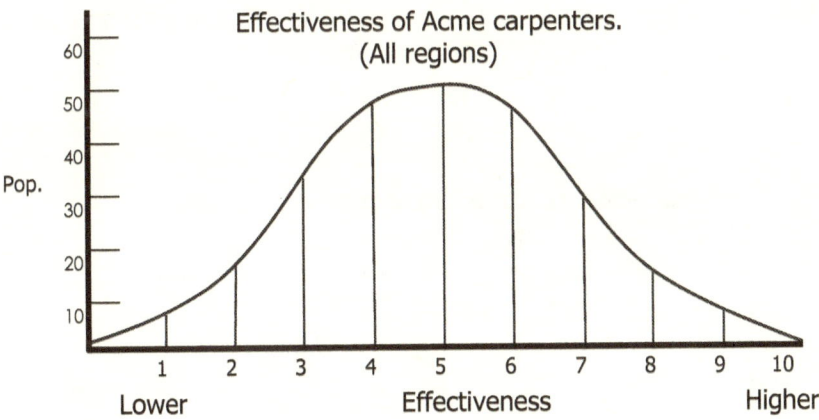

Later he added the figures for the non-integer ratings – the 1.5, 2.5, 3.5 etc. but the curve stayed roughly the same shape – it retained its 'normal curve' profile. Harry knew that he could have done the whole exercise on his computer with a spreadsheet. However, he had been attending a creativity training workshop recently and was keen to do it 'the old fashioned way' as a means of exercising more of his brain than usual. This included using his left hand as much as his right. 'Brain Gym' – he remembered the term used by the workshop facilitator.

Harry realized that it was getting late and it struck him that he was alone in the abandoned office. *'One more piece of the jigsaw and I'll pack it in,'* he thought as he rummaged on his desk for the staff costs report he had gotten from HR earlier in the day. This time he put the figures into his computer and with swift elegance, the software produced the normal curve he had so painstakingly built by hand earlier. Next, he keyed the staff costs figures into the model and constructed the table of data to incorporate all the figures giving a breakdown of profitability on a carpenter by carpenter basis.

With a few key stokes, he had a new graph on his screen – this time displaying levels of profitability across the population of carpenters in Acme. He noticed three distinct groups. The group on the left were non-profit making – his analysis showed that, for this group to operate, under current circumstances and costings, it needed ongoing subsidy from the company's resources. The group on the far right were contributors to the company's profit. The in-between group were more or less independent – they produced enough income to cover their costs but no more. Harry was a little surprised as he examined the new graph:

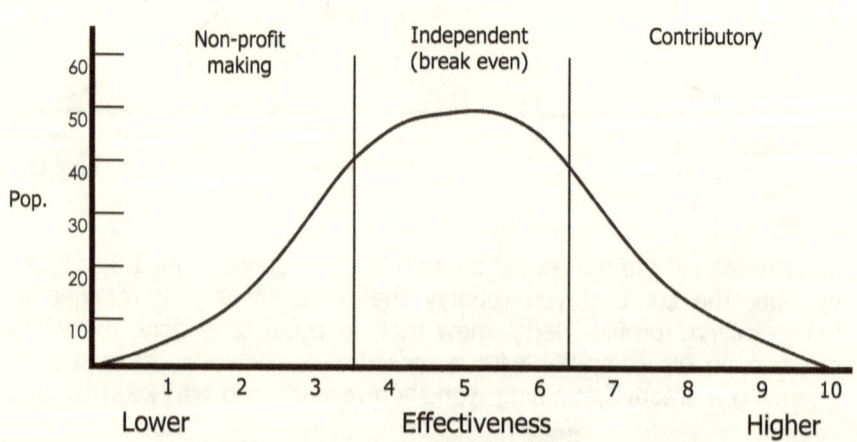

# Aiming for the Pinnacle

Harry remembered that he did not want to leave work too late. He will have missed the worst of the traffic so if he got moving now he would have some time with the kids before they went to bed.

*'Non-profit-making, Independent, Contributory, Effectiveness?'* he thought aloud, as he leaned back on his chair and watched the computer begin its shut-down stages. *'NICE!'* he added with a feeling of satisfaction as he pushed himself up to a stand.

As Harry drove home, he contemplated the figures he had collated. At this early stage, they suggested that the company might well be operating way under its potential. He naturally found himself thinking about how things might be if the 'N' group (non-profit making) and the 'I' group (independent) could be brought up to the same level of effectiveness as the 'C' group (contributory). *'This must be a management issue surely'* Harry thought to himself.

Just then, a black limousine pulled into his lane on the freeway without any indication or warning. Harry braked hard and held his hand on the horn for a few seconds. With no-one to hear him, he felt freer to shout a few expletives at the rear of the smoked-window stretch limo.

*'THINK YOU OWN THE ROAD!'* he shouted, as his heart rate rose somewhat.

Within seconds, the limo had left the highway on the next exit. Harry went back to his thoughts on the NICE curve - this time feeling quite impatient. *'Bloody dead wood!'* he thought, as he contemplated all the non-profitable carpenters jumping out at him from the graph. *'Damn shake up – that's what needed.'* Harry then noticed how his perception of the graph seemed to change with his mood. One minute this was a management challenge – how are the 'C' group being managed? Perhaps with more effective communication and management inspiration, things could be improved with the others. The next minute, after the limousine encounter, he was thinking in different terms. *'Sheila will find that interesting,'* he thought. *'Her being all into feelings and stuff.'* His attention slowly left the graph - and work in general. He was a few minutes from home and he found himself thinking about his wife and kids. A warm glow of appreciation began to nose its way up to his consciousness. Psychologically, Harry had clocked out of work and was looking forward to the evening at home.

**NICE Context.**

Harry had examined one group of people, carpenters in Acme, and he used specific criteria for measurement – staff costs, timber consumed and products manufactured. He knew that his analysis did not cover all variables. These might include measurables like administration and marketing overheads. They might also include variables such as staff morale, informal coaching & training and varying levels of equipment maintenance costs at different levels of output and use. He was to realize that actually measuring performance was not as simple as he initially thought. Harry had access to whatever management information systems (MIS) the company had in place. Indeed, he was also well placed to implement further MISs if he felt it was warranted. The issue was going to be an ongoing challenge. Meantime, he might be well advised to avoid pigeon-holing any of the staff on one of his own whims or those of his colleagues in Acme.

Remember Susan, the imaginary coach at the beginning of the chapter? She assumed that Tom, Bart's line manager, had accurately assessed Bart as under-performing and she let herself believe the same – 'the most natural thing in the world' some might say. Yet, in the light of further information, we discover that Tom, and others in Acme, had not been accurately measuring performance. Bart's skill was making really high quality furniture – a skill which neither Tom or Susan could claim. Tom, however, was claiming to be an effective manager – something in which Bart had no interest. Is it not reasonable to suggest that it was Tom who was under-performing? This could be with reference to managers in Acme, managers in the furniture manufacturing business, managers in general, or just some absolute idea of what a manager should be doing if their job is to make best use of resources under their stewardship. And this is just Tom. There is also Susan. To what degree was she performing? Just as we might choose a context for Tom in considering where he might lie on the NICE curve, we could also do the same with Susan.

If Susan's stated role was to re-enforce the Acme management assessment of Bart, then perhaps she had performed quite well. Bart increasingly 'accepted' the assessment of himself as not reaching expected results. Even though he was somewhat confused, and at times stressed, about all this, he would never have considered that the data being used in these assessments were incomplete. Bart assumed that those in management of Acme were as good at their job as he was at producing completed high-quality chairs – a 'positive projection' you might call it. However, if Susan's role was to help Bart become more effective without re-enforcing any assumptions that he had accumulated as a result of his contact with Acme management, Susan might well lie at the left end of the NICE curve. Her need for certainty, to be in control, to appear knowledgeable, to appear to be a performer, to believe that she is okay despite any unconscious thoughts to the contrary, the need to be seen as a successful coach, with clients, – all these needs may well have rendered her impotent in her capacity as a personal growth agent for Bart and may even have been a significant contributor to her wanting to take on the contract in the first place. Again, in putting herself somewhere on a NICE curve she will first have to decide on the criteria to be used – the context of the NICE curve. Alas, she might not use criteria that would put her to the left end of a NICE curve. This is, for example, what Nancy, as in the case of Nancy, Ian and Cathy earlier, would have done too. Ian would have been using a different NICE curve and Cathy a different one again as they considered where Nancy might fit.

## NICE Generally.

Of course it can be tempting to start plotting everyone we know on the NICE curve. However, at this early stage, it would be wise to note that we who might find ourselves considering where others might fit on a NICE curve actually do so using a NICE curve designed by us and based on our own perceptions. In turn, our perceptions are the product of our current needs. We unconsciously design our NICE curves based on where we are, not where we think we are, on another NICE curve! Perhaps this other NICE curve is, conceptually, one designed by someone with access to more information than we have. In turn, they might be being observed by someone with even greater information.

Imagine a perfect MIS. Imagine a management information system that factored in all variables – for everyone. Imagine it even factored in the relationship between our way of working and our use of resources and how we affect the resources available to future generations as well as the challenges future generations will face because of the decisions we made throughout our lives. Imagine if this MIS measured and collated the resources used by all individuals and was able to plot us all, objectively, on a 'Great Universal NICE Curve.' Those of us who like to talk about people reaching their 'full potential' might find value in considering the existence of this virtual optimal NICE curve. If it were to exist, if we were to accept it conceptually, as we might the inherent logic of math, we might find ourselves somewhat humbled. It is in this very humility, I suggest, that we are offered the opportunity for greater human effectiveness.

**NICE Children.**

A common early response to the NICE curve concept is the notion that it suggests that children are in-effective. Whilst I can appreciate the temptation to interpret it this way, I would like to introduce another number of variables that I believe help build the robustness of the model. The first is very relevant to children and adolescents but the essential principle applies at any age. It has to do with inputs and outputs.

If a fifteen-year-old boy wants the freedom that normally goes with say being eighteen years old and, at the same time, wants the privileges of childhood, it can be worth looking at it in terms of effectiveness. If Neil (15) wants to be able to drive a car freely and, at the same time, is not yet able to do so safely, we might find an effectiveness issue. If Nadeen (15) wants to be able to have sex with her boyfriend but is unaware of the psychological implications for her in doing so, or is totally unprepared emotionally to deal with the responsibility of motherhood, you might argue that she is at the low end of effectiveness - in a NICE curve of a population of fifteen-year-olds.

At the far right end of the curve you might find fifteen-year-olds that do not engage in activities for which they are not ready or do engage in activities, such as driving a car or having sex, and are already mature enough to accept the responsibilities that go with those activities. I suggest that, in embracing the mechanics of the NICE curve in this context, you do not allow yourself to be distracted by a debate as to what constitutes responsible activity, e.g. teenage sex. Instead, park the stories for a while – as you would in coaching – and seek out the essence.

A second issue that is of relevance to children is time-scale. Let's ignore the first issue of privileges and responsibilities for a moment and assume that we measure need and contribution only. In this context, we could say that parents work hard everyday to provide for their children. The children, on the other hand do little to contribute. Their time is taken up having a good time and, the parents hope, investing in their education. Token house-work is done grudgingly with a sprinkling of normal teenage martyrdom and is seen by parents, sometimes clutching at straws, as part of their attempt to build their children's life-skills. Can you call the children in-effective or non-contributory? If you take the timescale into consideration, you might embrace a broader range of inputs and outputs. Say the children grow up and move into employment of some type. They create value in some way and pay taxes. These taxes are then put into the social pot and are used to subsidize others at different stages of development, the next generation of school-going children for example.

If we take a very narrow time-scale into consideration, we might conclude that teenagers, for example, are needy and non-contributory. If, however, we take their life-time into consideration, we will be left with a different interpretation. We may even take legacy issues into consideration. Imagine a disabled writer, subsidized all her life by the assistance of others, whose writings were before their time and which challenged and inspired later generations to commit to higher levels of justice, creativity and productivity. How would we fit Helen Keller into the NICE curve? How would we fit an academically mediocre teenager by the name of Albert Einstein?

A third variable, when considering NICE children, is the subtle, even invisible, emotional support children bring to adults. Even if we cannot measure it, any aware parent will tell you that raising children is tough at times but represents a meaningful, growthful and rewarding journey for them as parents and human beings. It is also worth considering the common syndrome whereby needy parents, at the left-hand end of the curve, were ill-equipped to do all they might have done for their children and one or more of the children 'held the show together' allowing their siblings to be children with some chance of 'normal' growth. Unfortunately, the legacy for those children who do, for whatever reason, step into the breach, is often at the expense of important parts of their own growth – as many psychotherapists will testify from their work with clients.

**NICE Retirement.**

In the same way that we might be inclined to dismiss children as needy non-contributors (in some quarters children are treated in this way – past and even present), we may also be inclined to do similarly with those that are old or infirmed. Again, if we take a broad time-scale into consideration, we see that when I am elderly, and physically weaker than when I was younger, I might have fewer options in terms of how I could contribute to my group, community, society. Not only do we not always take into consideration an older person's life-time contribution, those 'in charge' can often be highly 'ineffective' in bringing out creative ways in which older people can contribute. This could be as simple as stopping long enough to listen – to words that might be telling us that it is wise to stop long enough to listen! Wisdom is a highly under-valued contribution. This analysis, of course, does not even include the basic human quality of compassion.

I have several times seen a humorous plaque on a household wall with the inscription: *"Teenagers – quickly, leave home while you still know everything!"* Perhaps we are all teenagers at some level!


**NICE Work.**

I believe that an examination of one's relationship with one's work using the NICE curve can be a challenging exercise for both managers and staff.

You will remember, from earlier in this chapter, that Harold ('Harry to his friends') began to examine the carpenters' activity in terms of effectiveness and then profitability. This was a fictitious example and was over-simplified in order to present the concept. However, I have seen the thinking applied to a variety of work settings and, more particularly, I have worked with a broad range of individuals as they rummage their way around their own work environment with the NICE curve as a pocket flash-light. In general, I have found it to be a powerful concept to 'play with'. At a simplistic level, it can be a practical way to assess levels of productivity, effectiveness or contribution of one person, or group, compared to others or to do the same with systems – measuring the effectiveness of several business processes. At a more sophisticated level, when an increasingly wide range of variables are factored in, it can provide a compelling route towards personal growth and meaning. It can lead to simple process changes at an operational or at a managerial level and, at a base level, is simple accountancy. Taken deeper however, and with open minded insight, it can provide a canvass upon which one's growth as a human being can be mapped and accelerated. It can provide an ever-expanding template within which we discover a path towards meaning – a path not for the faint-hearted, and one which is strewn with conflicts and apparent impasses. In doing so, however, it nudges us towards ourselves and out of our comfort zones – as we break the shells of selective reasoning and peep out into a world of beckoning, but barely tolerable, freedom. Sometimes this gives us new wings with which to lead and to inspire others within our organization or community. By its nature however, the process waits for no man or machine and it may corral us into a corner and out through the bars on the window of our office, factory or service center – even of our most cherished alliances.

Whilst knowledge might be the accountancy of personal growth, courage is the currency and not everyone in your group will want to open their purse at the same time as you brave your way to the next foothold on your NICE curve and inch your way to your pinnacle.

**NICE Politics.**

The nice curve is designed with the suggestion that movement from left to right is desirable in the context of personal growth – as a life direction. Any assumption by an observer that there is a parallel between the left-right axis in the NICE curve model and the concept of 'left and right', as in politics, is flawed thinking.

Any attachment to seeing robust thinking in such a parallel is, in my opinion, most likely an expression of selective interpretation on the part of the observer. It is a 'coachable unproductive dependence'. In the snakes and ladders of personal growth, it is a silky python ushering any who step on its square the swift slide downwards to the lower regions of the drawing board made of recycled humility. This is the often the case with forced dichotomies.

**NICE PAUSE.**

You may remember from chapter two that I presented a definition of personal growth with the acronym 'PAUSE.'

'**P**ersonal growth is
**A** process by which we replace an
**U**nsustainable, unproductive or unethical dependence with a more
**S**ustainable, productive or
**E**thical dependence.'

Moving in this way from dependence to dependence offers stepping stones up the NICE curve. I am not suggesting that this process of replacing dependences in necessarily easy but, once we understand the essence and can discern our various dependences, we can build momentum and direction with at least a modicum of confidence that we are moving in the direction of growth towards our full potential – towards genuine 'self-actualization', to use a term associated with the famous psychologist Abraham Maslow.

Without some sort of reliable compass like the NICE curve, I believe it is probable that we will do one of two things. The first avenue is to avoid growth altogether. This avenue is a cul-de-sac of complacency, a dead-end of denied drudgery. If we do grow, in this context, it is despite ourselves and it is because life has other plans – we are chosen – worse still we are not! We might be offered the opportunity to face our fears and step outside of ourselves but we decide to take a rain-check and snuggle back into our duck-down comfort zones – our reliable dependences.  Or, we might believe that we are growing but actually we are simply replacing one unproductive dependence with another one - one just as limiting as its predecessor – albeit dressed in new clothes and with the fleeting shimmer of novelty. Even in the self-help field there is no shortage of emperors' new ensembles waiting to be tried on by keen searchers eager to sign the next testimonial before the synthetic fabric wears thin. With discernment, I believe it is possible to build ourselves into a more meaningful life. Without discernment, we live by chance. We are leaves in the wind subject to the whims of the next gust with little say about where we might be carried. Whatever chance we might have of being authors of our own destiny, it atrophies in the neglected petrie dish of 'an unexamined life.'

## GLADs & CUDS.

It can be tempting sometimes to consider that all dependences are 'bad'. Indeed, I have been so tempted. If we go down this route, however, we can find ourselves aiming to not have any dependences. I have yet to meet anyone with *no* dependences – anyone alive that is!

Even the most independent people I know will be stopped in their tracks if certain dependences are rendered absent. The chief executive whose wife leaves him. The middle aged mother whose children flee the nest. The teenage Romeo whose Juliet had other plans. The confident 'YUPPIE' faced with sudden redundancy.

I will present arguments later for the idea that some of the most significant 'coachable' dependences are, in fact, clusters of beliefs that are built on cognitive sand. At this point, I would like to look at just one - a cluster of beliefs around perceived *independence*. In an effort to create the illusion of freedom, we sometimes 'blank-out' the reality that we are actually dependent on someone or something in a way that we prefer not to admit. We then compare ourselves to someone else, without consideration of their dependences. We tell ourselves we are 'okay', or 'safe', or 'secure', or 'acceptable' – whatever we are currently clinging to – because we are as effective, or more effective, than them. We don't consider DOVE (Differentiate Output Versus Effectiveness) and, even if we do remember to, we are selective in our appraisal of the inputs, i.e. the resources being relied upon.

Food is a dependence – and everyone has it – the dependence, that is – not everyone has enough food - unfortunately. If we don't eat, we fizzle out. We cease to function. Chocolate can also be a dependence. If you are like me and have a taste for chocolate you might just know what I mean here. However, food and chocolate are different types of dependences. In a context where we have a basic amount of nutritious food, chocolate is something we can live without. Its absence will not prevent us from thriving. I know there will be those who passionately wish to believe that chocolate is one of life's necessities but, 'trust me, I am a coach', your dependence on chocolate is coachable! Your dependence on food, on the other hand, is another matter.

Food is a 'growthful' dependence. In fact, with a healthy diet, with the avoidance of unhealthy food – let's park the chocolate issue for the moment, a little managed collusion – I believe that we can be more *emotionally* able to face and out-grow our limiting dependences.

Food is also a 'life-enabling' dependence. Without food, we run out of life. I accept the fact that a period of fasting might 'detox' us leaving us more open to our growth. In fact, I recommend it to those who know what they are doing – with the usual disclaimer about seeking medical advice! However, once past the initial detoxifying period of a fast, without food, our body will begin to dip into its medium term fat resources and eventually will use up its longer term vital protein building blocks. It can only go for so long. 'Here lies the body of Mister Lean, he tried to live with no cuisine!'

Another feature of food, as a dependence, is that it is 'accepted.' By this I mean that after any rational discussion about food, no-one will be told that they should 'give it up' or that they are being selfish or self-indulgent in aiming to obtain enough food to live. In this context, I am not talking about pavlova or crème broulé or premium ice-cream, with the possible exception of the triple chocolate flavored variety, – these are unlikely to be lying in wait on the bread line.

The key feature here is that the universal dependence of basic food is not up for debate – it is *accepted*. Whilst *how* people obtain food, buying, stealing, controlling world commodity prices, might present room for argument, the *need* to eat will not be seen as a personal growth issue. No business manager will hold out for union agreement for the banning of all lunch breaks and eating opportunities for staff. No doubt there are those who have wanted to implement such policies, but common sense tells us that there will be implications for productivity, sick-leave, morale and staff turnover – not to mention the law suits. Multinationals are not putting out tenders for team-building workshops designed to rid executives of their irritating habits of going home to their families to eat! Or are they?

In summary therefore I suggest that food, as a dependence, has the following characteristics. It is a:

**G**rowth enabling – a healthy diet supports personal growth,
**L**ife-enabling – try living without food,
**A**ccepted as a reality – the need for food cannot be coached out of you,
**D**ependence.

## Aiming for the Pinnacle

Food therefore is a 'GLAD' and represents a type of dependence that is just part of life. As a need, it is as persistent as gravity. You can disagree with gravity. You can vote against gravity. You can write a treatise on the injustice and brutality of gravity in a modern so-called democratic society. You can even produce a moving Hollywood 'docu-drama' on how governments are standing idly by whilst the scourge of gravity reeks havoc on ordinary people's lives on a daily basis. But, if you are to reach your full potential as a human being, if you are to climb your way up towards the dizzying heights of your own self-actualization, you are probably going to have to come to some level of accommodation with the reality of gravity as a limitation to human endeavor. Our need to eat will line itself up shoulder-to-shoulder with this limit. You will not be coached out of your need to work around gravity. Neither will you find a coach qualified to coach you out of your malnutrition without embracing some role for food, of some sort, in the equation.

Sleep is another GLAD. Try giving wise, inspired, emotionally generous support to a friend when you are severely sleep deprived. Have you ever seen an article in a magazine entitled 'Ten Ways to Eliminate Your Need for Sleep.' At least, if you did, how much credence will you attach to it? I concede that some genius in the scientific community may someday invent a pill that will finally liberate mankind from the universal need for nocturnal re-charging. However, I doubt it and, to be frank, I hope not. A world without duvets and Saturday morning lie-ins?

*'Ah!'* I hear you say..
*"What about a few cups of 'Roasted Java Blend' – ground and filtered to perfection?"* Coffee, however, does not eliminate sleep. It just defers it and at a price.

At this point, some readers will be reminded of Abraham Maslow's 'Hierarchy of Needs' or possibly William Glasser's 'Choice Theory' and 'Reality Therapy'. I do believe that an examination of human needs is indeed valuable in the exploration of the terrain of personal growth. However, I have vivid memories of Maslow's 'Hierarchy of Needs' being presented to me and my fellow students in college many years ago. It was offered as a tool with which consumers could be categorized and 'managed' in a way that would allow crafty marketers maximize sales and achieve 'market penetration', or even 'domination.' In my naiveté, all those years ago, I thought I understood what Maslow was onto and I ignored a 'still small voice' within me that tried in vain to niggle me.

Some years later, I encountered the same theory whilst undertaking psychotherapy training. This time, it was offered as a tool with which we could understand how people can have a need deficit in their development and can be helped to bridge that deficit. These deficits were seen as the type that can leave people vulnerable to the manipulations, penetrations and dominations of crafty advertising types! The tables were turning – for me anyway. The ignored niggle folded its arms and glared at me with distain – 'I told you so!' rested unapologetically on its lips.

Abraham Maslow was interested in human potential, his study was around 'self-actualization', people becoming 'all they could be'. I believe the same can be said about William Glasser and others of like mind. I doubt if either Maslow or Glasser lay awake, night after night, pondering on how the market for underarm deodorant could be segmented for the purpose of price discrimination and profit maximization. I believe Maslow's passion was about notions of humanity that transcend even the height of market share analysis and vertical integration. My college lecturers and I, however, I conclude in retrospect, had a 'need' to focus on elements and implications of Maslow's hierarchy of needs, and his suggestions in the area of self-actualization, as they related to *our own needs* at that time! The lecturer had a *need* to interpret *needs* in a certain way and we, the students, joined in with reckless abandon.

I suggest that using the writings of Abraham Maslow to help university college students to get people to buy a product is a changeable need and therefore it is a *coachable* dependence (unlike food). In addition, the lecturer's need for their selective interpretation of Maslow's theories is unproductive – at least relatively. I would also say that it is an unsustainable dependence – if everyone operated on its premises, there would be no-one left to exploit! If the ongoing application of the theory is sustained by the profit, created through exploitation of other human beings, unlucky enough not yet to have made it out of the needy end of the NICE curve, I might even go so far as to suggest that the marketeer's dependence is an unjust or unethical one.

This marketing selective interpretation of Maslow's hierarchy of needs is a certain type of dependence summarized as a:

**C**oachable (in theory - once there is an opening of course),
**U**nsustainable or unproductive (at least relatively)
**D**ependence

This is now a different type of dependence – a CUD versus a GLAD. Personal growth is about working with CUDS until, in theory at least, all that are left are GLADS. All unproductive dependences are replaced with productive ones and the individual moves from the left to the right on the curve.

**Fear to Faith.**

As we progress through this book, I will be laying down a theory. It is that, in order for any human being to move towards their full potential (to genuinely and authentically do so, as distinct to being seduced by a counterfeit version draped in 'SHAM' hype – '**S**elf **H**elp **A**ctualization **M**ovement), that they will inevitably proceed through a progression of moments of PAUSE. The cumulative effect of these moments of PAUSE will be to transform their experience of themselves and their relationship with life. A key milestone of this process will be when they notice that they have moved from a life confined by the bindings of fear to a life elevated by the wings of mature faith. This movement is not about inculcating ourselves with a self-serving doctrine of wishful-thinking shimmering with shared mythology – historically accurate or otherwise - that is re-inforced by the collusion of a group of similarly imprisoned adherents. Under those circumstances, we cling to a formula in order that we do not have to face the unknown and certainly not the abyss!

Quite the opposite - this movement takes us through a journey of voluntary interrogation of our most cherished beliefs. It entails the stripping away of our self-serving subjective reasoning and the exposing of our insecurities – to ourselves primarily and others if we chose. We face and outgrow our CUDs. We learn to move to GLADS alone.

A second product of this journey towards genuine faith is an increasing trust in, and understanding of, the very process of growth – that organic, and self-sustaining transition from neediness to contribution. It is the natural evolution from survival to thrival, from ego-centrism – in its subtle and not-so subtle forms – to ethical intelligence and living. It is the shedding of the 'me' and the embracing of the limitations of my humanity. In involves the acceptance of the 'gravity' of our mortality whilst at the same time shuffling off the heaviness of our morbidity. It is about learning to care enough to learn when and how not to care – to be purposefully carefree. This is a journey that takes no prisoners of delusion. Again, it is not for the faint-hearted.

The journey of ongoing personal growth is, I believe, a mandatory journey for anyone presenting themselves as a coach. Its soaring importance leaves perfunctory tools and tricks in the embarrassing spotlight of impotence. Its authority sooner or later asserts itself to all who chose to open their eyes to it. Funnily enough, it takes us to the highest levels of our effectiveness – to **H**abits **O**f **M**aximum **E**ffectiveness. For the acronym addicts amongst us, it takes us HOME – and back to where we started – with fresh eyes!

## Coaching In Context.

In Chapter One I briefly looked at coaching and suggested that it could be described as a way of being with someone that is designed to help them to get more out of what they have. I also suggested that at the heart of coaching is *who the coach is* – as distinct from *what the coach does*. Finally, I suggested that the creation of that being, on the part of the coach, is about the coach's own growth and their relationship with life – with living.

In Chapter Two, I explored understandings of what personal growth is and suggested that there is a difference between personal growth and personal development. The implication is that you might have one without the other.

In this chapter, the third, I have put forward some concepts that I believe need to be embraced if we are to create soil out of which growth can sprout and sustain itself. This would be as distinct from the type that starts with great promise but runs aground when the 'low hanging fruit' has been gobbled up with help of a few tools and exercises.

In the next chapter, I would like to revisit the concept of coaching having laid the preceding groundwork. However, before doing so, I would like to look at one more feature of the coaching context. It is about where coaching fits in to a person's reality – if at all.

**Elucidating with Examples.**

**# 1 - Elaine.**

*Elaine (20) is feeling quite unmotivated generally. She is frustrated about her work situation – working for a radio station. She has a passion for working in the media. However, she hates the way her boss treats her and feels alienated from others in the office. Her boss has been 'on her case' for the last two years and Elaine suspects that her boss covertly uses her as an example of how not to perform.*

*Elaine took the job as she liked the sound of the company – dynamic, young and with great opportunities for development. In taking up the job, she had forgone an opportunity to go to college that would have been paid for by her parents. She took the job despite her parents' concerns about the decision and decided that she would do her media studies degree at night after she had settled into the job. She has not yet managed to complete the degree programme.*

*Elaine's confidence is at an all time low. She feels she is in a vicious circle which started some time back when she had had a rough month after a break-up with her boyfriend and the coinciding appearance of her new boss. Her boss appeared to have written Elaine off on the basis of what she saw in her in those early days. Nothing Elaine had done in the meantime, and there have been great achievements, including a modest industry award, seems to be capable of changing the boss's opinion of Elaine. The fact is that Elaine's boss has a blind-spot (upon which she is dependent to sustain her own perception of herself) and this blind spot leads to a consistent de-valuing of Elaine's work. The cumulative effect of this is that Elaine is hanging on by a thread to her dream of a career in the media. Elaine's boss has a blind-spot and all the power. The result, whether the boss is aware of it or not, is that Elaine is being bullied and is suffering the disempowering symptoms that are associated with this.*

I accept that a situation like this may call for a debate on what is bullying and what is not – what responsibility Elaine might have in the situation and how she might be contributing to the problem. However, on this occasion, I am pinning my colors to the mast as follows: When one person has substantially more power than another, and that power is used in certain ways, it can leave the less powerful person finding themselves in a position of psychological oppression. The oppressed person can be making continuous intelligent reasonable decisions but experience high rates of failure only because of the way the person with power exercises that power in the context of those decisions. Once this starts, it is very hard for the oppressed to break out of it without an inordinate amount of pain and loss – far more than the oppressor would have to experience if they were to let go of their dependence on their way of exercising power.

In addition, the oppressed breaking out may leave a legacy of injustice which is like a scar that lingers for a long time - sometimes years. The oppressor breaking out brings with it a sense of remorse and liberation and, even if it also brings with it an amount of lingering guilt, this is nothing like the scars of the oppressed. Guilt of this nature tends to dissipate relatively easily and will probably bring with it a degree of growthful humility.

The point about Elaine's situation is that, in general, intervention is what is needed to break the cycle. Not doing so is extremely costly. I have come by situations where coaches, and counselors/therapists, have worked with clients as if sensitive coaching or therapy will provide a breakthrough for a victim of bullying. However, the client is so deep in survival mode that this approach is largely a waste of time – at best it is a band-aid.

In addition, and crucially in these situations, every day that goes by without the matter being addressed at a power level, i.e. intervention, leaves the victim more and more vulnerable to illness or disastrous failure – requiring extended recovery time. In short, Elaine has an environment to deal with.

Of course Elaine may end up taking a bullying law suit against her employer – if she survives long enough to do so.

## # 2 - Philip.

*Philip (35) has a rewarding job as a civil engineer. He is married to Patricia and has three young children. In the last twelve months Philip has been finding himself somewhat low in energy and a little forgetful. He has also a reduced interest in Patricia sexually – something both of them are surprised by and about which Patricia is more than a little concerned.*

*Philip wondered if he was going through an 'early onset mid-life-crisis' and decided to work with a coach to get some focus and renewed energy. Having looked up the yellow pages, he did several sessions of coaching over a few months but felt that he was going around in circles – getting nowhere. He began to feel that much of what he was living on was the presumption that the coaching would get him back on track and that this 'crutch' was beginning to wear thin.*

*Then, Philip received a birthday present of a book about nutrition and health. He placed it aside with the intention of reading it someday when he had more energy. However, Patricia began browsing through the book and thus began a sequence of events which led to Philip being diagnosed as having food allergies. The allergies were playing havoc with his physiology which in turn adversely affected his energy levels, his sleep and his motivation.*

The relevance of Philip's story is that a person's physiology can and does affect their output and their level of motivation.

When a physiological problem is underlying a person's functioning, coaching is likely to be of questionable value until the physiological problem is sorted.

With an under-functioning nervous system...
(1) a person can be inhibited in how they engage with the coaching and
(2) even if they do engage in the coaching, the results are likely to be short-lived. The client will wonder why others seem to get a lot out of coaching but they don't seem to be getting very far. It can even set up a

dynamic where they blame themselves and move towards a subtle cycle of dependence on the coach – a cycle with huge potential for collusion with a coach who appears to have skills but is actually blind to such dynamics.

## # 3 - Eddie.

*Eddie was feeling pretty unmotivated and 'out of sorts' and his doctor suggested that he did some work with a coach. Eddie worked in a job with practically 100% job security. As he said himself, you would have to be a right idiot to get fired from this job and, even then, the union would be behind you. At the age of forty-two he had made his way up a few rungs of the promotion ladder. Even though the organization he worked for claimed to employ a fair and transparent decision making system for promotion, Eddie claimed that he knew 'how the system worked' and who worked it. By his own admission, he had manipulated the system and gotten into a cushy number. 'It's who you know' he claimed with, literally, a nod and a wink.*

*Eddie was lucky in my opinion. Not because he had a 'cushy number' but because he had found himself working with Martina – a coach of substantial insight and presence. On top of that, his employer was paying for it – it is unlikely that he would have been sitting there on his own time and money. Eddie found the coaching increasingly challenging and, despite the odd periods of waver, he stuck at it. He found himself discovering a lot about himself that he never even considered before. Within a few focused sessions with Martina, he found himself jolted out of his comfort zone and this was to be a pattern.*

*After a year, Eddie was struggling with whether he could tolerate 'that place' – what had been known as the 'cushy number'. The relevance of the story here is that Eddie, again in this book a composite character, obtained value from coaching because there was room for 'voluntary interrogation' of his cherished beliefs and comfort zones. His experience of himself changed – for better or for worse – he somewhat reluctantly assessed it as for better. After the coaching he felt he saw 'stuff' he did not see before. Not only that, but he could see why he couldn't see the stuff before and cringed at his past selfishness and arrogance. His 'experience' of himself and his environment had changed.*

If we take Elaine, Philip and Eddie as representatives of three elements of the context within which coaching might fit, and put them together, we could look at them as follows...

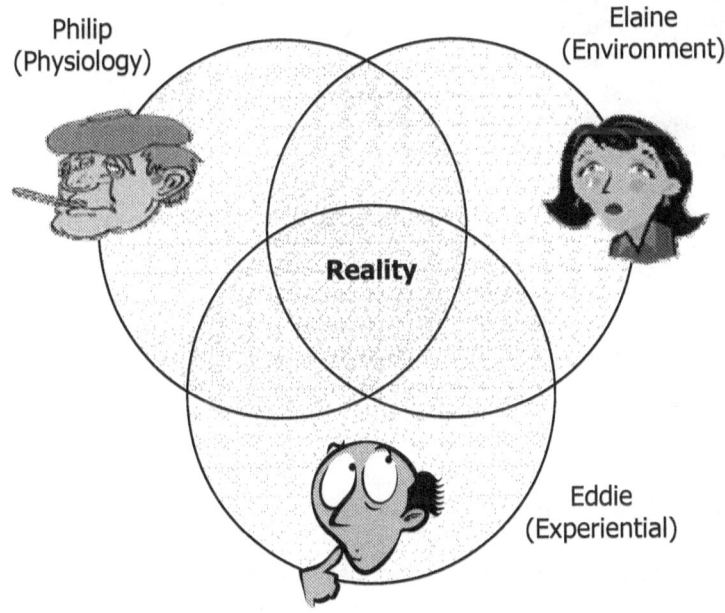

- Philip represents the fact that people are physiological.
- Elaine represents the fact that they live and work in an environment.
- Eddie represents the fact that we experience things in different ways.
- Reality is where all three of these overlap for any of us.

Again, for those of us with a questionable dependence on acronyms, like me, we have 'PEER' – the **P**hysiological, **E**nvironmental and **E**xperiential aspects of our **R**eality.

I believe that the reason for the great debate on treatment for symptoms of psychological distress – in short, whether the answer is to be found in pharmacology or in the 'talking cures' – centers around the nature of these three elements of our reality. It seems eminently sensible to me to keep a very open mind as to the relationship between all three and not allow ourselves to get over-attached to any one.

Consider...

- The doctor who doesn't want to consider the possibility of buried emotional trauma, attempting to be surfaced and resolved, as a root cause of illness.

- The psychotherapist whose one solution is interminable therapy for every ill and all their friends.

- The activist who is certain who is to be lined up against the wall come the revolution.

- All of us who think we have the solution but ignore the all too common ugly injustices and inequities in our society.

A coach would be wise to approach their work with humility.

**A Note on the Experiential.**

I use the word 'experiential' to describe everything pertaining to how we interpret and make sense of what we notice. It is the software with which we create form out of a barrage of data. Within this, you can contain the psychological, the spiritual, the existential and the philosophical – all as experienced and interpreted. I don't propose even trying to differentiate these terms at this stage. I am not sure I even see value in doing so in this context. I do, however, recommend that before we do spend time dissecting the possible components of the Experiential, that we look first at unpacking the implications of PEER in our own attitudes, in our choices, in our lives.

Philosophizing can be an enjoyable activity – even very fruitful.
It can also offer an abundance of avoidance opportunities!

# Aiming for the Pinnacle

**Chapter bullets:**

- There is value in pinning down the meaning of language used in presenting coaching.
- Assumptions made preceding contracting can have significant implications for the direction of coaching.
- Coaches can collude with clients and sponsors even at a business exploration stage.
- Susan coached Bart.
- 'Terminal enmeshment' is a coaching cul-de-sac.
- Remember 'DOVE'.
- It rhymes with 'love!'
- Sam coached Don.
- Effectiveness can be looked on in terms of a continuum.
- Nancy, Ian and Cathy are in a coaching peer group.
- The effectiveness in, and of, a group can be plotted on a graph.
- The Pareto principle can be a feature of group effectiveness.
- Harold considered the effectiveness of his carpenters.
- Harry noticed his perceptions changed with his emotional state.
- Mal-measurement of effectiveness is in-effective management.
- We use our own NICE curves.
- There are different categories of dependences.
- We interpret models of needs in accordance with our current needs.

- Growth takes us from fear to faith.
- Coaching features in a context.
- There are three key components to that context.

# Chapter 4
# Coaching Revisited.
*Generic or Otherwise.*

A few years ago, I was in my local bank and the young teller noticed the account name – 'Séamus Scanlan trading as Lifecoach'.

*'Do you teach people to swim?'* the teller enquired.

I assumed from this comment, and was pleased to consider, that I might look fit enough to pass for a swimming instructor! However, it was a reminder that the notion of a coach for one's life was a concept known only to a relatively small number of people, albeit a growing number.

Since then, the idea of a Life Coach has spread considerably with regular mentions in the media - in some of which I admit to having had a hand. Every year, I notice new coach training schools popping up and more and more people out there with a desire, if not necessarily with matching levels of readiness, to set up their stall as the next professional coach on the block. In addition, over the years, I have had hundreds of conversations with people interested in either entering the profession or availing of the services of one of its number. Through those conversations and the other hundreds, or even thousands of hours exploring coaching and its related issues, with trainee and practicing coaches, I have managed to organize my thoughts and, at least to some degree, map out the territory which I believe has been gradually colonized under the flag of coaching – or, perhaps more precisely, under the flag of the *word* 'coaching'. This conceptual organization process has culminated in my desire, amongst other things, to write this book.

Some statements which I believe to be true in relation to coaching:

1. Not all people using the word coaching are describing the same thing.
2. Not all coaches are doing what they claim they are doing.
3. Not all of these coaches realize this discrepancy.
4. These statements apply to internal and external coaches.

In addition, there are a number of things I believe to be the case in relation to books about coaching (and self-help books generally):

5. There are books written by people who have *grown* into wisdom.
6. There are books written by people who have read a lot of books.
7. All else equal, books written by people from their own growth offer the most insightful and applicable help to their readers.

These might seem like sweeping statements. I would not, however, make them without considerable thought. Furthermore, I believe that the more experienced coaches – and I do not mean this in terms of number of hours spent 'coaching', however interpreted – will know these statements to be true. In addition, I would say that quite a high proportion of the members of *the market* for coaching, the buyers if you like, especially in the corporate sector, are more aware of 1 and 2 than some within the profession.

In the opening words of the first chapter, I suggested that coaching, in the context of this book, is a word describing a way of being with people that invites them to make better use of what is available to them. However, this alone is not precise enough – I suggest it merely as a starting point.

A bank manager could be described as someone that helps people to make better use of what is available to them. So could a builder. If I have some money, perhaps I could get a loan and employ a builder to construct a house for me. Both the bank manager and the builder could be described as helping me to make better use of what I have. The purest in me wants to suggest that coaching is a way of being with someone that invites them to make better use of what is available to them *without, permanently or temporarily, giving them any other resources.* This last bit is the key. A coach's true value is in how they help a client see things differently and therefore do things differently.

In Shakespeare's 'Hamlet', when Polonius gives advice to his son Laertes his parting shot is:

*"This above all: to thine own self be true, And it must follow, as the night the day, Thou canst not then be false to any man."*

## Aiming for the Pinnacle

It is interesting that Polonius thought it of value to advise his son to be true to himself. Polonius' advice suggests that it is possible to be 'untrue' to oneself – that we can be '*false*' to ourselves.

Coaching, the purist in me wants to claim, helps clients to discover the ways in which they could be truer to themselves and to deal with the accompanying challenges. A big part of that, of course, is discovering that it is possible to be living in a way that is *untrue* to ourselves, whatever that means. Some readers might share my belief that achieving this discovery is one of the greatest challenges of all.

This issue is at the heart of effective coaching and it is because we can be 'being untrue' to ourselves that the terrain can be complex, confusing and even appears at times to be contradictory. Everyone who examines 'coaching' does so from a position of their own level of 'true-to-self-ness'. We interpret 'coaching' with the very mental software that 'coaching' would be working on if we availed of it. The cleaner our software, the more effective we are at sourcing effective coaching. Equally, the cleaner is the software of the coach, the more effective he or she is likely to be.

You may now begin to detect the possibility of a kind of circularity in how people end up with certain coaches. The more discerning we are, the more discerning the coach we choose. The more discerning the coach we choose, the more discerning we end up as a result of the quality of coaching we receive! Such is the terrain of growth.

One of the aims of this book is to help people sit back and get a better feel for the terrain. My belief is that, in doing this, those considering availing of coaching will do so with more precision than they might have otherwise. The same applies to those who are already availing of the service or have already done so. My hope is that they will be better equipped to assess past value and access future value. If this precision does ensue, it will of course 'raise the bar' for many within the profession. I hope the book also helps those coaches to raise their bar further or contribute to a productive debate.

In aiming to build a definition of coaching, I have found myself moving in a certain direction. I was seeing coaching, at its essence, as about challenging others to acquire new perspectives that lead them to change their behavior and this in a way that they have more of what they want. However, this wasn't quite enough for me. I looked around and I saw this process happening in a variety of settings but I could not satisfy myself that this was what I saw as coaching. There were ingredients missing.

I saw people walking away from conversations with coaches, and salesmen, therapists, managers, leaders, politicians, writers and others, with new perspectives. These new perspectives seemed to lead to new behavior on the part of the 'coachee.' This behaviour, in turn, seemed to allow the coachee, at first glance anyway, to get more of what they wanted. I saw people make interesting decisions about their jobs, their careers, their staff, their boss, their marriages, their health, their education, their home entertainment systems, their choice of automobile upholstery, their voting patterns, their sex life - the latter tending to be more in the way of hearsay I admit!

However, I also found considerable evidence to suggest that a lot of these decisions were regretted later and, most importantly, on retrospective review of those very conversations, the 'coachee' felt that they had been manipulated or seduced into seeing something a different way. I was interested in why people would do these things and later feel this way. I looked into a variety of areas most of which I had had an interest in previously – areas such as philosophy, psychology, psychotherapy, spiritology, shamanism, cultism, consciousness. I looked afresh at these areas, this time with a specific interest in mind. Why do people change their minds as a result of having contact with others? My re-rummaging gave me little pieces of the jigsaw. The clearest insight that presented itself was that the more we know, the more we realize that there is so much more that we don't know!

> *The clearest insight was that the more we know, the more we realize that there is so much more that we don't know!*

For the purpose of building a workable definition of coaching, I would like to suggest an additional ingredient to the definition I offered previously i.e. coaching, at its essence, is about challenging others to acquire new perspectives that lead them to change their behavior and in a way that they have more of what they want (and now adding) *ethically*.

There was, however, a further feature which I thought I saw in the area of 'coaching' - or 'selling' or 'leadership' or whatever word is used to describe the process of engagement leading to change in behaviour. This was that the engagement was usually a mixture of things. Apart from conversation, the 'coach' might do other things. He or she might give advice. They might agree to deals or discounts, advancement or advances. They might promise to do something (in the context of a level of enforceable accountability or none) or promise not to do something. The coach might threaten, overtly or covertly. They might lie! They might 'educate' or might even blind the coachee with science. These activities just didn't fit into my understanding of coaching and so, in building a definition, I needed to screen them out. I thought coaching, as I understood it, was the sole activity of the relationship - that no other activities encroached into the coaching.

I ended up with a slightly more cumbersome definition but one I was comfortable with. It had now evolved into a claim that coaching, at its essence, is about challenging others to acquire new perspectives that lead them to change their behavior in a way to have more of what they want - ethically and (now added) *solely*. This last piece highlighted a key feature – that real coaching, as I saw it, did not have the escape route of some other activity when the going got tough. The 'strong' coaches, in my opinion, could stay the course when the coaching seemed to be in a cul-de-sac and could resist drawing on their, sometimes extensive, knowledge or other skills. In this context, both the coach and coachee are challenged to dig deep to find answers - answers that offer incremental pieces of that very special jigsaw – two jigsaws in fact. The first jigsaw is the picture of the degree to which the coachee is 'to his own self being true' and the second jigsaw is the very same but for the coach. This I felt was coaching.

As I mentioned, my definition was not quite as elegant and snappy as I might have liked but I felt it did hold together nicely. In addition, it was considerably lighter than other definitions such as: 'Being with a person, or group, in a responsible, ethical and sustainable way, that is designed to stimulate them to take prompt optimally effective action towards the achievement of their prioritized goals when they are not with you!'

True to form, and to aid my questionable retentionability, I needed an acronym. My definition became one of coaching being about:

**C**hallenging
**O**thers to
**A**cquire new perspectives that lead them to
**C**hange their behavior in a way that they can
**H**ave more of what they want,
**E**thically and
**S**olely.

Or **COACHES**!

The acronym-averse amongst us will no doubt cringe. Here is the definition without the acronym... and there is always Tippex for the space above!

> *'Challenging others to acquire new perspectives that lead them to change their behavior in a way that they can have more of what they want, ethically and solely.'*

It is my firm conviction that, in order to deliver coaching in accordance with this definition, a coach has to be totally committed to their own personal growth and to have achieved certain 'critical mass', a certain maturity, in this growth. Without this commitment and maturity, no amount of knowledge or skills will compensate. On the contrary, the more skilled and knowledgeable an immature coach is, the more adverse can be their effect on the growth of their clients.

**Professional Eyesight**

I will look shortly at some of the market offerings that might 'compete' within the market for coaching. First, however, I would like to look at the notion of what I call 'Professional Eyesight'.

## Aiming for the Pinnacle

In college, in a 'previous life', I was introduced to the concept of 'Marketing Myopia.' It is an idea which I associate with a writer by the name of Theodore Levitt. Marketing Myopia is a condition which ails many a business and the results of which has the corporate patient not fully clear of exactly what business they are in. As a result of a re-think of their 'myopia', a word borrowed from the ophthalmic condition of short-sightedness, many businesses changed their perception of what they do in the market. A classic example is the DIY product supplier, who used to sell drills, and who set up their new stall as a seller of 'holes' – in wood, concrete or whatever you like and by whatever means prevailing technology invites.

Another enterprise went from photo-copying to 'document management.' No doubt there are others who went from jeans to 'coolness' or oil drilling to 'energy management solutions'. I previously revealed to you that I sometimes, admittedly tongue-in-cheekily, claim that that I am in the sales business – I aim to sell a premium product within the commodity called 'clarity'. As with any vendor, I will have my better days and my not so better days.

I suggest that to understand personal growth coaching, a good starting point is to understand what it might be delivering and the context in which it is sold. By the way, whether you are a coach in professional practice, being paid irregularly by clients, or you have 'coach' on your job-description and are getting paid a reliable monthly salary, you are presumable aiming to deliver something and that something is what you are selling. In this light, therefore, what would be a myopic approach to coaching? Perhaps you could just say that you are selling 'coaching' and follow it up with a description of the things you do when you are with a client. You could explain to a prospective client that they will pay you money and you will 'do' coaching – measured in hours and in this way you will be fulfilling your contract. You may meet a client, or a decision-maker within an enterprise, interested in bringing coaching into their organization. The client might have a simple enough approach to it all. They are looking for someone, who calls themselves a coach, to show up at agreed times and 'do' coaching until the agreed time is finished. Then everyone can tick a box on a page somewhere to confirm that 'X' hours of coaching has been conducted as per the strategic plan and everyone is happy. The coach gets paid and the paymaster can now be safe in the knowledge that they, individual or organization, can now slot themselves into the category headed up 'those who have been coached' – no longer a member of the great unwashed – what a relief. Next value-added-service-offering, please!

Alternatively, you might decide that you are in the 'increase your effectiveness' market. In this case, you might study psychology, philosophy or perhaps do a Masters in Business Administration – the coveted 'MBA'. You might then present yourself as a consultant – a consultant on, amongst others things, 'coaching.' Of course, in doing your psychology degree or your MBA you might get a taste for the academic and become a teacher of business philosophy. Penultimately, you might decide to set up a training company and be a subcontractor to a consultancy practice – or, of course, be a consultant to a training practice – or you might teach a class on how to be a contracting consultant to the training profession – and with a 'coaching ethos'!

Finally, you might decide that you want to make a contribution to mankind by training yourself in psychotherapy and help 'the walking wounded' to get more out of life. In this decision, of course, you behold an array of courses and models of therapy to choose from. In an effort to avoid 'professional myopia', you choose 'the best' and never look back. On second thoughts, perhaps not never. At least you don't look back for a few years, at which time you do a short course in 'coaching' and continue to do what you always did but replace the word 'therapist' with the word 'coach.' Phew, what a roller-coaster – would it not be easier to train as an electrician? But then you might want to set up your own contracting firm and get some coaching on it – we're off again!

Is it any wonder that the public is more than a little confused and sometimes understandably downright skeptical when the word coaching slithers out of someone's professional portfolio and up the leg of an unsuspecting and pressurized HR manager or a frazzled mother-of-four? Is it any wonder that we hear debates on radio phone-in shows where some people complain that they paid hundreds to a coach and still can't figure out what it was all about or, worse still, feel ripped off? At the same time, just to confuse everyone, someone else comes on to tell how their life is so much better as a result of working with a coach.

I believe that it is for the benefit of all that those of us with an interest in the coaching profession have our professional eyes tested and get personalized lenses. As with ophthalmic eyesight, we might encounter fewer headaches, greater clarity and a lot more focus.

Coaching, as I present it, is about helping people, in a certain way, to grow. Just as a gardener would be wise to learn something about nutrients, different soil types and their suitability to different plants as well as the process of growth and even the notion of seasons, so too, I believe, should a coach know the equivalent. It's no good knowing *how* to use a watering can when you don't know *when and where* to use a watering can. The same applies to coaching – it's no good being a good listener when you don't know when is a good time to listen and when is not a good time to listen – or when is a good time to question and when is not a good time to question. The secret to personal growth coaching is actually in timing. The path to good timing is, guess what, one's own growth.

I believe that those with a sustained involvement in coaching will sooner or later see that the only approach to true optimization of a person's potential has to embrace a robust and applicable understanding of personal growth. Without that understanding, coaching is vulnerable to going around in circles. It will be regularly adjusting its language to sustain itself and its dependences – all the while colluding with willing compatriots aligned to a shared reality. That 'reality', however, simply offers a safe fortress within which people of like mind can trade vocabularies without any real movement.

One of the problem areas facing both coaches and the buyer of coaching is the area of language – both in terms of negotiating the possibility of working together and in the actual process of the work. Let's look at an example.

*Michael is looking for a coach. He phones a number of coaches and decides on one of them – at least to begin with. He meets Matt. In the interview Matt talked about self-actualization and personal development. He talked eloquently about effective goal-setting and the enhancement of 'soft skills'. He used words like 'alliance' and 'co-creative'. Michael found this language to be familiar and comforting and was looking forward to the coaching. However, after a few meetings, Michael came to the conclusion that Matt was not the coach for him.*

*'To be honest,' he said to his friend over a beer, 'The guy seemed to be all talk.'*

Michael then arranged to meet Barbara. The language used by Barbara was about finding 'a safe space' so that Michael could explore new perspectives. She said that the essence of her work was 'relational' and that she would hope to help him tap into the more passionate aspects of himself. This was new language to Michael and he was a little wary of it. He gave Barbara a go anyhow. Unfortunately, Barbara turned out not to be quite right for Michael. 'A bit all over the place,' he confided to his friend over another beer, as he brought his buddy up-to-date.

Next, Michael met Celine an experienced coach who happened to be pregnant. She was a little like Matt in her language and Michael again took some comfort in this. He encountered a little bit of cognitive dissonance when he thought about Celine. She looked so feminine and cuddly with her big bump and loose dresses. He felt quite protective towards her. After a few sessions with Celine, Michael began to feel a bit stretched.

'Sharp cookie that one,' was how he described Celine to his friend, as he waited for his ball to return at the bowling alley.
'Pity she is taking maternity-leave. Mind you, she had warned me'.

Frank was Michael's fourth coach. He was soft spoken and said things like 'your true self' and your 'calling'. He spoke about getting a sense of 'your path'. He talked about 'checking in with yourself' and 'perhaps facing some hard-to-face stuff'. Michael was a little wary of this type of talk after his experiences with Barbara. However, working with Frank turned out to be quite an eye-opener. Frank had an uncanny habit of eye-balling him just when he might have preferred to not be eye-balled.

'And that bloody non-judgmental expression!' Michael quipped as he and his friend set out towards the first tee.
'I have to admit' Michael conceded.
'He's making me look at stuff I would never have considered and I can see the connections. Damn, I hate to admit it - I underestimated him at the beginning.' Michael revealed.
'You... admitting something like that Michael?' His friend exaggerated his incredulity with mocking affection.
'This coaching stuff might be doing something after all.' His friend looked him in the eye with a slight air of puzzlement before taking a brand new golf-tee from his pocket and bouncing it briefly in his hand.

Here are four fictitious coaches and one fictitious client. It is probably unlikely that one client would have experience with so many different coaches – at least in such short a timescale. But this vignette might surface a usually subtle aspect of the coaching landscape. That is that you can have people using language but not necessarily understanding the origins or the essence of the language. The result is that the timing and delivery of their engagement is different to that of someone who does understand the underlying principles.

This is a major issue in coach accreditation. How can you present a transparent coach accreditation system and, at the same time, show its appropriateness and fairness to independent assessors? If you use the traditional systems of assessment such as essays you just get to see that the coach can write essays on the subject of coaching. You may or may not be able to discern maturity through this, but in any event, it runs the risk of being hit and miss. Recorded 'vivo' sessions can be rehearsed or selective. An interview needs to be conducted by someone who knows what to watch out for. What they see is notoriously difficult to point out to anyone who has the same blinkers as the interviewee!

One way to gaze into this issue is through what I call 'The CLING Matrix.' Think of the idea that we sometimes 'cling' to the familiar.

## The CLING Matrix

Coaching

| Growthful? | Language identifiable | Language Novel |
|---|---|---|
| Yes | Growthful with language identifiable to client. | Growthful with language novel to client. |
| No | Non-growthful with language identifiable to client. | Non-growthful with language novel to client. |

You can see here that you can have four different types of coach. It might be worth knowing by what criteria we might assess them if we are to get the best coach for ourselves.

So where might Michael's four coaches fit into the CLING matrix? Let's try this.....

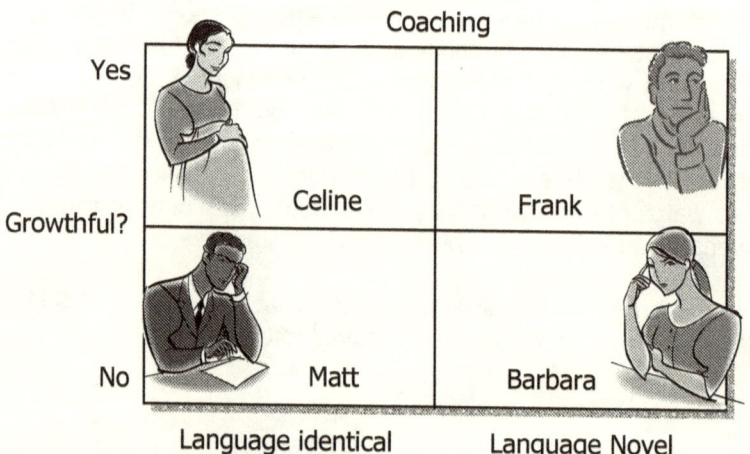

If coaching is about acquiring new perspectives, working with someone who has the same perspectives will be of questionable value. The coach may well dress their perspectives in exciting new language, and that may seduce the client, and indeed the coach, into thinking that they are coming from different perspectives. The woman whose teenage children are preparing to flee the nest meets the knowledgeable 'transformational coach' not knowing that she, the mother, has learned more from parenting than the coach has from their training. Or you might have the stressed executive who finds uplifting the rousing words of their articulate and dynamic coach but continually forgets within days of the latest weekend workshop. Life slouches back to its usual empty crawl or gets swept onto its frenzied but meaningless gallop - whichever is their particular pony on the merry-go-round of life.

**Market Offerings.**

The last few years has seen the rise of what is questionably termed as 'Reality TV.' I have a proposition for any budding reality TV producer. Fit out a room with live cameras and microphones and advertise to make up the following group:

A psychologist.
A psychiatrist
A counselor
A psychotherapist
A consultant
A career-guidance counselor
and, last but not least... a coach.

I believe it would make interesting viewing...if nothing else for chronic philosophers like me.

The first core competence of any coach, I believe, is the ability to clearly explain what exactly coaching is and in a way that can differentiate it, as required depending on the circumstances, from similar offerings. That competence cannot be delivered with just one sentence, or even a menu of 'just one sentences'. I don't believe that it can be enough to be able do an 'elevator speech' – unless it is designed for use in a building, in which the elevator is operating, is quite a sky-scraper and your listener is prepared to go all the way with you and back down to earth.

Rather, I believe that this competence is delivered through a conversation – even a wide sweep of conversations depending on the circumstances and the parties involved. How that conversation will go is as unpredictable as a coaching session. It will depend on the perceptions, needs, desires, mood and circumstances of the listener(s). It will also depend on the rapport between the presenter and the would-be client and this is often influenced by the environment in which the two meet. In order to deliver this competence, the would-be coach needs themselves to understand what it is they are selling with a multi-layered comprehension. I believe that this contains two broad types of understanding. The first is simply a cognitive familiarization of relevant facts. Depending on learning styles, it can be researched and absorbed through a mainly academic approach. The second, more challenging, one is the 'integration' of these facts. This integration is normally only achieved through experiential learning – wrestling with the implications for oneself. It involves seeing up-front the subtleties and consequences of a mindset that takes us out of the consensus reality and into less trampled paths – paths strewn with irritating pebbles, inconvenient brambles and sometimes seemingly insurmountable boulders. It contrasts with the well worn trails of the familiar – with the carved out routes to where others have already gone and the nature of which may or may not have been accurately conveyed to us.

In an effort to home in on a robust description of what coaching is, or perhaps more specifically, what personal growth coaching is, I would like to look at some other market offerings that might, in the minds of the stakeholders, present a discernment challenge. I will look at each case in terms of the 'give a man a fish' metaphor. This, I believe, has its origins in the orchard of Chinese proverbial wisdom. The common version is usually something like 'Give a man a fish, and you feed him for a day, teach him to fish and you feed him for life'.

Let's go on a fishing trip!

**Teaching.**

If you asked someone what they did for a living and they answered that they were a 'teacher', how would you imagine them at work? I have asked around and the picture with which I am presented is quite consistent. Most people imagine a classroom of children and an adult at the front with a blackboard, or more often nowadays, a white-board.

Most people's pictures will be informed by their own experiences as children in school and possibly their understanding of their children's experiences of teachers. Many people can remember one or two teachers that stood out as being fair and tolerable, if not quite uplifting or inspiring, to have as a teacher. They might find themselves reflecting on how such teachers managed to bring out the best in them and how, somehow, learning with them was verging on the effortless and how they had left a positive lasting impression on their students. Most people also remember one or two teachers that, with luck, they never had to tolerate or, possibly worse, remembered attending school with a kind of 'sub-terrainian' fear that they would have such a teacher someday - that they would finally have to face the dreaded bullet in the Russian roulette

## Aiming for the Pinnacle

of teacher allocation. Finally, and sadly, there are those who sat in the classroom run by a teacher who would have ranked amongst the dunces of their own profession.

Whatever about the origins of the word 'to teach' or its noble highpoints, of which it has many, for the purpose of this exercise, I think it is useful to look at it in terms of *how it is understood by consumers.* In this day and age, teaching is associated with the transmission of knowledge and in an academic setting. It conjures up the image of books, assignments, lectures, projects and exams. It suggests a person who is well versed in their subject. They may even be a professor or university lecturer and present large volumes of material to high IQ scholars.

Having conversed with four-year-olds, fourteen-year-olds and twenty-four-year-olds, and having myself cumulatively attended, as a learner, for more than two decades, environments with substantial reliance on lecture delivery, I am not fully convinced that teaching, as we know it, really teaches a man to fish. I believe that it more likely teaches a man to sit exams on fishing, speaking figuratively of course, and sub-optimally prepares the learner to discover what it is really like to step onto the wobbly dingy of life and set off onto the river whilst still trying to find the right hook, line, and sinker required for the job at hand. Some do well following their sojourns through the academic corridors and are thankful for the privilege. Many, I believe are corralled into a pre-determined path designed to fit in with the needs of others rather than elicit the full potential of the learner. With a growing demand for personal growth coaching, I can't help but believe that there are many out there who feel that the teaching they received from 'the system' could be augmented with something else. 'If only *they* taught us what that something else was!'

At this point, I wish to pin my colors to a political mast. I believe that education, even if it itself is not operating to its full potential, offers the single strongest deliverable for the generation of a 'self-actualized' society. Providing *the right learning environment* to children, from the outset, will maximize the chances of them developing into 'whole' people who can contribute to that society. Of course the ingredients of an education system need to be right for this to happen. The nurturing of Hitler-youth showed us a different approach to education with a result that went somewhat wide of the self-actualization ideal and could be described as a catastrophic own-goal for humanity.

In summary, teaching, as it is understood by most people, is about the delivery of knowledge, and certain understandings. I am reminded of an English teacher who was keen to persuade one of her students that his interpretation of 'To Kill a Mocking Bird' was not the 'correct' interpretation of the story. I thought the student's interpretation was intriguing and insightful and worthy of unpacking – presumably I suffer from the same delusions as the student and, in time, will come around! I have met inspiring teachers with whom I would very comfortably entrust my children. I have met teachers who, in my opinion, are simply in the wrong secure and pensionable job and who subliminally imbue their own fear of uncertainty in life into their innocent and as yet forming charges. I have met brilliant and talented fishermen, and fisherwomen, with little or no formal education. I have met college graduates and PhDs who have not yet grasped the essence of fishing. By the way, I have also met people on either side of the academic hedgerow who have yet to befriend the full power and value of metaphor!

Personal growth coaching is not teaching as described here. That is not to say that a teacher will not be in a position to contribute to the personal growth of their students – I have no doubt that many do.

## Consulting.

Somewhere out there, a man with a deep voice, is being paid, presumably well paid, to provide the voiceover for what seems to me to be the vast majority of movie trailers. Perhaps my reticular activating system is somewhat over-exercised, but I can't help thinking that ninety percent of these voiceovers are provided by the same man and that ninety percent of his voiceovers contain the words 'in a world' as an opening phrase. I am tempted to imagine a surreal script along the lines of *"In a world of dog-eat-dog competition for guttural voiceover performers, he who says 'in a world' best is the only survivor. There are no second places."*

*In a world* of highly competitive market dynamics, specialization and simply increasingly high levels of complexity in life, personal and organizational, a good consultant is worth their weight in gold. Well, given that many consultants help organizations to become 'leaner and meaner' one might expect that consultants would not be carrying around too much excess weight – valuing them by their weight in gold might suggest somewhat circular reasoning! That aside, a consultant is someone who has expertise in an area and makes him or herself available to clients on the basis that the client believes that they themselves do not currently have aspects of expertise that would be relevant and useful to their objectives.

Anecdotally, I suggest that many organizations, and individuals, get value from consultancy services. The small company experiencing rapid growth employs a management consultant to help them restructure their business process so that they can upsize in response to their new found territory. The large multi-national company, struggling to compete against an increasing number of 'niche players' picking off the profitable segments of their market, employs a team of consultants to help them down-size and re-structure to a more flexible operation. The family who suddenly find themselves having to deal with a railway company, that wishes to run a new line through the family's manicured garden, employs a consultant to advise them and act as their agent. These are examples of how a person or an organization might use the services of a consultant. The temperament and modus operandi of the consultant may vary – say from traditional 'leave it with me' to a more collaborative and two-way-consultative approach. The core service is, however, that the consultant has made herself appropriately familiar or expert in the relevant areas. The client has not had time or may not have the inclination to go back to college and make themselves expert – so they seek out the consultant for the job in hand.

In terms of fish, does a consultant feed a man? If so, is it for a day or for life? He might do – and perhaps for a bit of both. Or, he might establish how to fish a particular river. A consultant might examine the river, do research into various fishing options and produce a report, with recommendations, on what the man might do next including cost benefit analyses on various fishing options (subject to the terms of reference in the consulting contract). The consultant may or may not factor in the sustainability of fishing in that river. He may or may not seek to explore other alternatives to fishing.

In availing of a consultancy service, the man may not have been challenged to discover how to establish these things for himself and this may or may not be what he wanted. It may or may not be in his longer term interests to be challenged in this way – who is to know and when? Perhaps a 'consultancy consultant' could be employed to do a detailed analysis of the consultancy services received and put forward a recommendation!

A coach does not need to be a consultant but it would probably be of great value to the interested public if the coach knew enough about consulting to differentiate coaching from consulting.

Personal growth coaching is not consulting. This is not to say that a coach could not act as a consultant. However, I have found that many coaches aim to work, as coaches, in areas familiar to them. This might be a parent of grown-up children presenting herself as a parenting coach. It might be the career-change managing director who wants to coach people in the business world. If these coaches are on a journey of genuine personal growth, I believe they will come to see that their motivations for doing so, and their understanding of the boundary between what they *say* they are offering in coaching and what they end up *delivering,* have been less clearly defined then they would like things to be if the tables were turned.

On the journey to being a personal growth coach, an aspirant will usually reach the limit of their capacity to help a client 'un-pack' their thinking. At that point, the coach will replace that process with another. For many, that other process is consultancy.

> *On the journey to being a personal growth coach,*
> *an aspirant will usually reach the limit of their capacity*
> *to help a client 'un-pack' their thinking.*
> *At that point, the coach will replace that process with another.*
> *For many, that other process is consultancy.*

Consultancy itself is a very valuable tool. However, this switchover is done often without the coach realizing it and just as often without the client realizing it. The agenda has changed and neither party has flagged or named it. Once the option to switch over in this way is reserved by the coach, the whole relationship and the coaching work done before and after it, changes in its personality. This may or may not be a good thing.

How you measure what is good and bad in this situation is notoriously difficult. One thing is reasonably measurable however – whether or not the coach and client are aware of the switch over.

Another matrix...

### The MUNCC Matrix

|  | Coaching Meeting | |
|---|---|---|
| **Named** | **Consulting Named.** Revised agenda. Collusion possible. | **Coaching Named.** Main agenda. Rarely needed after contracting. |
| **Un-named** | **Consulting Un-named** Outside of agenda. Collusion likely. | **Coaching un-named.** Main agenda. Reasonable expectation. |
|  | Consulting | Coaching |

The MUNCC matrix can help identify some of the dynamics of a coaching meeting. (**M**eeting, **U**n-named, **N**amed, **C**oaching, **C**onsulting).

In the upper-right-quadrant of the matrix, the URQ, you might have an acknowledgement of the fact that the coach is responding as a coach. An example of this might be when a client asks the coach for advice and the coach responds with a question like:

*'If I gave it to you, what value would that be to you?' The client then, perhaps jokingly, 'names' the coaching with a response such as: 'I should have known you would answer me with a question – typical coach!'*

In the lower right quadrant, the LRQ, the coaching hasn't been named. However, in this context it is assumed that the meeting is a coaching one and the coach is simply operating out of that contract. The degree to which the coach is sticking to the client's agenda, in terms of content, is a separate issue - they are still operating out of a coaching approach rather than a consulting approach. This is probably the normal mode of coaching. Both parties have contracted to coaching, neither needs reminding that this is so and this is what is happening.

The ULQ, upper left quadrant, is one not uncommon in coaching. Encountering the need to operate within it is usually an indication that the coach has come to the edge of their comfort zone in coaching. In this case, the client has asked for advice, information or guidance and the coach has responded with advice, information or guidance. They have, however, named that that is what they are doing and that, in doing so, they are not coaching at that moment. Sometimes a coach will literally gesture that they are swapping hats in front of the client. The degree to which this course of action is an expression of the coach's limitation as a coach, and the degree to which the coach sees this accurately, are separate issues and worth exploring perhaps with their own coach or Peer Consulting Group – 'PCG'.

Finally the LLQ, lower left quadrant, is the trickiest one. This is where the client has asked for advice (or even didn't ask), the coach offered it and did not name or flag that this is what they had done. In this case, and again assuming that the coaching service was sold to the client as a service designed to help the client find their own answers and surface any limiting beliefs etc., the coach has changed hats and has not noticed it or has not noticed the significance of doing it within such a contracted meeting. (I accept that, on occasion, a coach may choose to defer naming it for a short while and for a constructive reason). If the client is to be helped be true to themselves, then the coaching process needs to be true to itself and it is the coach's responsibility to 'keep it clean'. They do that by naming any potential discrepancies just as an airplane's navigation system checks continually to ensure that the vessel maintains the right bearing. Not doing so might have the plane approach the wrong destination!

Personal Growth Coaching is not consulting. However...

1. A coach might act as a consultant to a small or large degree.
2. This may or may not be within the terms of the contract/the coach's job description.

3. A client or coach may employ the services of a 'personal growth coaching consultant' – someone who is expert in the area of personal growth coaching and be in a position to advise on the subject – e.g. the selection and assessment of coaches in the case of clients, or 'how to do it better' in the case of coaches.

4. A consultant's modus operandi may support their clients' personal growth.

**Mentoring.**

It is difficult to see how life would exist without mentoring – even if the word was never used.

I believe the terms 'coach' and 'mentor' are often used interchangeably or, at least in the eyes of observers, are not always distinguished from each other with great clarity. I believe it is worth making that distinction.

A mentor could be described as someone who is familiar with some of the specific challenges of the mentee and has a greater degree of experience and expertise in those areas but, unlike a consultant, a mentor tends to be an 'insider' – they could be a parent, a more senior employee or an older youth club volunteer. The mentor might not be familiar with the technical nature of the mentee's challenges but be very experienced in the culture or politics of the environment in which the mentee operates. Usually, but not always, the mentor has little direct influence over the mentee's path – e.g. promotion recommendations.

Mentors would tend to have a lot of advice to offer. Mentors may use some coaching as they provide mentoring. A mentor will tend to be already acculturated into the organization/family/group – by the same token, they are likely to have similar blind spots. Mentors tend not to write reports but they may give feedback to the mentee. A mentor may or may not be referred to as a mentor – parents, for example, mentor their children regularly but are usually not referred to as 'my mentor'.

A mentor won't give a man a fish but can tell him who to go to about it, in what order, and how many copies of the fish order form should be submitted!

It is not uncommon for a line manager in an organization to have, as part of their job description, a responsibility for 'mentoring' the members of their team. This may be loosely described with little or no structure to it. Alternatively, mentoring could be a carefully recorded management deliverable with regular reviews and measurable milestones. The degree to which this structure and delivery of mentoring will enhance the effectiveness of the team, or contribute to the personal growth of any or all is, in my opinion, a function of many variables. I do not believe it is safe to assume that a large 'volume' of a certain type of activity, identified by management to constitute 'mentoring', necessarily equates to progress. Having said that, I believe that a well designed mentoring programme can be of significant benefit to an organization – or even a family! Good mentoring programmes can accelerate the learning and adjustment of new staff and those ripe for advancement.

A common approach to structured mentoring is to provide it through the use of a suitably experienced individual *who is not acting as line-manager* to their mentee. The thinking behind this is that the day-to-day demands of the line delivery too often take precedence over the mentoring activity. Another reason has to do with power.

Try this:

## The 'PACE' Matrix

Environment

| Advice/Info Giving | | |
|---|---|---|
| Low/None | **Low advice, High power** (E.g. In-line coaching) | **Low advice, Low power** (E.g. LOGOSE® Coaching,) |
| High | **High advice, High power** (E.g. apprenticeship manager) | **High advice, Low power** (E.g. consulting, possibly 'off-line' mentoring) |

High      Power over outcomes      Low/None
(Coach/Mentor's Power)

## Aiming for the Pinnacle

This, the PACE matrix, **P**ower **A**dvice **C**oaching **E**nvironment, helps discern the vocabulary from a couple of the essential elements.

In general a mentor does not necessarily need to have technical expertise in the area in which the mentee is operating. Mary, a finance executive, could act as a mentor for Joe, an up-and-coming IT project manager. Mary's expertise is in how the organization works. The assumption is that Mary's understanding of how the organization works is of value to Joe and should assist him in his job – even if they never discuss any IT technical problems and solutions. Mary might help Joe approach the training & development department in order to enhance the technical skills of his team. Alternatively, she might be able to give him advice on how to obtain funding for new hardware for his section.

Let's assume that Mary has no power over Joe's promotion/job prospects within the company – she has no power over Joe's ability to keep or increase his power. With in-house mentoring, this may or may not be the case of course – Mary may play squash every week with Stewart, the IT executive down the corridor from her office - Joe's boss, or boss's boss, and there is no guarantee of a 'firewall' between Mary and Stewart. Let's also assume that Joe *believes* that Mary has no power over his path in the company – other than the value of her mentoring. In this case, the relationship could fall into the LRQ of the PACE Matrix. Mary gives Joe lots of advice but has no power over him. Mary is seen as a more senior figure in the organization whose wisdom is worth hearing. Mary may use a coaching approach to how she relates to Joe but the core of the relationship is about her greater knowledge and understanding of the cogs of the organization and how they work. There may even be a parent/child-like element to the relationship. This could be conscious or unconscious to either or both.

In my experience, in-house mentors are rarely devoid of power over their mentees – consciously or unconsciously. Mentees might accurately believe that, in certain circumstances, mentors will put there own opinions into the advancement decision making pot, but the mentee may be in denial about this belief. This denial is usually related to their dependences on, and perception of, the organization – the most common is a dependence on being 'loyal' to the employer organization in some way. This then clouds the relationship. The clouding may or may not serve the conscious objectives of the organization but it is likely to be part of its culture. An effective personal growth coach will help a client to: (1) discern any such dependences, (2) evaluate their costs & benefits and (3) consider options for informed choices.

You could of course have the word 'mentoring' being used in the context of the line manager's job description and this could be defined in a way that might be called 'coaching' in another organization. In this case, the manager who is coaching or mentoring has high power and is low on advice - except when they are 'instructing' the staff member to do something a certain way – as part of the line-manager's other duties.

As you can see, I am suggesting that, in real life, the vocabulary used can vary. However, it is of great value to understand the essence of the different relationship environments – particularly if one is aiming for personal growth.


**Training.**

Another word that can make itself comfortable in the nest of terms associated with coaching is 'training'.

Again, in asking people how they might interpret the word 'training', I believe there is more than a little consistency. People think of training as related to a skill or job. The trainer may or may not be very accomplished in the skill or job but will usually have gotten a minimum of experience in order to do justice to the training. Hopefully, however, the trainer will be quite skilled in the job of training itself.

A skilled trainer will be able to make effective use of delivery modes such as demonstration, exercises and presentations in their provision of training. Whatever mode they might be using at a given time, most experienced trainers, I suggest, make use of well-timed coaching interventions to augment the training. The job at hand, training in the particular skill, will take precedence over any personal growth breakthroughs that might otherwise have presented themselves. Training in people skills, however, often provides for some level of personal growth. A trainer in personal growth coaching for example, would need to have skill, often subtle to the trainees – even appearing counter-productive at times, in eliciting new levels of personal consciousness and facilitating its integration. A trainer in simple skills-based coaching may not need such elicitation and facilitation skills.

A useful way of looking at training is in terms of the STATS matrix....

## The 'STATS' Matrix

|  | Training Skill Low | Training Skill High |
|---|---|---|
| **Subject Accomplishment High** | Subject Skill High<br>Training Skill Low<br>Some learn much | Subject Skill High<br>Training Skill High<br>Many learn much |
| **Subject Accomplishment Low** | Subject Skill Low<br>Training Skill Low<br>Few learn much | Subject Skill Low<br>Training Skill High<br>Many learn some |

The **S**ubject **T**raining **A**ccomplishment **T**raining **S**kill matrix, the 'STATS' matrix shows the two dimensions.

Looking at the STATS matrix, we can see that the ideal training situation is where the trainer is both accomplished in the subject of the training and skilled in the business of training. I have seen situations where people have completed a training course in coaching and been immediately recruited to deliver the same training course to a new group of trainees. The novice coach may or may not be skilled at the delivery of training. In these circumstances, you might have many in the new class learning some but few in the class learning a lot – in the case of a trainer who either has a natural talent in training and/or has done effective training in training.

Of course, if the trainer has limited experience in coaching *and* limited ability to deliver training, none of the trainees may get much out of the training. They might enjoy the course. They might even provide good evaluations but they run the risk of not knowing what they don't know –

with implications for when they approach the market or delivery point. I have also seen excellent coaches try to apply themselves to training with little understanding of training as a discipline. In this situation, certain people within the class, with certain learning styles and levels of maturity, will pick up a lot from the coach-trainer but others will take longer and may even feel left behind for a while. Coaching however does have an inbuilt mechanism to help identify the needs of the learners. A plasterer, with great skill in plastering but little skill in training, may not have the same advantage.

Sometimes we see the 'Sit-by-Nellie' approach to training in the business world. A new entrant sits beside their trainer as the trainer actually does the job and, hopefully, will learn how to do the job – as Nellie does it – for better or for worse.

In business, and elsewhere, a common complaint is that staff sent on training courses are often not in a position to apply what they learned to the new job at hand when they return to the work-place. The tight demands of a production or service unit, dealing with unforeseen sick-leave or technical breakdowns often just cannot afford to put the trainee into a position to take advantage of the new training. In fact, the trainee may have to deal with the back-log of work left behind for them as a result of their being away on the training course!

As in most areas of life, you 'use it or you lose it'. New learning not consolidated with on-the-job practice has a comet's tail – and a short one at that. It could be a while before it comes around again, if ever. Of course, if the trainee's mindset is proactive they may well make sure they get an opportunity to consolidate the learning when back at the job. However, even the most proactive has the same number of hours in the day as anyone else and, workaholics apart, will likely want to spend some time with their family!

And the fishing metaphor? I suggest, tongue-in-cheek, that a trainer will carefully take the man through the steps of fishing just before he gets transferred to the poultry division!

The movie 'The Guardian' (2006), starring Kevin Costner and Ashton Kutcher, contains some interesting angles on training.

**Counseling and Psychotherapy.**

Many years ago, during a time when I was training in psychotherapy, I attended an open-evening arranged by a healing centre in Dublin, Ireland. A member of the audience enquired as to the difference between counseling and psychotherapy. My now abbreviated version of the answer then offered is that "psychotherapy went 'deeper' than counseling."

Way back then, the latent coach in me wanted to ask what exactly was meant by 'deeper'. Somehow, I didn't seem to want to ask that obvious question and, as far as I can remember, no-one asked it on the night. With hindsight and a certain amount of honing of my perceptual antennae in the intervening years, I believe that there was a 'sub-surface' anxiety within the group that this statement might turn out to be somewhat simplistic and that, if that was so, many in the room might have to review their perception of counseling and psychotherapy. Perhaps, more significantly, they might be required to review their perception of themselves within the context. I suspect, given the literature issued on the night, and the general conversation, that those involved in the centre thought of themselves as at the deeper end of the implied continuum. The question I would be inclined to ask now, with the thinking of a coach, is not so much, where are we on the continuum? but first, what if the continuum, as it was seen, is an illusion in the first place?

In the intervening years, I have not really satisfied myself that there is a reliable distinction between counseling and psychotherapy. There are people describing their work as 'deeper'. I haven't heard any practitioner yet describe their work as 'shallower' although I have heard some describe others' work as 'more surface'. However, I still haven't seen a reliable pattern – none that would invite me to suggest to a member of the public that a service with one label 'works deeper' than the other. Explaining what 'deeper' means in the context would of course be another matter.

From *a consumer's point of view*, I believe that there are a number of key aspects of the counseling and psychotherapy marketplace worth noting:

1. As suggested above, the terms 'counseling' and 'psychotherapy' do not offer reliable labels to discern two different service offerings. They might be reliable terms to an experienced practitioner in assessing other practitioners, using their chosen criteria, but I do not believe the man or woman in the street can use the terms reliably in searching out a practitioner.

2. The term 'deeper' is sometimes used by practitioners. It would be of value to a consumer to clarify what a given practitioner means by the term – both in terms of the process of the work and the results.

3. There are different models, or modalities, of 'therapy'. Therapy is a term I will use in the context of this book to describe any form of 'talking cure' and, as I do not include coaching as a healthcare service, I exclude coaching as such a cure.

4. Not all practitioners, who have trained in a given modality, will deliver their service in an identical way.

5. Some practitioners describe themselves as 'eclectic' meaning that they draw on several modalities in their work. In my experience, few therapists describing themselves as eclectic have received professional training in all the modalities they claim to use. This may or may not influence the value of their service.

6. Many professional bodies in the therapy market have a mandatory or non-mandatory requirement of therapists to attend 'supervision'. This involves meetings with a more experienced practitioner, usually working from the same modality as the therapist. The meetings are specifically for the purpose of helping the therapist reflect on how they are working with their clients. Frequency of supervision meetings is often determined by the number of client sessions the therapist is doing.

7. In addition to a supervisor, a therapist will often attend their own therapist. Sometimes an 'issue' arising in supervision will be 'processed' in the therapist's own therapy. Both of these supports are designed to add value to the client work.

I will be briefly looking at some of the more common modalities and will attempt to unpack the differences between them – again from a consumer's perspective. However, before doing this I would like to suggest that all modalities have two main features. The first I would call the cognitive element and the other is the emotional element. I accept that there are those who will suggest that there is also the 'spiritual' element and I not sure that I would be inclined to disagree with them – especially if we could find common ground on what 'spiritual' means. However, for the moment, I would like to suggest that the cognitive and the emotional can be seen as the hammer and chisel of therapy (delicate and sensitive ones I might add) and the spiritual, amongst other things, represents the material and its characteristics in a given context.

In looking at an approach to therapy, and/or perhaps more productively, at a particular therapist's way of working, I believe it can be useful to examine at it in terms of the TECI matrix – see below. I believe there will be therapists who will say that insight isn't the objective of therapy, and that simply being 'in the process' is of value in itself, but even the notion of something being of value in itself is an example of an insight. It might appear as a simple 'eureka' experience, with a feeling of mild contentment, or it might appear in the context of a painful emotional breakthrough. Either way, it is an insight that will effect how the insightee sees their world – if only for a while.

## The 'TECI' Matrix

Therapy (any modality)

| Cognitive Insight | Low Emotional Insight | High Emotional Insight |
|---|---|---|
| **High** | **Cognitive Insight** Useful but incomplete 'Heady' or 'disconnected' | **Cognitive & Emotional Insight** 'Integrative' |
| **Low** | **Neither Cognitive nor Emotional Insight** Waste of time or abusive. 'Blind leading the blind.' | **Emotional Insight** Useful but incomplete Unreasonable? comfortable discomfort? |

TECI Matrix - **T**herapy **E**motional and **C**ognitive **I**nsight matrix.

In the LLQ – the lower left quadrant – the client is gaining neither cognitive insight nor emotionally insight. The 'talk' is neither cognitively grounded nor emotional liberating. There may be complex talk in it but the talk is fantasy-based and founded on ideas or believes that have little or no grounding. A discussion about the imminent alien invasion from outer space, when there is no reliable evidence of such an invasion, is an example. There might be complex discussion about hyper-drive propulsion systems and photon torpedoes and it might sound very intelligent but the underlying beliefs have yet to be accurately tested and agreed as grounded or not.

Equally in the LLQ, there is no emotional insight. The work is not leading to the client facing emotions in a way that would free them up to engage with reality more resiliently. There may be emotional experiences and expressions but they are circular and often self-perpetuating. Any 'deep' emotions experienced by the client, fear and apprehension for example, are most likely generated by their perception of the situation – 'the aliens are coming.' There is also the possibility that the emotions are 'comfortable discomfort zones' – they might appear to the therapist to be the expression of healing emotion but they are, in fact, a way of avoiding other emotions. More often, in this case, there is no real emotional engagement and cognitive engagement is of flawed integrity. In certain circumstances this type of engagement might be a precursor to insightful therapy – it might form part of a rapport building process. However, if this is so, it is important that it is named as such and not mistaken for actual therapeutic work.

Moving to the ULQ, we see that the engagement is leading to cognitive insight. This could be, for example, *'I realise that, when we get onto the subject of my boss, I feel disconnected – like I am not in touch with my feelings.'* The client can see something that is happening and, so far anyway, it seems like a fairly grounded insight. They might go a step further and say that they wished that they could connect with their feelings around their boss. Another example might be *'Ah. I see that this business of the alien invasion is a load of rubbish. How could I have been so blind?'* In a case like this, the client might have already been getting emotional insight previously and just needed the final penny to drop. Alternatively, they may simply let go of one fantasy in favor of another – *"No aliens coming – but those giant spiders are about to appear from under the ground."*

In the lower right quadrant, the LRQ, the client obtains genuine emotional insight. They 'discover' how they really feel about something. There is no real emphasis on reality other than accessing emotions that may have been avoided up to that point – those emotions are seen as the relevant reality. The client might start a session discussing her father and be quite matter of fact about how he used to use physical violence on her and her siblings when they were growing up.

As the therapy progresses, the client finds herself becoming angry about her fathers actions and realizes that she was terrified, as a little girl, that she would be rejected by her father. The emotional insights are as a result of accessing the emotions themselves – complete with fast breathing, changes in body language and facial and tonal expression. Later, within the therapy, or on reflection afterwards, she may ruminate on the situation and settle on a new cognitive understanding of her relationship with her father – this could be described as a new cognitive insight that she allowed herself after she had 'processed' the emotional content.

The key here is the accessing of emotions as distinct from the challenging of perceptions. If, for example, the client's father had died when she was a baby and there had been no mention of a step-father, the therapist might be tempted to challenge the discrepancy. This would be working on the cognitive side of the equation.

However, the therapist might be fully aware of this discrepancy but also notice that the client is moving into an emotional state as she told the inconsistent story. The therapist might ignore the inconsistency and encourage the client to allow the feelings to be accessed. Afterwards, the therapist might reflect back to the client any inconsistencies he thinks he sees and thus challenge the client towards a new cognitive insight.

Combining these two can take the client to a point of 'integration'. They see things, like the childhood violence, from new perspectives. They might move to a position of forgiveness or they might discover that they were imagining the violence and, somehow, that that imagining took them in and out of emotional territory they had not yet colonized or at least had hitherto avoided.

The general idea is that by wrestling with the emotions, irrespective of the groundedness of the perceptions, it will be a move forward. In theory, this process leads to a development of the client's emotional intelligence and this, in turn, allows them to see themselves and their environment with a higher degree of groundedness and resilience. The emotional insight comes first and makes way for a cognitive insight.

Of course, this type of untrammeled emotional work can lead to retrospective imaginings on the part of the client and may be the basis for 'False Memory Syndrome' when it exists.

False Memory Syndrome is a term sometimes used to describe situations where, for example, a therapy client claims to remember being abused as a child but the alleged perpetrators claim otherwise. As to who is presenting the truth of the matter, this is not known.

## Mind & Body.

Another dimension worth exploring, in the world of therapy, is the debate around the origins of the human condition and its 'dysfunctions'. It is a debate that also has relevance to coaching. Therapy has its roots in the medical profession or at least it sprouted out of adjacent soil. It was offered, originally, as a talking cure and as an alternative to a medical approach to mental illness.

A long-term debate has run along side the development of therapy over the years. The debate centers on the nature of what was being called 'mental illness' and the most appropriate remedy for such illness.

A key underlying principle behind any from of therapy is that the illness, or dysfunction, is, at least partly, as a result of psychological functioning of a certain kind that can be treated in such a way that the illness or dysfunction can be 'cured'.

In my experience, I have found that different therapists have different beliefs around the issue of the mind-body connection.

Firstly, I propose looking at the issue with the aid of the 'COD Matrix.'

## The 'COD' Matrix
Cause of Dysfunction (Perceived)

|  | **Psychological** No | **Psychological** Yes |
|---|---|---|
| **Physiological** Yes | **Purely Physiological** e.g. Brain-Damage alone | **Combination of Physiological & Psychological** |
| **Physiological** No | **Neither Physiological nor Psychological** | **Purely Psychological** e.g. Post-traumatic Stress |

The ULQ of the matrix might contain such things as Brain Damage, either congenital, or acquired through accident or illness. Depending on a therapist's views on what does and does not constitute 'dysfunction', they might slot different conditions into this quadrant. Some might say that brain-damage is a condition that cannot be helped with their particular mode of therapy. On the other hand, a speech therapist might be confident to work with someone with brain damage.

A common issue in coaching is motivation. Clients often work with a coach to, amongst other things, get themselves more motivated. Sometimes, they describe a certain sluggishness to their life in a way that might come close to what some medical professionals might categorize as 'sub-clinical depression'. Depression, of course, is a condition that therapy is commonly seen to treat – successfully or not. A therapist's approach to depression is generally that its root cause is psychological – that unearthing buried emotions will cure the depression.

I have encountered considerable credible evidence that accessing emotional states of a certain kind can alleviate the symptoms of depression – at least temporarily – and leave a person more motivated and alive. I have also encountered stories of people who have attended years of therapy and found no significant change in their struggle with depression. The reason they stuck at the therapy was because they hoped it eventually would make a difference.

If therapy doesn't work for a given condition what explanations might suggest themselves?

- The cause was physiological and would never be cured by therapy?

- The therapy was not delivered correctly?

- The therapy was delivered 'correctly' but just didn't work?

Of course the other issue sometimes raised relates to when the client/patient does seem to shed their condition – be it depression or otherwise. The question sometimes posed here is *was it the therapy that provided the cure?* or would the condition have cleared up anyway in the absence of therapy – 'spontaneous remission', as the medics might say. These are questions more related to therapy than coaching but I believe they are worth some thought.

Another layer of the body-mind analysis is the degree to which the therapist 'gets it right' in their discernment of the causes of a condition and therefore its relevance to therapy.

## The 'DOC' Matrix

Discernment of Causes

|  | Physiological (Actual) | Psychological (Actual) |
|---|---|---|
| **Perceived: Psychological** | Physiological mistaken for Psychological ('Interminable Therapy') | Accurately perceived as Psychological (Best fit for talking cure. E.g. Post-traumatic stress.) |
| **Perceived: Physiological** | Accurately perceived as Physiological (Effective pharmacological or alternative physical therapy) | Psychological mistaken for Physiological ('One Flew Over the Cuckoo's Nest') |

If the therapist 'gets it wrong', they could end up either working with a client beyond the useful life of the therapy or could infer to the client that the condition cannot be cured by therapy and would, for example, need medication administered by a psychiatrist. If they get it right, they will presumably find themselves either working effectively with the client or saving them the time and expense of therapy that has no possibility of success.

I have already alluded to the possibility of a client attending therapy without any value to them. The other side of this coin is when a person's condition is treated with medication when it could be cured through a talking cure. Jack Nicholson, in the 1975 movie 'One Flew Over the Cuckoo's Nest', comes to mind when I consider this quadrant. The lines between sanity and insanity, of the inmates and of the staff of the asylum, were cleverly blurred in the screenplay. Of course, the movie also takes us into the realms of environment and power. These are highly relevant to personal growth.

The key question here is how does a therapist make this discernment? It is not within the scope of this book to deal with this question but is this not a question somewhat relevant to coaching?

**Therapy Modalities.**

As I mentioned above, I am using the term 'therapy' as a broad term to include counseling and psychotherapy – the talking cures. Any therapy will presumably involve a way of engaging with someone that is somewhat out of the ordinary – otherwise the client would already be experiencing it in their ordinary life and there would be no point in paying for it. This 'extra-ordinary' way of engaging can come in many forms or modalities – therapy is not a generic commodity. Even within one modality, you can have differences depending on the experience and the temperament of the therapist as well as the way in which a particular client might act and respond to them. However, even in the context of different temperaments amongst therapists, I do believe it is of value to consumers, and coaches, to be somewhat familiar with the different modalities and to be able to discern the differences and similarities they might have with coaching.

## Psychoanalysis – The Freudian Slipstream.

The old joke goes as follows: 'A Freudian Slip is when you mean to say one thing and you end up saying *amother*'.

**Sigmund Freud** (Austria, 1859-1939) 'invented' psychoanalysis and the 'psychoanalytic hour' – actually a fifty-minute hour. He developed his ideas towards the end of the nineteenth century and rolled them out to the scientific community, to Vienna and to the world, as the twentieth century got under way.

Freud confronted existing sensibilities by claiming that conditions such as hysteria existed as a result of unresolved unconscious feelings and conflicts. He suggested a range of explanations mostly related to patients' relationships with their mother and/or father and proposed certain common dynamics such as 'Penis-envy' and the famous 'Oedipus Complex.' His approach is sometimes referred to as 'psychodynamic'. In practice, Freud used techniques such as dream interpretation and word association to explore repressed emotions and conflicts. He also interpreted the patient's resistance, to his interpretations for example, as well as their 'transferences', as a way to help patients free up psychological energy for better quality relationships.

Transference, in this context, meant the feelings that clients had about the analyst. Freud suggested these were really expressions of feelings for a parental figure, or other, repressed at an earlier age. He also proposed the concept of counter-transference – this is where the analyst transferred his or her repressed feelings on to the patient.

Psychoanalysis often comprised several fifty-minute meetings per week with the analyst over several years. The client, referred to as the 'patient', reminiscent of the approach's original association with the medical profession, or the 'analysand', usually lies on the couch and the analyst, often taking notes, listens to whatever the client expresses. Periodically, the analyst offers an interpretation such as:

"*You see your recurring dream of cutting down ze large oak tree in your parents' garden tells us of your overwhelming jealousy of your fawzer – that you repressed when you were a small boy – as well as your desire to kill your fawzer and have your mohzer to yourself.*"

Not all psycho-analysts have Austrian accent!

Freud's psychoanalytic theories generated more than a little debate when they were first released and still do to this day. A common criticism is that the approach is not scientific enough – too subjective. Another is that its emphasis on sex, particularly as a powerful drive influencing almost everything we do, is exaggerated. Longitudinal research over the years seems to have produced inconsistent findings as to the results and value of psychoanalysis.

The other big name that comes to mind, when I think of psychoanalysis, is non other than Woody Allen. Allen was once asked if he thought sex was dirty to which he replied: *'Yes, if done properly!'.* I wonder was this comment made before, during, or after a stint in therapy!

### *Jungian Analysis – Pastoral Dissention.*

**Carl Jung** (Switzerland, 1875-1961) was a contemporary of Freud's and for a time was one of the Austrian's disciples. However, with a passion for spirituality not shared by Freud, Jung broke away and developed what he called 'Analytic Psychology' and 'Psycho-analytic Therapy'. The latter also came to be known as 'Jungian Analysis.' Jung saw *meaning* as a key component of the human psyche and that the analyst should ideally avoid putting anything into the work that is not of the patient's. Freud's interjections with sexual explanations of patients' inner conflicts were unacceptable to Jung. Jung believed these to be more about Freud than the patient. Jung went his separate way, convened a following of his own and left a legacy comparable to that of his erstwhile Austrian master.

Jung stressed such concepts as the individual unconscious and the collective unconscious – the latter being a realm of consciousness accessible to all. He also propounded the existence of 'archetypes' within the unconscious. Archetypes are our own personal versions of aspects of the psyche that we share with all of humanity but which we have a tendency to avoid or disown at the expense of our wholeness. Therapy involves, amongst other things, exploring our inner world and wrestling with these archetypes if necessary. The most significant archetype is probably 'The Shadow'. This is a catchall realm containing the aspects of ourselves we would rather not admit to and yet, in confronting the dragons and demons of this disturbing wilderness, we can find the freedom to be ourselves.

Jung was wary of Freud's reliance on diagnosis and prognosis and believed that the analyst should approach work with patients with humility and without pre-suppositions or judgments. He also suggested that it was impossible for the analyst to be totally objective but that knowing this was at least some help. In common with Freud, Jung felt strongly that a key part of an analyst's training was their own self exploration and, to Jung, this included the integration of their shadow. He likened it to a doctor ensuring that he was free from infection before performing surgery. The other main archetype is the Anima (male) or Animus (female). This archetype, Jung suggests, represents our true self as well as our connection to the collective unconscious. This concept takes us back to Shakespeare's Polonius advising his son to *'thine own self be true'*.

Jung took psychoanalysis into areas resisted by Freud. I often wonder did anyone serve as analyst to Freud and explore with him his resistance to Jung!

Freud's work, whilst the subject of much debate, garnered considerable credibility from early on. His 'science' was seen by many as highly authorative and there were those who took it on with religious fervor. The same could be said about Jung's teachings and yet, on some aspects, the two men were diametrically opposed – God being one. This divergence of opinion between the two, deservedly or not considered giants of credibility in their time, is itself a lesson in humility for any coach. A model of understanding of the human psyche can be powerfully compelling – we need to beware of our potential dependence on making it the whole truth.

### *Cognitive Behavioral Therapy – Dogs to Doctorates.*

Whilst Psychoanalysis and Psycho-analytic Therapy fall into one class of psychotherapy, Cognitive Behavioral Therapy, CBT, is a second class of its own with an approach quite different to the psycho-dynamic models.

Not always quoted as part of its history, I tend to associate the origins of CBT with Pavlov and his dogs as well as Skinner and his rats. Around the same time as Freud was molding his Oedipus complex, his Electra complex, his Id, Ego and Super-ego, **Ivan Pavlov** (Russia 1849-1936), a Russian priest turned scientist, was feeding dogs and ringing bells. Initially, Pavlov noticed that his dogs would salivate when they saw a man in a white coat approaching them. The reason for this, he concluded, was that, as the dogs had been habitually fed by men in white coats, the dogs' automatic response to seeing a man in a white coat, even when he had no food for the dogs, was to salivate. Pavlov experimented with other stimuli, most famously by ringing a bell at feeding time and found consistent results. He termed as 'unconditioned' responses the inbuilt responses, such as salivating when given food. The learned responses, such as to the bell or the white coat, he termed 'conditioned' responses.

Burrhus **Frederic Skinner** (USA, 1904-1990) came a little after Pavlov and achieved a doctorate in psychology in Harvard in the 1930s. His work suggested that organisms 'operate' on their environment and learn behavior based on what happens in response to their actions. He called this 'operant conditioning', a term for which he is probably best known. Skinner worked extensively with animals using 'reinforcement' to condition a range of behaviors – from rats pressing pedals to be fed, to teaching birds to bowl! He experimented with a variety of reinforcement patterns and wrote extensively on his findings.

The thrust of Pavlov's and Skinner's respective conclusions is that we build patterns of behavior as a result of the pleasurable and not so pleasurable experiences which we encounter as we motor along through life. The extrapolations of this are that we can change our behavior by engaging in new actions designed to replace the previous conditioning. The child who is afraid of dogs, as a result of previous experiences, can be helped to replace their cynophobia with more positive responses to dogs by gradually exposing them to pleasurable experiences with gentle dogs. The man who is afraid of his boss, because of his negative experiences of male authority figures in the past, learns to overcome his fear by working with a relatively non-threatening figure such as a male therapist.

The idea of conditioning was later introduced to a therapeutic intervention perhaps most notably by **Mary Jones** (USA 1897-1987). She spent her working career studying developmental stages and, whilst associated with a behavioral approach to therapy, in latter years took a more eclectic (multi-modal) perspective to the human condition.

The cognitive side of Cognitive-Behavioral-Therapy began to emerge in the 1950s and 1960s. Its proponents included therapists such **Aaron Beck** (USA, 1921- ). Beck was a psycho-dynamic analyst who took an interest in the internal dialogue that his patients seemed to invariably conduct and most of which they resisted revealing to him. He suggested that many emotional problems are the result of thinking patterns that are flawed or are based on 'dysfunctional assumptions.' Beck moved from the psycho-dynamic approach which theorized that problems could be solved by going 'back' to old repressed experiences, to a more 'in the moment' approach. He operated on the theory that emotional problems persist to the degree to which flawed thinking is sustained. Beck's approach would have a patient examine their assumptions and test them against reality. This testing usually includes 'homework'.

Another prominent name in the field of CBT is **Albert Ellis** (USA, 1913-) who developed an approach he called Rational Emotive Therapy (RET) latterly Rational Emotive Behavior Therapy (REBT). Ellis suggested looking at problems using the abbreviation 'ABC'. 'A' stood for the activating event in a situation. 'B' stood for the beliefs that a person has at the time of the event – especially their irrational or dysfunctional beliefs. Finally, 'C' stands for the consequences.

Similar to Beck, Ellis stressed the creation of emotional states through our distorted thinking. Ellis used expressions such as 'musturbatory thinking', describing an irrational belief that we 'have to' do something and 'awfulizing' describing the way in which we might blow something unpleasant into a debilitating and self-generated emotional state. He later added D & E to his ABC model. D stood for the process of 'disputing' the irrational beliefs and E the enjoyment of the positive effects of shedding such self-destructive patterns. Ellis recommends that we concentrate on identifying our self-destructive beliefs, replace them with more realistic ones and, all the while, aim to accept ourselves rather than measure and evaluate ourselves.

One more name I believe worthy of note in the field of CBT is **Alfred Adler** (Austria 1870-1937). Whilst spending some time in Freud's 'circle', like Jung, Adler also broke away from the Freudian approach and did not subscribe to Sigmund's emphasis on sex as a driving force in the human psyche. Some may argue that Adlerian Psychotherapy falls into a category of its own, or perhaps straddles more than one school, but I am comfortable that his approach has a strong cognitive element and is also action-oriented in a way that is not generally found in the psycho-dynamic arena.

Adler's approach would include a robust process of questioning to surface flawed thinking as would be found with Beck's and Ellis' system. In addition, Adler would include processes designed to facilitate emotional breakthroughs and reinforced new behaviour as well as the adoption of new, more socially conscious perspectives. Adler was interested in helping people reach the full potential of their functioning.

### *Humanistic Psychology – Pyramids to Potential.*

The Humanistic school of psychology, sometimes referred to as 'the third force' when considered in a psychotherapy context, psycho-dynamic and CBT being the other two, probably has its roots in classical philosophy. Its modern flourishing, however, is considered by many to have been sired by the renowned psychologist **Abraham Maslow** (USA 1908-1970).

Maslow had a passion for understanding what the peak of human potential might be and how that might be 'actualized' or, more precisely, to use his favored term, 'self-actualized'. He suggested that the route to self-actualization involves the understanding and attainment of certain hierarchically mounted needs.

This 'hierarchy of needs' is commonly presented in management or business training and educational programmes as a way of understanding employee or consumer behaviour. As I mentioned previously, I suggest that the stakeholders in such programmes will interpret the hierarchy in ways that will be influenced by each individuals own profile of met and unmet needs.

In brief, Maslow suggests that, as each layer of needs is met, the next one tends to kick in. For example, if I am close to starvation I might be inclined to take a risk to my security, I might be prepared to stalk a dangerous animal or climb a tall coconut tree. In these circumstances, I might not be too concerned about who loves me, who thinks I am great or how I can ensure that I register for a watercolors class.

Having established a reliable supply of food and drink, I might begin to think of how I can protect myself from danger. Once I have a secure environment, I might notice that I have a growing desire for some 'quality time' with my family. Once this social need has been met, Maslow suggests that a new need will kick in – recognition and esteem from my community. Finally, when I have gotten all my subsidiary needs met, I will find myself prompted by a drive to be 'all that I can be' – to work towards my self-actualization.

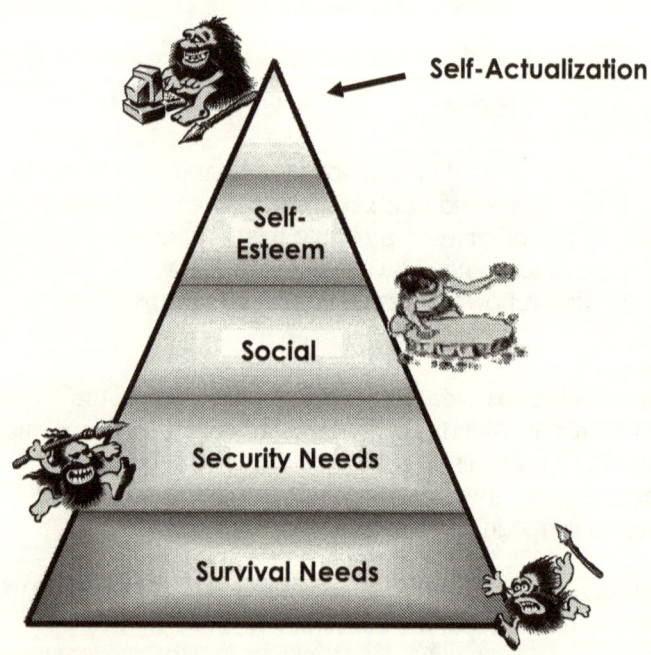

A representation of Maslow's hierarchy of needs.

Whilst the psychology arena and, perhaps more particularly, the psychotherapy profession, were traditionally concerned with illness and helping people to be 'normal', Maslow took an interest in the other end of the spectrum. He examined individuals who he judged to be at the high end of peak development and, whilst many argue that the criteria he chose to measure had to have been subjective, the qualities he cited included realistic perception of oneself and one's environment, creativity (in how one responds to life), detachment, sense of humor and a capacity to have peak experiences – not of the drug-induced type! He suggests that self-actualizing people approach life with an aliveness and openness to new perspectives. This contrasts with an approach to life on auto-pilot and conditioned responses, stereotyping and redundant categorization.

A key element of the whole humanistic school is *awareness*. In fact, the approach is often termed 'phenomenological'. This is a complex term but, in this context, it can be taken to mean that the subjective experiences of the individual are of value in themselves and do not necessarily fit into a scientific or rational analysis. The key to growth towards self-actualization lies in the uncovering, or surfacing, of feelings and thoughts – no matter how irrational or fantastical they might be. The theory is that, with time, those experiences teach us something about ourselves, about who we are and about what self-actualization might be *for us*. Humanistic psychology tends to resist categorizing people as normal, abnormal, sick, healthy, right, wrong, good, bad etc.

**Carl Rogers** (USA, 1902-1987) is probably the best known writer in the application of humanistic psychology to psycho-therapy in practice. His approach to therapy is often referred to as 'Client Centered Therapy' or 'Rogerian Therapy.' Rogers' work in training 'lay' people (non-psychiatrists) to work as therapist resulted in the adoption of the word 'counselor' in order to allay the concerns of the medical establishment at the time. Rogers put forward the idea that 'troubled' people will move towards resolution and self-actualization when certain core relationship conditions exist. He suggests that when a client is in relationship with a therapist who is real, caring and empathic that these conditions are sufficient to facilitate the client to new levels of self-discovery. Effectively, the therapy provides a 'safe-place' in which the client can allow themselves to be emotionally vulnerable and thus 'name' buried emotions – i.e. they allow themselves to feel emotions previously inaccessible for them or inaccessible for them in the context of certain issues. This in turn liberates the client to consider new interpretations of their environment, and their needs, thus freeing them up to move along the path to self-actualization.

If, for example, a child needs a sense of security before they can really feel loved, security might be a need that the adult therapy client needs to explore emotionally if they grew up feeling insecure and never had opportunities to 'process' the feeling. Therapy could assist them to discover the parts of themselves they 'cut-off' in order to survive or move on to the next stage whilst growing up. The need to be accepted by parents or peers can eclipse any lingering unaddressed security needs. The theory is that the optimal environment is one where children get to catch up on their daily experiences and gradually grow into the emotional challenges that these experiences bring with them. In that optimal environment, ongoing facilitation and support, by family or community members, provides children with the equivalent of therapy but in a flowing and natural way and without years of backlog and the resultant dysfunctional ways of getting needs met.

If this model of understanding is robust, it is interesting to consider how many of us grow up in such an optimal environment. A quick scan of the history of the human race suggests that a constant barrage of challenges and difficulties have to have left families with what must have been less that optimal conditions for the self-actualization of their members before their often relatively early demise. War, murder, famine, dangerous animals, disease, bereavement, tsunamis, earthquakes, volcanoes, slavery and oppression appear to be consistent bedfellows of humanity as far back as records show. Even in relatively good times, greed, fear of loss (of achieved lifestyles, whether ill-gotten or not), carelessness and engineering failures with loss of life, and a range of modern ailments, such as heart-disease, cancer and addictions, provide daily suggestions that life by no means guarantees optimal conditions for self-actualization.

The core relationship conditions, authenticity, caring and empathy, are key to Rogers' approach. The notion of being 'real' or 'authentic' or 'congruent' has shades of Polonius' advice to his son – '...to thine own self be true!' The idea is that the therapist is not playing any games with their role or putting up any type of façade. Rather than an 'expert' Freudian type sitting out of view of the client, who is lying on a couch, and the analyst providing authorative interpretations, a client-centered therapist will sit opposite their client face-to-face, on chairs of equal height (or for example bean-bags), and in a non-threatening way. Anything revealed by the client will be reflected back to the client uncontaminated by the therapist's theories as to what might be happening. With quality listening and objective reflection along with that subtle quality of emotional empathy, the client is given a relationship environment that allows for non-defensiveness and deeper self-acceptance.

Another name that appears in the realm of humanistic psychology is Frederick **'Fritz' Perls** (Germany, 1893-1970). Having trained with Freud, he also parted from the psychodynamic approach and he developed what he called 'Gestalt Therapy' – the German word 'Gestalt' signifying a kind of synergistic wholeness. The emphasis in Gestalt therapy is again realness and the present moment. It has much in common with Rogerian Therapy but will tend to be somewhat more structured, employing exercises designed to accelerate the client's engagement with themselves. Perls would stress the difference between talking about past experiences and being 'in' one's present moment experience. In Gestalt therapy the experience of the process is the key and not so much any conclusions that can later be interpreted - potentially interminably.

A further school of therapy, which I propose sits within the Humanistic domain, is 'Transactional Analysis' or 'TA'. Developed by **Eric Berne** (Canada 1910-1970), TA was another disillusioned deviation from psycho-analysis. In fact, Berne's outspoken views may well have contributed to his not being allowed to qualify as a psycho-analyst – the suggestion being that he needed a few more years' analysis before he was 'right'.

Again, Berne stressed the intrinsic value of people for who they are, ill or otherwise – 'I'm Okay You're Okay' being the title of one TA book. A key element of TA is the idea of the three 'ego-states' – Parent, Child and Adult. Berne's model suggests that people tend to play games in their relationships and often adopt a role of Parent or Child when the optimal relationship would be of Adult-Adult. A TA therapist would be trained to identify and confront 'transactions' that reflect more a power game than a genuine intimacy or equal collaboration. A friend withholding information relevant to you might indicate that they are behaving like a parent to you. You suspecting it but not facing it might suggest you are acting like a child. If you were aware of it and made a conscious decision not to confront it you might be behaving in a parent mode to them. A man or woman treating their spouse as if the spouse has an unrealistic responsibility to 'mind' them like a parent, rather than be an equal adult sexual partner, might be another example. Berne also proposed the notion of 'life-scripts.' These are patterns of behavior and perception accumulated through childhood experiences – problematic when they were heavily weighted towards survival and away from peaceful co-habitation or healthy inter-dependence. TA therapy would aim to identify these life-scripts and re-write new more constructive ones.

Another term closely associated with the humanistic psychology field is that of transpersonal psychology. This is a branch of psychology with a particular interest in 'non-ordinary states of consciousness' in which people experience a much deeper sense of who they are and their connectedness to...well everything...other people, nature, collective unconscious archetypes (as in Carl Jung above) and states of being often described as falling into the realm of spirituality. Transpersonal psychology has as its aim the exploration and understanding of these states of consciousness but does not propound any particular religious or spiritual set of beliefs. Whilst peak states and alternative realms of consciousness were of interest to Carl Jung, Abraham Maslow and others, I believe the work of **Stanislav Grof** (Czechoslovakia, 1931- ) presents a poignant example of this approach to therapy.

Stanislav Grof has spent much of his life researching the area of non-ordinary states of consciousness and has written extensively on the subject. In the early days, as a psychiatrist, he explored the use of psychedelic drugs in the treatment of severe mental illness. These were administered in facilitated 'sessions' as opposed to being prescribed as an ongoing control over symptoms. During these sessions, he found that patients entered into states of consciousness that allowed them to access powerful repressed emotions and he claims that this process provided a potent means for the healing of conditions hitherto considered treatable only with ongoing medication.

After LSD was banned in the sixties, Grof, having moved to the United States, explored non-drug based mechanisms for inducing similar states. His research into age-old processes practiced by tribal societies led to the development of what he termed 'Holotropic Breathwork' – Holotropic coming from the Greek words for 'wholeness' and 'towards.' Through a combination of fast paced deep breathing and rhythmic, percussion-dominant music, often 'tribal' in nature, in an environment of supportive facilitation, Grof found that patients were consistently accessing therapeutic altered states and claiming healing effects. Over time, more and more facilitators trained in the delivery of the breathwork and its use broadened to the treatment of milder conditions, addictions and has even been seen by some as a tool for accelerated self-actualization without the prompting of any particular ailment. The theory is that the altered state allows us to by-pass our normal selective perception of ourselves, the one that defends us from deeper insight into ourselves and reality.

By wrestling with the emotions and experiences that we encounter without the strait-jacket of our ego, we develop our ability to deal with deeper levels of reality on a day-to-day basis. An example might be Mary, in her early thirties, reasonably accomplished but now addicted to alcohol and prescription sedatives. In her Holotropic Breathwork sessions she encounters powerful emotions of deep grief that seem to relate to preverbal stages of her childhood. She describes the experience as discovering that when she was a baby she had a positive expectation of the world and the people in it but, at an early age, was traumatized when she encountered the dysfunctionality of the world that was unfolding around her. Repeated ventures into this difficult emotional area of her psyche allow her to chip away at the backlog and integrate more of her true feelings into her conscious world.

Grof presents considerable theoretical material around the origins of emotional problems. He suggests that the Freudian notion of exploring one's relationship with a parent is not a reliable or complete remedy to such problems. He suggests that much of who we are can be influenced by our experience of birth and offers theories under the heading of pre- and peri-natal psychology. Grof suggests, for example, that there are four stages in the birth process and that a complication or problem in one or more stages can lead to trauma and ongoing patterns of perception. In turn, if this trauma is not healed, with the nurturing of infancy and childhood, it can form a foundation for problems or health or psychological or behavioral tendencies later in life. The four Basic Peri-natal Matrices (BPMs), or stages, listed by Grof are:
(1) Pre-contraction, or 'amniotic bliss'. The fetus floats comfortably in the womb with a strong sense of connection to the collective unconscious.
(2) Contraction has begun but the cervix has not yet opened.
(3) The journey through the birth canal after the cervix has opened.
(4) The emergence into the outside world.

Grof theorizes that an experience during birth, that is emotionally overwhelming to the baby, will be 'cut-off' and, unless resolved, will generate what he calls a 'Coex' or collective-experience. This is effectively a pattern by which we tend to experience life in a way that mirrors the cut-off experience. If, for example, a baby finds the contraction of the womb before the opening of the cervix as overwhelmingly oppressive, she will be vulnerable to finding situations, that might threaten to limit her movements in her life, too much for her to bear. If a mother during pregnancy was the victim of violent or aggressive experiences, the baby in later life may avoid conflict or engage in unnecessarily aggressive responses to situations. If a baby found the journey through the birth canal to be an exhilarating and adventurous experience but found the delivery room to be cold, over-bright and crushingly disappointing, they may be set up to strive for accomplishment but never be able to savor their achievements.

Grof goes even further with this and posits the possibility of 'cellular memory.' This is where consciousness is carried in the cells of sperm and eggs and provides a blueprint for temperament and a psycho-spiritual legacy within the newly conceived person. Healing states of consciousness offer opportunities for what could be termed 'redemption' of these legacies. One could be forgiven for considering that, if Grof is correct in his idea of cellular memory, it might be congruent with the notion of 'the sins of the father being visited upon the son' and the notion of 'generational deliverance'.

One final name worthy of mention, before finishing this brief and highly abridged tour of consciousness theory, is **Ken Wilbur** (USA, 1949 - ). Wilbur has written extensively on the subject of consciousness and appears to have aimed to weave different schools of wisdom, both East and West, contemporary and ancient, into an integrated tapestry of understanding. Whilst at times highly complex and conceptually exercising, his work offers perspectives characterized by breath and depth.

## Therapeutic Models – Different Strokes for Different Folks?

Establishing what Wilbur's work might contribute to coaching, and this could be said for any school of psychology or therapy, will be 'up to the individual church-goer' to borrow a phrase from the world of religion. Each coach will be drawn in different measures to different understandings at different times depending on their own journey of self-discovery. In the next chapter, I will look at what effective coaching dialogue could be and how it might use understandings also utilized by other types of dialogue.

And the fishing trip? Some models of therapy might help a man to learn to fish. Others might simply help him discover he is hungry!

**Chapter Bullets:**

- Coaching is not generic.
- '..to thine own self be true.'
- Discerning clients find discerning coaches.
- If clients 'raise the bar', coaches will be challenged to do likewise.
- One can be influenced and later feel manipulated.
- COACHES offers a definition of coaching.
- A precise business definition can help 'professional myopia.'
- Good timing is at the heart of coaching.
- The CLING Matrix is about growth and language.
- A teacher can have a coaching oriented delivery style.
- The MUNCC matrix is about coaching and consulting.
- The PACE matrix is about power and advice.
- The STATS matrix is about accomplishment and training skill.
- The TECI Matrix is about cognitive and emotional insight.
- The COD and DOC matrices are about causes of dysfunction.
- Freud and Jung were of the psycho-dynamic school of therapy.
- Beck, Ellis and Adler are of the CBT school.
- Maslow, Rogers, Perls & Berne are of the humanistic school.
- Grof and Wilbur examine the transpersonal arena.
- Coaches may be drawn to different theories at different times.

# Chapter 5
# Coaching Dialogue.
## Seen and Unseen.

*'Effective psycho-therapy can assist a person to move from being abnormally dysfunctional to being normally dysfunctional.*

*Effective coaching can help a person move from being normally dysfunctional to being abnormally functional!'*

This is an answer I sometimes offer, tongue in cheek, when I am asked to explain the difference between psycho-therapy and coaching. Given the non-generic nature of both coaching and therapy, I suggest that the statement not be taken too seriously. The essence of a continuum running from abnormal dysfunction right the way to abnormal function is, on the other hand, something that I think is worthy of consideration irrespective of how movement along that continuum might be facilitated.

Professional coaching is a market offering and is presented to the market in language such as follows:

Coaching...
'helps you to achieve your goals'
'helps you to be more effective'
'helps you to improve work-life balance'
'helps you to live your dream'
'helps you to get more focus'
'helps you to find direction'
'helps you to manage your time better'
'helps you to move to a new career'
'helps you to be more successful'

Again, I suggest that the recurring theme here is that coaching is offering itself as a way with which clients can make better use of the resources available to them – to help them become more effective – remember DOVE.

## Aiming for the Pinnacle

In the training of coaches over the years, I always propose that the prime competence of a professional coach must be their ability to explain what coaching is to a potential client. Unless that important step is covered competently, the relationship runs the risk of moving into the same type of dynamics that the client normally encounters in their everyday life – or worse. The whole idea of coaching, as we present it, is to help clients to achieve more clarity. If the first transaction, i.e. the initial discussion about what coaching is, is not characterized by clarity, it does not auger well for the coaching proper. Of course, this competence is not about rattling off the same one-line sentence to every query. It is more about being able to conduct a conversation with potential clients, each unique client having their own distinct mindset, reservations, desires, blind-spots, fears, strengths, ways of engaging and expectations of coaching – realistic or otherwise.

So, what is it about effective coaching that contributes to an increase in a client's effectiveness? From here on, when I use the term 'coaching', I will be referring to 'effective coaching' unless otherwise indicated. Please remember that coaching is not a generic commodity – what I am describing might not be what someone else calls coaching.

If you decide to get physically fit, you might choose to go to a gym and commence a fitness programme in order to achieve your goal. As you get fitter, your stamina and strength will likely improve. You will be able to do more with what you have. You might have more energy and be able to achieve more in a day. 'Achieving' might include having more energy to spend quality time with your family at the end of a demanding day's work or indeed spend more time at work. In summary, you will be able to do more with what you have. You haven't added a 'second you' to the equation, although you could argue that there is more of you available – perhaps more muscle mass. It is likely of course that you would loose weight, fat, as a result of getting fit. You might be of small build to start with so your strength might not be the same as that of a bigger person. It might not even match that of a bigger person who is less fit than you. However, you are still making better use of what you have – than you did been before you got fit – 'Differentiating Output Versus Effectiveness.'

When you engage a professional coach, you will not be doing physical exercise when you are with the coach. I am not talking here about a sports coach but even when you work with a sports coach you do not do *all* your exercise when you are with them and they do not do *any* of your exercise for you. In professional coaching something new happens in the time the client and coach spent together – new to the client and often new in some way to the coach. Also, something new happens when the client and coach are not together. Whatever happens in the coaching session, the client walks away, does something different and gets new results. This doing something different could be as overt as asking for that long overdue raise or as subtle as mulling over new perspectives that lead to a different type of engagement with the coach at the next meeting – without any major changes in behavior in the intervening time. Remember, of course, I am assuming that the coaching is effective.

So how do we tell if coaching is effective? This might seem a simple question with a simple answer – ask the client. However, I suggest that discerning the effectiveness of coaching is not that simple. Here are a few variables:

- The coaching helped the client to achieve what they wanted in the short term. The client claimed the coaching was effective.

- The coaching did not help the client achieve their goal in the short term. The client claimed that the coaching was ineffective.

- The coaching helped the client to achieve their stated goal but the client was disillusioned with the outcome. The client claimed that the coaching was ineffective.

- The coaching did not lead to the client achieving their stated goal but, in their efforts to achieve, and their reflection on the experience, including the failure, facilitated by the coaching, they attained useful insight into themselves. The client claimed that the coaching was effective.

- The coaching led to the client achieving their goal and they then claimed the coaching was effective. However, a year later, following other experiences, with or without coaching, they reflected on the coaching, and now regretted that they had achieved their goal. They now saw the coaching as manipulative, collusive and instrumental in their avoidance of important blind-spots. With the benefit of hindsight, they can now see both their own over-enthusiasm and the coach's lack of objectivity. At that stage, they claim that the coaching was ineffective.

- The coaching was precise, grounded, objective, insightful, non-collusive, appropriately challenging and supportive, and in the moment of the coaching, of compelling power. However, the client's way of dealing with potentially transformative engagement is, as soon as they are out of the coaching, to blank it all out and avoid integrating the insight. The client considers the coaching ineffective. They may even deny this to themselves and continue with a few more sessions without revealing their thoughts to the coach.

- The coaching left the client with compelling beliefs about new ways of being in relationship with others. However, those ways were self-serving and blind to the vulnerabilities of others in the client's life who have less power – e.g. children, employees, trusting friends. The client considers the coaching to be effective – the coach might not.

- The coaching had the effect of compellingly challenging the client's self-limiting beliefs and facilitated a movement towards healthier ways of being inter-dependent with others. Initially, the client was tempted to opt out, finding it a bit too difficult, and claimed to their friend that the coaching was not effective. Still, they stuck at it in the hope that it would offer something and because they had a niggling feeling that the coach had 'something'. In time, the client changed their mind and saw significant value in the coaching. The client claimed then that coaching was effective. Meanwhile, the client's spouse, who was finding the challenge of a revised marital relationship tough, was claiming that the coaching was ineffective!

If the above statements are reasonable, and none of them is incongruent with what I have encountered in coaching over the years – from a variety of sources – then it seems compelling to me to drill into the issue of what defines effective coaching and understand any implications, subtlies and even paradoxes. I accept that there will be those who say that there is no need to look at this beyond the simple question of asking a client if they are happy or not. However, I will be presenting a case that, in order to give maximum value to a client, from a personal growth and self-actualization perspective, a coach needs to go beyond this simplistic approach. If they are to help clients to live in alignment with their values, a coach needs to learn to live in alignment with their own values.


**Results.**

Two important dimensions in this exploration are 'results' and 'delivery'. A not uncommon claim made about coaching is that it 'Helps you to achieve your goals'. This is what could be termed a results oriented approach. In my experience, a coach who sets up their stall with this particular claim can limit the effectiveness of their coaching from the word go. Whilst it might seem a reasonable claim to make when you are offering something to the market and a potentially effective way of selling your wares, I believe that such a claim sets up expectations within the coaching relationship that are likely to be sub-optimal and potentially dysfunctional.

How can I know why a client is not already achieving their goal? More precisely, how can I know that the reasons for a client not achieving their goal already are such that coaching can overcome them? Also, if I have presented this as the objective of coaching, what happens to me when the client shows signs of failing to achieve their goals? Do I find myself emotionally attached to 'delivering' what I said I would and is this, for example, only because I don't want to see myself as failing? If I claim one thing when offering my service, and suggest otherwise when things don't go quite the way I would have liked, I could reasonably be accused of changing the goal-posts mid-game. I might be skillful in certain areas of coaching but changing my pitch *after the contracting* runs a very high risk of compromising trust in the relationship and introducing a new 'elephant in the room'. This is something both client and coach expend energy avoiding – the very thing coaching is expected to dissipate.

I suggest a simple adjustment to the claim about coaching helping someone to achieve their goals would include 'or discover why you are not achieving your goals'. This addendum can free the coaching up to be what it can be. This is not to assume that the client is guaranteed to be able to achieve this goal but it less likely to draw a client into an unrealistic expectation.

One last tweak can also help. Instead of claiming to help a client achieve their goals, or see why they are not achieving their goals, it can be worth suggesting that coaching 'aims' to help. One of the common themes in coaching is the notion of responsibility. The effect of good coaching is that the client steps 'into the driver's seat' of their own life. As they make that move, either quickly or gradually, they usually discover the ways in which they have been avoiding being in the driver's seat of their own life. The usual discovery is that, in some way or other, they have been allocating responsibility to someone else – effectively blaming others for their lack of success. (This is not to be confused with appropriately holding others accountable for *their* behavior.) If this is the case, and the coach is not careful with the language they use, they could collude with this mindset from early on and make it difficult to model a compelling argument for a more refined understanding of responsibility – an area inextricably linked to personal growth.

Another aspect of the results issue, in the context of accurately explaining coaching to potential clients, is to consider the goal itself. If the goal I am considering is 'to increase my income by 50% in the next six months', that's one thing. If the goal is 'to increase my self-awareness' or 'to achieve a greater sense of direction', it is another. The former is an achievement goal and the latter are examples of personal growth goals. It is possible to achieve an increase in my income of 50% without any personal growth. By definition, increasing my self-awareness is a fruit of personal growth. However, looking at how I seek to achieve an increase in income can take me into potential personal growth territory.

## Delivery.

Another way to explain coaching to a potential client is to describe the process of coaching – what happens within coaching. On its own, without reference to the aimed-for results of coaching, describing the process of coaching is of limited interest to clients but it usually features in the negotiating conversation. *'What does the coach actually do during the coaching?'* is not an uncommon enquiry.

Just as with claiming results of coaching, a coach would be wise, for the sake of their client and themselves, to think carefully about how they might answer this question. A superficial answer is easy but rarely enough to satisfy a client – particularly the more discerning.

Here is an example of a telephone conversation between a potentially interested client and a coach:

**Coach:** Good afternoon – Synergy Coaching Services.

**Client:** Hi, I wanted to talk to someone about coaching.

**Coach:** Hi, perhaps I could help you. My name is John and I am one of the coaches here.

**Client:** Oh great. Can you tell me a little about coaching. Em...I wanted to...em.. just find out what it's about.

**Coach:** Sure. Had you any particular question in mind? Sorry, I don't know your name...

**Client:** Yes... eh... sorry my name is Cleo.
Yeh... well I kinda wondered would it be something I could try... Is it suitable for someone? ...em...I'm thinking about looking at a few things in my life and I wondered would coaching be of help.

**Coach:** It may well be Cleo... but let me ask you a question. What do you know about coaching at the moment?

**Client:** Well, I ...is it something to do with goals?

**Coach:** Yes – that would be part of it.

**Client:** I am a bit lost after that...I read an article in a magazine recently about coaching and it sounded interesting but to be honest I don't know much about it.

**Coach:** Okay. Fair enough.
Well, coaching is about helping people to look at what they would like to achieve in their life and how they might set about applying themselves to that. It's about...

**Client:** But I don't know what I want. Does that mean that coaching wouldn't be any use to me?

**Coach:** No. Far from it Cleo. Part of the process would involve teasing out what might be suitable avenues for you to look at and then what options might be appropriate. Actually getting some clarity about what 'floats your boat', so to speak, is a key part of it all.

**Client:** Okay... well that sounds good.

**Coach:** You could say that your first goal is to figure out what you would like to do next.

**Client:** Okay...yeah I'm with you.
So what would the coach actually do?

**Coach:** Well the coach's specialty is about listening and questioning in a way that opens your thinking and helps you identify self-limiting beliefs, for example. The coach will get you to test the robustness of your current strategies and help you piece together a picture of yourself moving to your full potential. Depending on what you want to work on and your particular learning style, you may also be invited to consider exercises for yourself that would take you into new territory in bite-sized chunks.

**Client:** Right...
I just feel kinda... a bit...I don't know...kind of in a rut.
I've been doing quite well in my job... I work in an office...and I'm just not that pushed about it any more. I kinda feel like I am missing something but I can't put my finger on it.

**Coach:** Well each coaching 'journey', if you like, is unique so I can't really say where it would take you but coaching aims to help you to see how you see things and to play with other ways of looking at things that might free you up to new horizons...if I am making sense.

**Client :** Yeah John... no that makes sense. Sounds kind of exciting...

*even a bit scary... Ha!*

**Coach:** (Chuckles)
*Can be challenging at times but in a way that supports you.*

**Client:** *That's comforting...and, you know, I am beginning to think I need a bit of a challenge to get out of this rut.*

**Coach:** *Well, we can't guarantee anything Cleo but it might be worth your while meeting up with a coach and getting a sense of what coaching might do for you. A half-hour meeting can give you a bit of an insight into how it might be to work with a given coach and it won't cost you anything but thirty mins of your time.*

**Client:** *Okay ..yeah ...I'll go with that... sounds good.*

**Coach:** *How would next Tuesday at 2:00pm suit you Cleo?*

Each initial conversation is different for each client and the style of each coach will vary also. Cleo and John is just one example. You will notice John did little or no 'selling' but did build a degree of rapport with Cleo even in that short space of time. All John did was to answer Cleo's questions as best he could without sounding like an encyclopedia. Cleo felt comfortable with his answers and felt no pressure to commit to anything. You will notice that John did not at any time 'diagnose' Cleo i.e. he did not suggest to her that there was anything 'wrong' with her or that she had 'issues'. The conversation was, as much as John could influence it, a dialogue between two adults who could make informed choices. Cleo may well have 'issues' depending on how you define such a term and, by the same token, so could John have similar or completely different issues. However, in the interaction, John aimed to be as objective and as transparent as he could. Apart from being important to him in terms of his own values, John knew from experience that it was important for him to start as he means to continue. He knew that authenticity, clear thinking and genuine care for Cleo would be vital ingredients for a quality coaching relationship.

## Content and Context.

In examining different approaches to therapy, the thrust in literature is normally on the interaction between practitioner and client – the content of the relationship if you like. The same has generally tended to be the case in offerings on coaching. I believe, however, that there is also another dimension that influences the experience - and that is the context.

If, within a society, availing of a particular service is generally accepted as 'normal' more people will be inclined to avail of it. Plastic surgery, in some communities, is considered to be self-indulgent and the privilege of those with more money than sense. In other communities, it is seen as almost as normal as getting dental work done. The values and perceptions of one's peers, as perceived by us, influences our perception of an activity.

In general, I believe that people tend to seek a therapist in response to a problem. In the early days of therapy, clients/patients tended to be referred by medical practitioners. This has changed over the years but I believe that most therapy clients see therapy as a temporary process to 'get them right' or sort out 'stuff'. The desire to feel accepted as part of our idea of 'normal' has, I am sure, influenced many a therapy client to abandon the process before they maximized the benefit of that relationship. I also believe that, in some communities, it is seen as abnormal *not* to have a therapist – perhaps Woody Allen might know some who could fall into that category. In that case, there may be the possibility that the client is attending therapy long after the benefits of the relationship have been maximized. Of course, an effective therapist will likely spot this and respond. How we measure the benefits of therapy is another day's work of course.

The cultural attitude people have to therapy, and their understanding of the role of therapy, provides the context within which therapy is provided. More specifically, it is the macro-context. The context within which the therapy is offered, by a specific therapist to a specific client, I term the 'micro-context.' These two elements of context influence the relationship before any therapy is done.

The same applies to professional coaching.

## The Psychological Contract.

Say I drive my car into a gas station, put $50 worth of gas into the tank, walk into the shop, hand the shop assistant the cash, take the receipt and walk out. I could complete that transaction without saying a word or signing anything. I did not need to enter into negotiation with the gas-station company or sign a multi-claused contract. However, there were expectations on my part and on the part of the shop assistant. These sets of expectations were both taken as given. I expected to find gas available having driven into the station. I expected it to be acceptable for me to put gas in my tank without asking anyone's permission and the shop assistant expected that I would then walk into the shop and pay him for the gas. If you asked me, and the assistant, why we had these expectations, we might just shrug our shoulders and suggest that it was obvious. We would probably wonder why you were asking in the first place. A key part of it would be that we would both consider it quite reasonable to have these expectations and to behave in the way we did. We did not need to sign anything or commit to anything either verbally or in writing. In addition, once complete, the transaction is closed and in the past. Neither party feels any discomfort with the transaction – no niggling thoughts or emotions lingering on. By the time I get into my car, the episode is over for me and the shop assistant is taking money from the next customer.

These sets of expectations represent the 'psychological contract'. In the case of the gas purchase transaction, it is simple and straight forward – all expectations were clear and known. The contract could be described as bi-laterally balanced – both sides had expectations of each other and the behavior of each matched the expectations of the other. However, not all transactions are that simple. Let's add a little extra to the gas transaction.

As I drive up to the garage, I see a sign that says 'Free Car-wash with every $50 gas purchase'. Great, I think to myself, I don't really need gas right now but my car could do with a wash so I'll go in. I put $50 worth of gas into the tank and pay the assistant. The assistant hands me my till receipt but no car-wash token. I quickly think to myself that the assistant forgot to give me the token and I politely remind him.
*"Oh I'm sorry, the car-wash is out-of order,"* the attendant informs me.
Now we are moving into a psychological contract of a slightly different color. I had an expectation of the assistant and it wasn't happening – no

car-wash token. The psychological contract is skewed or unbalanced. If I leave now, I won't have the same closure as I would have had in the previous situation – without the car-wash sign. At this point, new expectations enter the equation. I now have an expectation of the assistant to do something about the situation. Let's say the assistant says something like this...

*'Oh I am really sorry, I thought the car-wash sign had been put away until we got the car-wash fixed. Look, I will deduct the price of the car-wash from your gas bill and give you a refund for that amount. I am really sorry – our fault – can I give you a newspaper too. I appreciate that it's not fair on you.'*

As the psychological contract was skewed for a moment, I generated new expectations of the assistant in new circumstances. I expected him to do something about the fact that I had been misled and he responded, in my opinion, admirably. Anyone can make a mistake, we're all human and, when he realized the mistake, he did what he could to make amends. I accept the refund, and the free newspaper, and walk out with complete closure having first wished the assistant a nice day. I might even have more than closure. I might have a little spring in my step as a result of the assistant's very reasonable (in my view) response. If only everyone could be so pro-active and non-defensive – there would be hope for the world! The experience might make up for a less than satisfactory previous event elsewhere.

The second scenario was a little more complex but was quickly brought into balance. Again, both parties had expectations of each other all of which they both considered to be reasonable – including that people can make mistakes. Let's add some more.

Let's say that the sign said *'Free Car-Wash with every $50 gas purchase... Subject to availability'* the last bit in very small print.

*'Sorry about that but the car-wash is not available'* says the assistant and looks over my shoulder to the next in line as if to say *'Next please'.*

We are now in a new psychological contract again. The assistant expects me to accept the explanation and go. But I don't believe that this is reasonable. How I engage with the assistant will be different. The shop assistant might think that it is reasonable to use two different print sizes for the two parts of the sign and expect that drivers read the whole sign. I might consider it unreasonable to use two different print sizes especially in a sign designed to attract people who are already concentrating on the road whilst they are driving. The situation does not make for an optimal engagement and certainly is not conducive to a relationship built on trust. But let's try another scenario.

Say there was no free car-wash sign when I drove up but I remembered that there was one last week and the car-wash unit is fully operational. I put the gas into my tank and hand my $50 to the assistant. I get my receipt and ask for my free car-wash. The assistant informs me that the offer ceased last week and so the free car-wash is not available. I then express my dis-satisfaction that the deal is no longer available and ask the assistant what he is going to do about it. In this scenario, I could be described as having an unreasonable expectation. The assistant doesn't know what to do. He considers my behaviour unreasonable but there is a line of impatient customers behind me. The assistant has a reasonable expectation of me not to be behaving like this but doesn't fancy his chances of convincing me of this. He looks at the situation as realistically as he can and decides to give me the free car-wash to get me out of his hair. His expectations of me were reasonable in terms of what he thought I should do but also realistic, one could argue, in terms of what I was likely to do. My expectations of him could be described as realistic because I could see his vulnerability with a line of impatient customers looking at him – I reckoned he would give me the car-wash - but unreasonable in terms of what he should do given the circumstances. In seeing this, as an observer, as unreasonable, I am operating of course from certain values and understandings. A great philosophical debate since time immemorial is, of course, about what constitutes reasonable behavior and by what criteria is it assessed as such. I approach this from a position of a particular understanding of personal growth.

One can see from the example above that psychological contracts can be simple, effortless and collaborative, or they can be complex, unpredictable and hard work.

As with the gas-station examples, psychological contracts exist in professional coaching relationships. Unlike the gas station examples however, I suggest that working with the psychological contract is actually part of the coaching. In other words, the gas station attendant expects the psychological contract with his customers *not to* get in the way of his transactions. The effective coach *expects* the psychological contract to 'get in the way' of the relationship as a means by which the coaching can offer the client greater clarity. Working with the psychological contract, and its pinch points, is part of the stock-in-trade of coaching. The gas-station assistant expects not to have to work on unbalanced psychological contracts with his customers. Even if a coach expects not to have to deal with unbalanced psychological contracts, they are likely to be engaged otherwise when working with clients. They may not make elegant sense of what is happening in the relationship. They may collude with the skewed psychological contracts They may or may not have heard of the term. However, if they are not alert to the dynamics of psychological contracts, whatever term they use, including their own part in them, I am certain that they will miss significant opportunities for growth and clarity.

**Games and The Psychological Contract.**

Psychological contracts can take many forms and every one of them has its own unique profile. If we were to examine the theories of Eric Berne's Transactional Analysis, as introduced in the last chapter, we can see psychological contracts at play. When one adult behaves like a child to another adult we get a psychological contract that says something like:

*'I expect you to do for me what a parent would normally be expected to do for a child even though we are both adults and you have the same adult challenges as I do. Furthermore, I do not want us to acknowledge this because then it might have to change and, if it did, I do not know how I would cope.'*

In this case, the 'child' is operating from a 'needs dominant' base – remember The NICE Curve? Berne used the term 'games' to describe ways of being in relationship that are *less than optimal* (my words). In effect, games allow people to avoid the most powerful level of relating to another adult i.e. authentically, or doing so in a way that is 'to thine own self being true'.

Personal growth coaching, amongst other things, will help a client to get greater clarity around what they are actually doing in their relationships (especially, perhaps, their relationship with themselves) and elicit more compelling ways of being as well as strategies for their development and application. To do this effectively, the coach has to be (1) Capable of not playing their own games or, if they are, to only be doing it consciously in order to surface unconscious games, and (2) be able to resist being pulled into the games their client plays. In practice, both parties will be vulnerable to playing games. Part of the added value the coach brings – in fact, probably the first element of added value the coach brings – is in not allowing themselves to be pulled into the client's normal games. The second is in not infecting the relationship with games of their own i.e. not pulling the client into any ungrowthful games.

In point of fact, operating on the assumption that all that is called 'coaching' is generic, and capable of facilitating growth, is in itself a type of 'game'. It usually involves a dependence on an irrational generalization about a group. The 'group' can then be perceived as a type of pseudo-family in which we can take psychological refuge. The forming of professional coaching bodies is a process which I believe can be vulnerable to these games. This is because those with the greatest need to be part of a group will generally be most inclined to get involved and least inclined to spot the elephants in the room. As these bodies tend to be 'democratic', the culture will tend to reflect the needs of those less independent – those at the left end of the NICE curve. This will be particularly the case with those who see no issues and wonder why others are jumping up and down or keeping their distance.

**Reasonable and Realistic Expectations.**

One way of unpacking the psychological contract is to see it in terms of certain types of expectations. Let's look at a couple of examples.

*Daniel has employed a coach - Marie. His stated objective was to improve his relationship with his wife, Betty. His main success criteria for this would be that they would be making love several times a month, at least, – as they had been when they first started going out years ago. He hoped that Marie's coaching would help him understand the relationship from a woman's point of view. His expectation was that Marie was not going to tell him what to do but that she would work to help him see the subtleties. Given Marie's promotional material, this was a reasonable expectation. However, during the coaching, he several times asked Marie* about her own sexuality - specifically questions like 'what turns you on' or 'would that turn you on'. Marie resisted answering him each time saying things like 'Well Daniel, it's not about me, it's about you and Betty.'

After a few sessions, Daniel began to get irritated with Marie's evasiveness – as he saw it. At one stage, he described a failed attempt to woo Betty the previous evening and Marie asked him to unpack his and Betty's behavior around that time to see if he could spot something that he had missed. Daniel described a point where he seemed to go from being quite romantic to being irritated and impatient with Betty. He suggested that, once that had happened, he had 'blown it'. Marie suggested that he looked at his beliefs around the situation and that they play with imaginary alternative outcomes – other options. After some exploration, Marie put something into the pot.

'You know Daniel, when you have asked me about my own sexuality on several occasions, and I didn't answer you, I sensed that you were less relaxed in yourself. Did I pick that up right do you think?' Marie asked.
'I wonder is that similar to what you are describing about last night.'

Daniel looked at her without saying anything. He was biting his lip and tapping his foot.

To cut a long story short, Daniel discovered that he had certain expectations of Betty and, when they did not come about, he became irritated and impatient. He came to see this with increasing clarity and began to look at new ways he might deal with this in future – including exploring with Betty what her expectations were of him. The psychological contract was what Marie used to throw light on the issue – to Daniel's advantage – and Betty's presumably. The first time Daniel asked Marie about her sexuality, she was a little taken aback and was tempted to respond with a teeth-gritted *'How dare you'* type retort. However, by keeping her boundary, noting that, from her perspective anyway, she considered his expectation of an answer from her to be unreasonable, and noting his responses to her when she 'evaded' his repeated questions, she was able to tease out a piece of the psychological contract.

Daniel's behavior was going to change but not because he found a list of steps to take to woo his wife – an 'action plan'. It would be because his perspective of the situation, and himself, had changed. Marie's acceptance of the reality of the situation, and her faith in the process of growth and 'revelation', allowed her to engage with Daniel in a way that was new to him. Daniel was not suffering from any illness that he was aware of and he had been quite successful in his career. He had once mentioned the relative celibacy in his marriage to a close friend over a drink. The ensuing conversation with his friend provided no more clarity as to how things might improve. Instead, it re-inforced his notion that all that was happening was that Betty was being unreasonable.

**Another Example.**

Jim is coaching Alan. On several occasions, Alan has appeared late to their meetings. Jim had generally continued beyond the original finish time to give Alan the full hour. One day, Jim began wrapping up and told Alan that they had five minutes remaining. Alan had been forty minutes late and felt like he had only just got there. He was taken aback when Jim told him the time was up and he went to his car slightly stunned. A week later he was back to Jim and on time. He said that he wanted to continue working on his goal of getting promoted. He said that he had been taken aside by his manager and advised to be more assertive with his team particularly on 'tea-break slippage'. Jim sensed something different in the way Alan was relating to him. It was as if they had gone from being buddies to being in competition with each other. There was a pause in the dialogue and Jim resisted the temptation to fill the gap - at least prematurely. He noticed Alan's eyes were watering slightly. Jim smiled softly.

"There's something getting in your way Alan – am I right?" Jim offered.

"What do you mean?" Alan answered.

"You're usually a pretty focused guy here......"

"There is something I want to get off my chest." Alan sat up a little.

"Yeah?" Jim suspected he knew what it was.

"Yeah...last week, I was pissed with you because you cut our meeting short." Jim said, looking a little more focused.

## Aiming for the Pinnacle

*"What was your expectation Alan?...about that last week?" Jim asked.*

*"Well I thought we would go on longer." Alan was softening a little.*

*"I certainly would have liked to Alan." Jim offered genuinely.*

*Alan stayed quiet for another minute. He was experiencing ambivalent feelings about Jim and the situation. He trusted Jim hugely – possibly more than he had trusted anyone. At the same time, he was confused.*

*"Would it help if I told you why I finished when I did?" Jim asked.*

*"Well...go on... I..." Alan softened a little more.*

*"I didn't want to keep my next client waiting." Jim explained.*

*"And I didn't want to be home late for supper with my family." He added.*

*"That's fair enough – I wish I had known before coming over here last week. Might have given it a skip." Alan was beginning to see something.*

*"I hate to do this to you Alan but we are running out of time here now." Jim interjected.*

*"God, where did that hour go to?" Alan sighed. As he left, he looked much more relaxed and somewhat pensive.*

Alan went on his way and started into the thirty minute drive home. As he drove, the dialogue with Jim went around in his head. He suddenly felt a wave of appreciation for Jim. Alan saw for a moment how he himself had been lax in his time-keeping and unrealistic with his expectations of Jim. He felt grateful for the almost artistic way that Jim had responded to the situation – frustratingly confusing – almost paradoxical. Alan just couldn't put his finger on what Jim had done but he knew it was something about timing and sensitivity. There was also a sense of firmness in the transaction. The key feature of it, however, was that he suddenly realized that something had changed in the way he saw the 'tea-break slippage' issue at work. It just looked different. Assertively reminding the staff that tea-breaks were fifteen minutes, and not forty minutes, seemed like the most reasonable thing to do. Logically, he thought that he and Jim had not had enough time to 'sort out' the work issue and yet, somehow, something had changed in his thinking.

Alan promised himself that he would ask Jim if he knew this shift would happen – in other words was it an intentional strategy? The next day at work, Alan mentioned the tea-breaks at the morning briefing and no-one seemed to resist the issue. Alan's manager noted the change. Alan was metaphorically scratching his head – puzzled as to how easily the problem had been sorted. This was one of many mini-modules in Alan's apprenticeship in leadership... and his move towards his self-actualization.

Whilst Jim could not have reliably predicted the exact shift in Alan's thinking after their meeting, he had operated from an intuitive sense and reckoned that Alan was close to a modest breakthrough in his thinking. He was not surprised to later hear what had transpired.

In the first example, Daniel came to see that, by reference to his own understanding of Marie's role as a coach, he did not expect her to reveal intimate details about her sexuality. In other words, despite the fact that he had asked her several times, he evaluated his own expectations as unreasonable.

In the case of Alan, part of his reflection was that his expectations were unrealistic – to expect Jim to automatically change his schedule because one client was late? Sure, he had gone over time previously, but Alan realized that he had taken Jim for granted in this. Alan reflected that, interestingly, the sequence of events had cornered him into seeing something about himself. And, and this was verging on the mind-blowing for Alan, being cornered into seeing his own self-centeredness seemed to lead to his being able to be more effective in his job. *"This coaching business is more an art than a science,"* he thought to himself. *"Might stick at it a bit longer."*

I find it useful to explore expectations in terms of their reasonableness and their realism. If they are my expectations, I look at them in terms of my idea of reason and reality. If they are a client's expectations, I co-explore them with reference to *their* ideas of reason and reality. Having done that, I then suggest looking at the expectations from the imagined perspectives of other stakeholders.

It will be of no surprise that this can be looked at using a four-quadrant matrix!

Aiming for the Pinnacle

## The 'RARE' Matrix

Expectations

|  | Unrealistic | Realistic |
|---|---|---|
| **Reasonable** | **Reasonable but Unrealistic** (Expecting a mugger not to take your wallet). | **Reasonable and Realistic** (Expecting your employer to pay you). |
| **Unreasonable** | **Unreasonable and Unrealistic** (Expecting someone to carry you indefinitely). | **Realistic but Unreasonable** (Expecting someone strong to carry you when you pretend to be hurt). |

Playing with the RARE matrix can help streamline our thinking and gain insight into the ways we might surface and shed some limiting beliefs. In particular, it can have us look at ways in which we might be operating at the needy end of the NICE curve.

Here are some expectations you might explore.
Where might they fit on the RARE matrix?

Expecting...
- people to fly
- cats to bark
- men to always be empathetic
- women to love engines
- all men to like football
- a friend to lie for you
- all women to be sensitive
- someone not to defend themselves
- your boss to be your psycho-therapist
- your mother to sell her house to invest in your business
- a bank manager to lend you money when your unemployed
- your spouse to figure out alone that you are having an affair
- to be paid without working
- someone to be your leader without asking them

- someone to follow you just because you want them to
- someone to tell you the truth when you can fire them
- someone to like you because you like them
- someone to love you 'for better or for worse'
- a child to understand marriage
- your spouse to understand love the way you do
- a disabled person to do what you can (when you're not disabled)
- an ambitious person to slow down so you can catch up
- someone else to be as motivated about something as you are
- someone to know what you want without telling them
- someone to know you want something when you have told them you want something opposite
- life to be wonderful all the time
- life to be awful no matter what you do
- life to be adventurous without taking any risks
- people not to walk around you when you are in the way
- people to vote for fair politicians
- a policeman to not arrest a rapist
- a cat to not notice a mouse
- a baby to sleep eight hours every night
- someone parenting small children not to be tired in the evening
- someone working in a very difficult job getting tired sometimes
- someone poor to pay all their taxes
- someone rich to pay all their taxes
- someone who is being bullied to be assertive
- someone who is bullying to be empathetic

Exploring our expectations in this way can help to distill what values underlie our perceptions and our behavior.

**Desires.**

Another approach to unpacking elements of the psychological contract is to look at any *desires* that are at play and their relationship with expectations.

Going back to Alan above, in his reflections, he realized that he had subconsciously felt that he had a right to Jim going over time because he, Alan, had arrived late and hadn't gotten the first forty minutes. He also had a *desire* to get a full hour worth of coaching. Jim had gone over time previously without bringing attention to it. Jim had considered addressing the issue the first time but his gut told him not to. To that degree, his strategy was deliberate but, as is often the case with intuition, he would not be able to predict exactly how things would pan out.

Alan discovered that he had been behaving in a way based on certain irrational beliefs. One such belief was that Jim could just go over time without any implications for himself or anyone else.

A second belief that influenced Alan was that he had a right to Jim going over time.

A third was that, just because Jim had gone over time before, this confirmed that Alan had been correct in his (internal) assertion that he had the right.

## The 'RUGED Matrix

Expectations

|  | Right | Gift |
|---|---|---|
| **Expected** | **Expected Right** (Expecting your spouse to be faithful) | **Expected Gift** (A birthday present from your partner.) |
| **Unexpected** | **Unexpected Right** (A thief to return my car) | **Unexpected Gift** (An act of kindness from a stranger). |

By exploring our beliefs in the context of the RUGED matrix, we can unpack our thinking and potentially distill some unproductive, unjust or unsustainable dependences - remember 'PAUSE'? Here is an example:

*Peter has been working full time for twenty years in the information technology (IT) industry. Particularly over the last ten years, his hours have become more demanding. In that time, he has also been promoted several times. Jenny, Peter's wife, left work as a nurse when she was pregnant with their twin boys who are now twelve years old. Jenny enjoys her lifestyle. There are times when she is quite busy but, overall, she has a lot of flexibility in her life and she enjoys playing golf and squash and watching soaps on the TV in the evenings. Having been plagued by a series of 'stress related' symptoms over the last eighteen months, Peter decided to take a redundancy offer that became available at work. His peers were somewhat surprised that someone at their level would want to do so. Peter wanted to set up as an IT consultant part-time and pursue his passion for writing and playing music.*

*When Peter revealed his desire to Jenny, she was thrown into crisis. As she dealt with the issue, she became more aware of her desires and her expectations of her husband. Peter and Jenny went through a rocky two years following Peter's decision to change his career direction. By the end of that time, they had adjusted to a somewhat simpler lifestyle, both working part-time and Peter's health was substantially better. The twins and Peter had begun to get to know each other and the couple was beginning to venture into a new tentatively more intimate chapter in their relationship.*

One of the key concepts Peter and Jenny used during this period of change was the RUGED matrix. In particular, Jenny came to see that her opportunity to spend so much time with her kids when they were young was a gift – even if she initially resented Peter for deciding that he was not continuing with his well-paid pensionable job.

**Dialogue.**

Professional coaching is a particular type of dialogue. As I mentioned before, if coaching is to be of value, it needs to provide something that is not readily available to the client on a day-to-day basis. Otherwise, the client would have no need for coaching. One thing that coaching does have in common with day-to-day dialogue is that signals are dispatched and received by the parties involved. These signals can be as simple as an offer of a glass of water – either verbal or non-verbal. If a friend

## Aiming for the Pinnacle

holds out a packet of chewing gum to you, the signal usually means 'would you like some?'

One legacy that Sigmund Freud, et al, have left us with is the notion of 'the unconscious'. It is not that the unconscious didn't exist before the beginning of the twentieth century but its existence was presented, by Freud and friends, as a scientific fact and it was given a new playground in which to dance. This was initially amongst the Austrian educated and later across a more global catwalk. The notion of someone becoming more aware of something about themselves has always, I believe, been axiomatic with human life itself. Whilst the concept of psycho-analyzing one's self, one's lover, one's friend's, one's enemies, had yet to become a popular sport, prior to Freud, ordinary people will have been getting older and seeing the next generation follow behind. No doubt, many an older person will have reflected on how they had been reckless and naively idealistic when they were younger and will see how they justified some of their actions by avoiding acknowledging their own true motivations for such actions. The notion of 'redemption' has had a long and exercised history. Even if the principle was hi-jacked from time-to-time, by individuals within a religious power structure to control the great un-washed, genuine redemption, as a process within which a person experiences a retrospective insight into themselves, appears to have sprouted regularly amongst the weeds of its pretenders – sprouts that could save 'a wretch like me' with amazing grace.

Having presented the notion of the unconscious as a vast unexplored territory, Freud, particularly, went to great pains to chart what he saw as the topography of this territory. In doing so, he offering a range of plausible explanations and dynamics to his audience – plausible, at least to those who found them plausible. But what if we look at the unconscious in a simpler way?

When my kids were little, from time to time, one of them would wander off in the supermarket. Something would catch their eye and, before they realized it, they were on their own. The usual procedure is that one of the other shoppers would see a little three-year-old on his own, bring him to the customer-service desk, and an announcement would be made over the public address system:

*'A little boy has been found in the store. He has blond hair and is about three years old. He is wearing denim dungarees and a lemon sweater. Would his parents please come to the customer-service desk to pick him up.'*

Meanwhile, myself or his mother, would already have been making our way to the desk to ask for help in retrieving our little treasure.

As we approached the desk, the toddler would put out his arms and attach himself, limpid-like, to his long-lost mother of father – long lost of about five minutes. And then would come the tears. It always struck me that the child would have a certain expression on his face when I approached him as he waited at the desk. It seemed reasonable to deduce that the tears were the expression of feelings that had been 'parked' until Mom or Dad were found. That expression told me something that the child did not yet know. Afterwards, as we walk away, it seems clear that the child had been afraid and seemed only to realize it when returned to safety – safety that is, in the child's mind – in the circumstances we never really felt that the child was 'unsafe' in that particular store. On re-unification with Dad, something moved to a new level of consciousness and was expressed in a new way – complete with tears and sobs.

The hypothesis I would like to propose at this point is that, when two people are in dialogue, say one is signally an offer of gum to the other – both verbally and non-verbally – that there is also the potential for unconscious signals being added to the transaction.

In fact, I believe that, in every area of our lives, where we aim to achieve something and somehow it turns out to be not as simple as we thought it should be, there will be unconscious signals and that these will explain why things are not working quite as we expected.

I also believe that the single most powerful feature of the most effective personal growth coaching is the process whereby *relevant* unconscious signals are accurately identified by the client and factored into their future decision-making. Sometimes this identification of unconscious signals totally changes the goal-posts and prompts a client to reconsider their goals. Other times, it just streamlines an existing process and assists effectiveness in the pursuit of a named agenda.

# Aiming for the Pinnacle

Consider Bart and Joe – you will remember them from when we looked at DOVE – Differentiate Output Versus Effectiveness.

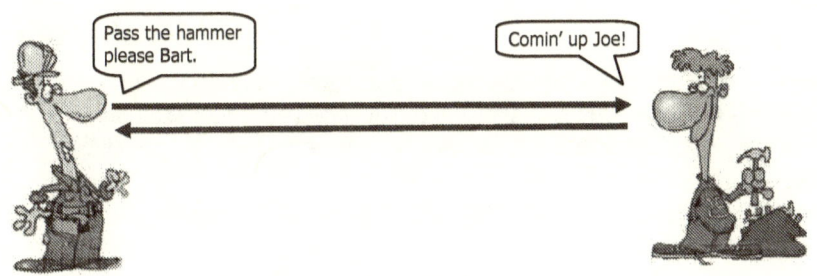

Here we see a simple conscious signal from Joe to Bart. Joe asks for a hammer, Bart picks up the signal and signals back to Joe. Everything in the transaction is conscious. Let's add more.

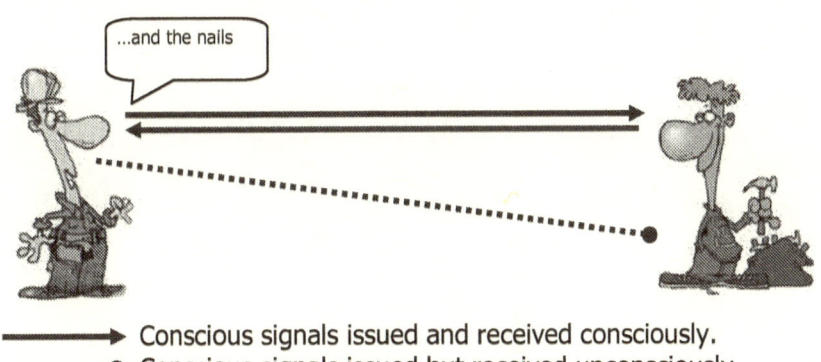

⟶ Conscious signals issued and received consciously.
┄┄┄•  Conscious signals issued but received unconsciously.

In this case Joe has asked for the nails but Bart does not hear it consciously. Let's say that there is a history here – and remember, I am using a simple fictitious example to present a point. Bart has forgotten to bring the nails as had been agreed. This is not the first time. He blanks out the fact that Joe has asked for the nails. Bart has received the message but he has done so unconsciously. He starts to get nervous – and, without realizing it, his leg begins to shake.

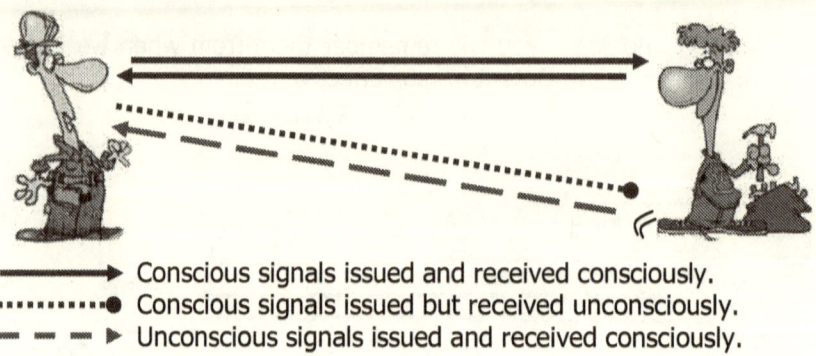

→ Conscious signals issued and received consciously.
•••••• Conscious signals issued but received unconsciously.
− − − ▶ Unconscious signals issued and received consciously.

Joe then picks up Bart's unconscious signal – consciously – i.e. he sees and is aware of Bart's nervous leg shake.

Joe's expression changes. He puts on a smile in the hope of putting Bart at ease so that they can deal with this problem – another conscious signal.

However, he also clinches his fist without realizing it. Bart does not see the clenched fist consciously but does pick it up unconsciously.

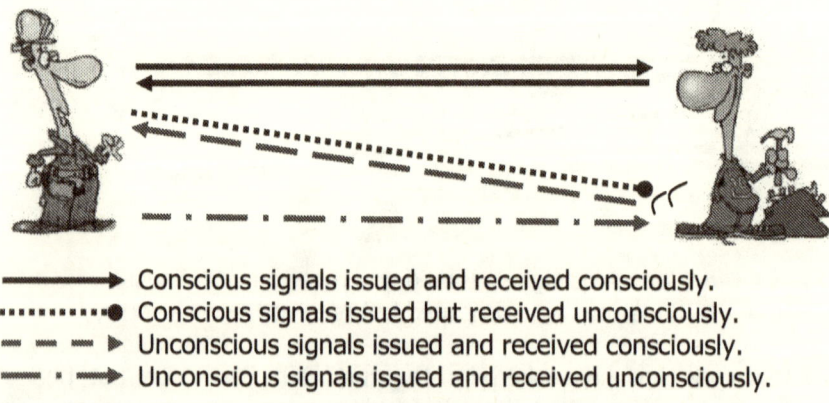

→ Conscious signals issued and received consciously.
•••••• Conscious signals issued but received unconsciously.
− − − ▶ Unconscious signals issued and received consciously.
— · — ▶ Unconscious signals issued and received unconsciously.

Without realizing it, Joe and Bart are communicating with each other in more ways than just the overt verbal signals and noticed body language. The dialogue is effected by conscious and unconscious signals. I call this 'The CAUSED Effect' – **C**onscious **A**nd **U**nconscious **S**ignals **E**ffecting **D**ialogue – and I believe it is possibly the most ignored and misunderstood effect in the area of coaching, leadership, parenting and relationships generally.

A key part of personal growth is about opening to the 'games people play', as suggested by Transactional Analysis theory, for example. In seeing what is really happening in dialogue, particularly substantive dialogue – dialogue that has the potential for impact on our dependences – we are empowered to make more precise decisions. Personal growth coaching is a form of dialogue that can surface hidden aspects of dialogue through focused attendance to the client's stated agenda. In theory, it does not matter what the agenda is. It could be the simplest goal or a profound one. It is how the coach conducts their side of the dialogue that will turn what would otherwise be a normal everyday conversation into something that can help a client chip away at their current constellation of perceptions towards a more effective and, whilst often challenging, ultimately liberating and empowering clarity of perception.

I once heard of a sculptor being asked how he produced such magnificent masterpieces in his work – how he starts out with a rough angular block of stone and ends up with an exquisitely curved statue of a beautiful woman?

> *"Well," replied the sculptor,*
> *"I start out with a rough angular block of stone and I chip away all the stone that is not part of the exquisitely curved statue of a beautiful woman."*

Perhaps this could serve as a metaphor for personal growth. By chipping away all the bits that are not me, perhaps I get to become me – to mine own self to become true.

In a coaching setting, in aiming to maximize the possibility of a client chipping away at beliefs and perceptions that limit or restrict their growth towards self-actualization, the coach's own set of beliefs and dependences will be relevant. If a client is operating on a need-based subjective belief, and the coach has a matching belief, it is likely that the belief will not be noticed for what it is. If, for example, a client says that integrity is important to him and yet he reveals that he is evading income tax, and, at the same time, I believe that integrity is important and I am also evading tax, it is likely that this potential inconsistency will be missed in the coaching.

It is important to understand that this is not to suggest that the coach needs to believe that tax evasion, for example, is always contrary to personal integrity. However, given its nature, tax-evasion would be a fairly obvious example of an activity that might suggest an element of self-deception – particularly if the individual partaking in it believes that they are a 'person of integrity' and wants to be such. A person that has been abused 'by the system' may well feel, and for all I know *be, justified* in evading tax until such time that they feel recompensed for the abuse. If, as a coach, I aim to be a conscience to the client, based on my set of perceptions and calculations as to what is right and what is wrong, I run the risk of hauling into the relationship a whole constellation of assumptions and selective reasoning that may well sabotage the growthful aspects of the relationship.

It is another matter, however, to respond to revelations that might suggest that the client is not being their own conscience *to themselves,* in accordance with their own values and their own history. In this event, I offer the opportunity to the client to constructively interrogate their own thinking to see if there is a possibility that they might discover a self-limiting dependence.

This gives us an example of how The CAUSED Effect might be at play. Let's look at a piece of dialogue:

**Coach:** *So Karen, you would like to continue where we left off at our last meeting. How would you like to do this?*

**Client:** *Well, I would like to look at the marketing strategy.*

**Coach:** *Okay. My memory of last time was that you were looking at the financial side and I am not sure we finished it off. Would that fit in with your memory of it?*

**Client:** *Actually, you're right. Yes, I said I would do the number crunching.*

## Aiming for the Pinnacle

**Coach:** So, which would you like to look at today – finance or marketing?

**Client** Finance. Absolutely. No point in going any further unless I pin that down. Thanks Richard. I do that all the time – go off into something before I have wrapped up another bit. Yeah...okay.

**Coach:** So...how did the number crunching go?

**Client:** Looks tight enough. But...
Well, if I am to go with this the way it needs to be done, I am about twenty thousand shy. Michael and I looked at all the budgets and, really, we'd be taking too big a risk by scrimping. It would just be a waste of time and money. We could string out the suppliers but we've already got some goodwill and, if we compromise that, we could find ourselves high and dry when things are tight.

**Coach:** Would that be something like with the other business... the one that you had to wind up?

**Client:** Yes...we really didn't attend to the cashflow early enough. Head-in-the-sand stuff...you know the story.

**Coach:** Okay, so, I am remembering you asking me to highlight any signs that you might be letting this area slip.

**Client:** Yep...I can see how I could do the same again...scary!

**Coach:** But if you stay on top of it this time, it should be fine...is that it?

**Client:** Well...here's hoping...God knows what else will come up. But if we don't have the cashflow right, we have only ourselves to blame.

**Coach:** Can I ask you to clarify as best you can, how I, as your coach, can best assist in this.

**Client:** Well, you could regularly remind me about the cashflow *tracking and projection.*

**Coach:** *To what degree will you be relying on me for that to happen?*

**Client:** *What do you mean?*

**Coach:** *Well, this is such a crucial issue...I wonder if there was a management process, for example, that you and/or Michael might put in place to cover it off. I am no finance expert but I would be slightly concerned that it would become part of my role as your coach and I am not sure that would be the optimal use of me – for your own sake.*

**Client:** *This is getting back to the thing about you always looking for ways to make yourself redundant? (Smiles).*

**Coach:** *Got it in one!*

**Client:** *(Makes a written note). Okay, I am going to talk to the accountant about this... I'll just put it on my to do list...there.*

**Coach:** *So...*

**Client:** *Where were we?*

**Coach:** *Twenty grand? Possibly?*

**Client:** *Yes...well.. we're about twenty grand shy.*

**Coach:** *Right...*

**Client:** *But...found a way to cover it.*

**Coach:** *Yeah?*

**Client:** *Well, you remember I sold the boat?*

**Coach:** *Yes....I seemed to remember you were happy with the deal.*

## Aiming for the Pinnacle

**Client:** Well... we had originally worked out the capital gains tax at around twenty grand so....

**Coach:** (Silent)

**Client:** There's no registration for those boats and it was a cash deal. Fran will give us a receipt for whatever amount we want – all in a days work for him. (Smiles wryly).

**Coach:** So... no tax.

**Client:** Yep......it is not as if we've been milking the system. Some people are creamin' it and paying hardly any tax. Michael and I have been paying into the system for years.

**Coach:** Any trade-offs in this decision Karen?

**Client:** What do you mean?

**Coach:** Any downside to it? Anything to lose?

**Client:** Well, the revenue people won't know a thing. We can use it to pay some expenses by cash. It'll just be blended into the trading. You're looking at me......(Shifts on her seat).

**Coach:** Well...I am interpreting my rôle here as...
...you said very early on..., quite assertively, that you value honesty and integrity in anything you do. I don't see it as my role to tell you what's honest or dis-honest, but I do think it's important for you to checkout any potential conflicts with those values.

**Client:** But everyone is doing it...tax...what a joke!

**Coach:** Are they? Would that be relevant?

**Client:** Well...not everyone...but.

**Coach:** (Smiles affectionately) I suppose the key is somewhere around how this decision is truly congruent with what is important to you. I accept that there may be lots of people

> evading taxes. I am not sure how many have promised themselves they will live a life of integrity and how it might be relevant if they did.

**Client:** Ouch!

**Coach:** What?

**Client:** Thanks a lot Richard! (jokingly) – you've just managed to burst my bubble. We had this all worked out last night. Now we're back at the drawing board. I thought this coaching was supposed to make me feel better!

**Coach:** Who told you that? (Feigning puzzlement).

**Client:** (Laughs...then sighs). Damn.

Whilst the words exchanged during this piece of dialogue were obviously an important part of the experience, much more was happening than just words. The words were being spoken in a context. Without that context, it is possible that the dialogue would have taken a different direction. Perhaps the most important part of that context is the existence of trust.

Karen opened up to Richard quite spontaneously. She trusted him enough to reveal her plan about the capital gains tax. One could argue that she might have expected him to simply see things the same way as she did – to simply agree with her that her plan was 'normal' or 'acceptable', or whatever word might fit, and that Richard was therefore no threat. You could argue, also, that their contract had stated that anything Karen revealed would be confidential. These may well be the case in a given coaching environment, but I suggest that when it comes to personal growth coaching the issue is far more nuanced.

Say ,for example, Richard had what we might call a 'creative' approach to income tax himself and, at the same time, he had a dependence on seeing himself as one of 'the good guys' i.e. not 'one of them' – those people who do 'bad' things. Let's say that, whilst he justifies his own tax evasion to himself, at the next level of consciousness down (or up –

depending on the graphic you use) he actually believes that to evade tax is wrong in the same way as shop-lifting is wrong. However, in order to maintain his current lifestyle, Richard has calculated that he 'cannot afford' to pay his taxes fully. He has what we might call 'competing commitments'. The commitment that prevails is the one suggested by his behavior at that time. Richard's two commitments are about honesty and maintaining his lifestyle. This could possibly be understood in terms of Maslow's Hierarchy of Needs – Richard has a strong current need for status, perhaps.

Richard's 'need' for honesty is a self-actualization need (in this case) and, for his self-actualization to progress, it will be necessary for this need to come into the foreground. When is does, Richard will be faced with a dilemma and will likely experience a degree of discomfort as this need will compete for his attention with a lower order need. Until this self-actualization need does come to the foreground, Richard will keep the conflict underground, i.e. subconscious. This subconscious tug-of-war will be part of his subliminal presence with Karen and will effect his dialogue with her. It is possible, and probably likely, that neither party will see the elephant in the room and there will be either avoidance – Karen will not feel safe enough (consciously or unconsciously) to reveal all – or she will reveal all and, through passive or active collusion, nothing will change.

Of course, Richard might have read a book on coaching and decided to bring the matter up. Even if this happens, the CAUSED Effect will kick in and the outcome will be effected. Either party, or both parties, will run the risk of becoming defensive and the relationship may be compromised by a type of awkwardness that is not accompanied by a compelling sense of growth. The matter might end up being a prompt to the coach to 'look inside' and deal with a layer of self-deception within themselves, but unless the matter is redressed with Karen fairly promptly, the growthful quality of the relationship is likely to be compromised in some way.

Of course, another possibility is that Richard is fully up-to-date with his taxes but has a subterranean anger at people who *'milk the system'* – *'those who do not pay their fair share'*. His anger might even have an ostensibly noble element to it – *'if those greedy tax-evaders paid their fair share, there would be more resources available for the socially deprived.'* This too will be part of the dialogue. In a later chapter, I will explore the world of emotion but, for the moment, I suggest that what Richard does with those feelings will be an important part of his effectiveness as a personal growth coach. If, for example, he has a strong need to believe that he is the type of coach that can provide a calm and safe environment to his clients, that is conducive to growth and insight, he might be tempted to avoid seeing that this unconscious anger is within him. However, consciously or unconsciously, Karen, and the quality of the dialogue, will be influenced by Richard's state – *particularly* if he is not aware of it. Karl Jung is reputed to have suggested that, just as a surgeon needs to ensure that they are not carrying any germs into the operating theatre, a therapist needs to ensure that they are not carrying, into the therapeutic relationship, anything that would contaminate the encounter. The same applies to personal growth coaching – the most important work that the coach does in coaching is done before even meeting a client. It is about the coach rigorously interrogating their own perceptions and needs in order to clear some ground ahead of the client. Otherwise, the coach is hoping to sell oil to the Arabs – good work if you can get it!

A third issue is when the coach's work ethic includes ensuring that their taxes are up-to-date and they are left with a potential ethical dilemma. No buried anger, no avoided collusion – Richard, for example, finds himself with a quandary. *"Do I want to work with a client who is living in a way that is in conflict with my ethics?"* This is an important issue for a coach.

One of the great challenges facing those, who are interested in building their effectiveness in coaching, is that frequently '*the words'* just do not work. *"I told the staff that my door is always open...and still they don't come to me to talk these things through"* is a not uncommon utterance from managers. *"I asked my client if their taxes were up-to-date and they said yes – so what's the problem?"* Usually, the key here is that the aspiring coach has underestimated the power of the context. Something as simple as the wording of a flyer can influence the coaching. This is not just in terms of client expectations but it can also influence *who* chooses to come to a particular coach.

## The Parallel Effect.

A useful concept to consider, in exploring the dynamics of personal growth coaching, is what I call 'The Parallel Effect'. Simply stated, this works as follows: when a coach approaches their work with a firm commitment to their own personal growth, they will tend to attract clients and issues that provide a 'next step' challenge to that personal growth. I have found this to be so prevalent as to appear at times to be miraculous! Time and time again, I have found myself working with clients who want to work on something just at a time when I am wrestling with a parallel issue. In addition, I have supported countless coaches over the years who find the same phenomenon at play. At times, it is enough to have the most committed atheist to doubt themselves!

*Jean, a coach, has been finding dealing with her teenage daughter tough going lately. Within days of a particularly tempestuous episode, Jean gets a call from a stranger – Maureen. Maureen says that she got Jean's name from a friend, Chris, who had worked with Jean before. Maureen starts the work by saying she wants to get fit, lose weight and write a music book. However, guess what, by the second meeting, Maureen reveals that of more importance to her is her relationship with Kate her teenage daughter.*

*Josh, a coach, has been working with Samantha for about six weeks. Josh's mother recently was taken into hospital and the prognosis does not look good. Within a week, Samantha reveals that her father has been taken ill and it may be terminal.*

*Anna had recently had to go to court over a land dispute. Her client, Julie, reveals that she is taking her employer to court in a bullying suit.*

These are typical examples of the parallel effect at work. It is important to note that it tends to present itself when the coach has made the commitment to their own growth. It is as if, when we acknowledge that our view of the world must be selective and self-serving in some way, but we don't yet know how, that somehow events conspire to show us how, and offer to us opportunities to move forward in our growth. In fact, the Parallel effect is so prevalent and powerful that I have come to the conclusion that there is much more value being transacted within a personal growth coaching relationship than the exchange of fees for a service. An open coach will know that each encounter with a client, if approached with humility and openness, offers the coach just as much opportunity for growth as it will the client. The exchange of fees is simply a contextual necessity that is logical given the circumstances. In fact, when the coach is pre-occupied with making money, at the expense of a passion for breakthrough on the part of the client within the coaching, this very issue can be paralleled in their practice. A client is stuck in their efforts to find a path in life that feels right for them. They are distracted by the opportunity to make money doing something that they really do not enjoy doing. Meanwhile, the coach is regretting taking on a contract last week with a client he just doesn't feel right about – *but the money is good!*

**Attitude.**

Coaching is often presented as something that can help people 'get into the driver's seat of their life'. Part of that process involves the client taking responsibility for their decisions and relinquishing excuses. One common excuse, that we use to explain why we are not happy, or why we are not achieving all that we might, is that it is other's people's fault. Of course, if we can blame someone for the decisions we make ourselves, it can really take us off the hook. If, on the other hand, 'life' gets in the way, it is more likely that we will accept its limitations and/or work around them. If a client is late every time with their projects, their employer may not be inclined to give them the big breaks. If they persist in maintaining their poor diet, they will only have themselves to blame if their health deteriorates. It is usually easier for someone to come to terms with the finite nature of life than what they see as the imperfections or the 'unreasonable' demands of others.

In aviation, the term 'attitude' means the orientation of a plane on two axes. One axis is the 'pitch', meaning the degree to which the nose of the plane is pointing above, at, or below the horizon. The second axis is the 'roll', meaning the degree to which the aircraft is banking if at all. The attitude of the aircraft will determine where it is going unless the pilot adjusts something. It will also effect the fuel efficiency. An airplane that has its flaps out in advance of landing will be able to pitch forward without necessarily losing altitude (height) as quickly as it would without the flaps – but it will be less aerodynamic while it is doing so.

# Aiming for the Pinnacle

A person's attitude will hugely influence where they will go in given conditions. In personal growth coaching, the attitude of both the coach and client will hugely influence where the coaching will go. The coach has little control over the attitude of the client. The coach has significant control over their own attitude. This includes the coach's attitude to the last statement!

A phrase attributed to Henry Ford is that, whether you believe you can do something or not, you are probably right. This is about attitude. One of the most powerful breakthroughs a person can make is to discover that they might just be able to achieve something they previously thought they couldn't. If a coach believes that a client can achieve something, this will be part of the CAUSED Effect in that relationship *(Reminder: Conscious And Unconscious Signals Effecting Dialogue.)*

If a coach believes that a client cannot achieve something, this too will be part of the CAUSED Effect. If a coach believes that a client cannot achieve something, but the coach deludes themselves by plastering over this belief with an un-integrated type of 'positive thinking', something the coach picked up from reading a self-help book, both these beliefs will be part of the CAUSED Effect.

So how does a coach develop genuine positive beliefs in a human being's capacity to rise to a challenge? The answer is for the coach to seek challenges themselves, in their own life, engage with those challenges, either succeed or fail, and learn to live with the consequences.

**Grounded Optimism.**

In an episode of the UK comedy TV series 'Red Dwarf', set in outer space, Lister, one of the main characters, contracts a 'space virus' one of the results of which is the manifestation of both 'Confidence' and 'Paranoia' as two new characters on board the ship. *Paranoia* is a dull, pessimistic, 'it'll never work' type character with the language of a man burdened by life's heavy tragedies. *Confidence*, on the other hand, is tall, well-postured, clean-cut, has a magnificent set of snow-white teeth, complete with occasional sparkle. This character is a *'can do'* type and, coach-like, energetically encourages Lister to take brave new steps into his own potential. Meanwhile, Paranoia continually lists the reasons why *'it'll never work'* in a drab self-defeating monotone. Red Dwarf is a British production and, by the way, Confidence has an American accent!

After some tortuous indecision, as he listens to both Confidence and Paranoia present their cases for life, Lister is persuaded to move out of his comfort zone into a new challenge. This is something he had been avoiding all along – a space walk out on the hull of the ship – scary! Each step of the way, Confidence cheer-led his apprentice to overcome his fears and venture out into the vastness of outer space – complete with magnetic boots and space suit. With the help of his all-American coach, Lister reveled in his achievement, as he took that *'one small step for a man, a giant leap for Listerkind.'* Confidence, never happy without going the extra mile, then invites Lister to take off his helmet. Lister is afraid. He puts up reasons not to do it. His coach eggs him on with more *'you can do it'* words of encouragement. 'But what about oxygen?' Lister asks, doing his best not to be self-limiting. 'OXYGEN IS FOR LOSERS!' booms his indominatable mentor. Lister recovers from his space virus.

The world of personal growth coaching lives within the solar system of all things coaching. The solar system of coaching lives within the galaxy of self-help. The galaxy of self-help lives within the universe of reality. How can personal growth coaching keep its life-line with that universe? Henry Ford may well have been right – for himself. Perhaps the father of the Model-T had a better than average grasp on reality than the average motor industry tycoon – or used car salesman for that matter.

Or, and whatever little I know about Ford cars, I know less about Henry, perhaps he was not lumbered with a need for oxygen, metaphorically speaking, like the rest of us mortals. Perhaps he had a single-minded approach to his goals that led to production of black cars for the masses but also made a major contribution to the western world's addiction to oil? Who knows – I don't. One thing I think I do know, however, is that I need oxygen – and no amount of positive thinking, no matter how powerful, has yet persuaded me otherwise. Alas, I am the victim of an intractable self-limiting belief – my aspiration for breathless living is domed to failure, no pun intended!

Abraham Maslow suggested that a symptom of self-actualization is an ability to face reality. No doubt this assertion caused ripples within the 'Con-federation Of Metaphysical Philosophers, Learneds And Illuminary

## Aiming for the Pinnacle

Neo-Thinkers' - COMPLAINT! History is replete with efforts to pin down reality. Even in this modern day, people argue over whether the creation of man was a seven-day carefully project-managed celestial roll-out or a multi-million-year evolution process, complete with amoebas and monkeys. I suspect this ship of debate will outlive me and may Darwin bless all who sail in her. Meanwhile I, and at least the majority of my clients, even the 'losers' amongst us, need oxygen. Oxygen is an example of reality – that needs little debate. Perhaps someday we will discover that the human need for oxygen is an illusion but I wouldn't hold my breath! Gravity is an example of reality. Anyone who wants to argue to me that gravity is an example of selective perception might make interesting company over a pint of Guinness but I will probably not be factoring their hypotheses into my walking trips around the Cliffs of Moher in the County Clare of my native Ireland.

Maslow also suggested that being 'solution-focused' is a feature of self-actualization. This means that a self-actualizing person will tend to look for the best outcome from a given situation. If complaining does not look like it will change things, complaining will be omitted as an option. If I can do nothing about an injustice done to me, the thing to do is to let go and move on.

I am not suggesting that I do anything to support a similar injustice – far from it. Every society has is begrudgers and its heroes. I once heard a rather tongue-in-cheek story suggesting the difference between an Irish man and an American. If you were walking with an American and, turning a corner, you spotted a beautiful house on the hill complete with spectacular view, swimming pool, tennis court and Ferrari, the American might say: "You know what, some day I am going to have a house like that."

If you were walking with an Irish man, the parable goes, and saw such a house he might say "You know what, some day I am going to get that bastard!" The story is suggestive of a streak of begrudgery said to have been not uncommon in Ireland in days gone by – some say as a legacy of colonial dis-enfranchisement. Alas, in the era of the economic Celtic Tiger, mother Ireland may well be outgrowing this particular foible. I hope, in a moment of pause, she has replaced this dependence with a more productive, just and sustainable dependence.

So, positive thinking is useful – as long as we remember that we need oxygen. A not uncommon challenge, in personal growth coaching, is when a client, or the coach for that matter, has chosen a set of beliefs that enable them to avoid feeling the existential 'slings and arrows' of real life but those same beliefs limit them from making reality-based decisions.

In his book *'Bush at War Part III – State of Denial'*, Robert Woodward (of *'All the Presidents Men'* fame) recounts a conversation he had with General Peter Pace in 2006. Pace was one of the key US players in the management of the war following the Iraq invasion of 2003.

The conversation went as follows:

Woodward: *"Is this going to happen in your lifetime? (Victory in Iraq)*

Gen. Pace: *"Yes, it is. Well, I hope, yeah. I don't know. I should retract that line. It can happen in my lifetime."*

Woodward: *"Do you have any doubts that this was the right decision to invade Iraq?"*

Gen. Pace: *"I have no doubt at all. None. Zero."*

Woodward: *"Isn't the process, though, you always have to have doubt? I live on doubt."*

Gen. Pace: *"I'm sorry for you."*

Woodward: *"Don't be sorry for me. It's a wonderful process."*

Gen. Pace: *"I do not have doubt about what we've done. We did not do this. When we were sitting home minding our own business, we got attacked on 9/11.*

(Page 476)

Perhaps General Pace had a positive psychology philosophy of life. His understanding of the rôle of doubt seemed to differ to that of Woodward. When Maslow suggests that self-actualization includes being in touch with reality, 'no doubt' Pace would say that *he* is operating from reality. Woodward, on the other hand, seems to be in no doubt that doubt is a wonderful process.

Which of these two perspectives, if either, reflects reality? Does either one have a gravity-like or oxygen-like quality to it? We always need oxygen. Gravity always applies (while on Earth in any event). Do we always know enough? Do we always have less than full information? If General Pace and Robert Woodward were operating as personal growth coaches, which of their mindsets would be most likely to facilitate the self-actualization of their clients?

A twentieth century Chinese revolutionary was once asked if he thought that the French revolution, two hundred years earlier, was a good idea. He replied that it was too early to say. He seemed to have no doubt about this. General Pace would, no doubt, feel sorry for the Chinese revolutionary. I suspect that Bob Woodward may well have felt sorry for General Pace, seeing him as less than blessed with the gift of humility. If so, such empathy and compassion in the corridors of world power is touching!

It is worth bearing in mind that one does not get to the rank of general in the US military without some capacity to produce results. Is Pace's mindset suggestive of a dependence on a belief that 'we were right' or 'we are the good guys?' Is this belief a need-dominant belief reflecting Pace's needs more than reflecting reality? If so, what would it take for Pace to let go of this dependence and what implications might this have for his other needs – e.g. esteem. How much courage would it take to let go of that belief and face the consequences.

Peter Pace's uniform jacket has a conspicuous array of medals and motifs reflecting, presumably amongst other things, what those who bestowed such awards on him saw as acts of courage under fire and elsewhere. I am not suggesting that I know whether or not it was a good idea to invade Iraq, but I am suggesting that it is a good idea to assume that we do not have all the facts when it comes to important decisions.

My experience in working in personal growth convinces me that the move from certainty to humility very often involves a significant emotional shift.

Again, this shift is not for the faint-hearted. I have seen people step into what is, to them at the time, an abyss of uncertainty as they open their minds to the possibility that they may have been living off a self-serving perception of something. When this happens, they see the door opening of a prison they did not even know they were in. When they walk through that door, and let their eyes adjust to the light, they report that living in a world of doubt and humility is 'wonderful' and liberating even though it brings with it new challenges.

If my hypothesis is robust, I have to wonder how someone who has survived through life-threatening bloody battle conditions, complete with bullets and mortars, does not have the courage to step into that abyss. One man's courage may well be another man's folly.

In personal growth coaching, the coach dances with two partners in a precarious affair. One is the solution-focused lover and the other is the reality-based spouse.

That dance can be represented by the OAR Matrix...

## The 'OAR' Matrix

Attitude

|  | Unrealistic | Realistic |
|---|---|---|
| **Optimistic** | **Optimistic Unrealistic**<br>I can be whatever height I like! | **Optimistic Realistic**<br>I can change my diet. |
| **Pessimistic** | **Pessimistic Unrealistic**<br>I can't change. | **Pessimistic Realistic**<br>I am not as good looking as I would like to be. |

Of course, a common issue is how do we know something is realistic or unrealistic? A simple answer to this is that a positive mindset, in the absence of evidence to the contrary, will assume that something is possible, rather than, in the absence of evidence to the contrary, that it is not possible. In other words, if you don't know what the reality is, you might as well assume the best – that the glass is half full rather than half empty. Nothing ventured, nothing gained.

An example relevant to the notion of grounded optimism is a term that has become quite common over the last few years: that is the concept of 'the abundant universe.' I have worked with people who have fervently claimed to believe that the universe is one of abundance but who seem, by their own analysis and not mine, to live a life of deprivation. They report a series of disappointments in their life but cling to a belief that things will be different – soon. As they courageously chip away at their real beliefs, they discover that their perception of the abundant universe is a house of cards. It is actually a piece of wishful thinking that allows them to cope with a life that they actually see as tragic, unjust and threatening. It is as if their belief in Santa Claus was never really outgrown but replaced with a somewhat less seasonal alternative. Again, this can be seen in terms of Maslow's hierarchy of needs. For people to grow, they need to feel safe enough to step into a new stage of maturity. Children who do not experience nurturance, security and love, find it harder as adults to exist at the contribution end of the NICE curve – to move close to self-actualization before their three or four score and ten years are up. However, if you believe you can make up for previous deprivation, you probably can and I have seen no shortage of evidence to support this. Equally, if you believe that you can't, you are probably right. We have the option to choose which attitude to take – optimistic or pessimistic. Free will exists whether we like it or not – like gravity and oxygen. If we want to be real to ourselves, we have no choice but to accept the existence of freewill!

**Empathy.**

In the last chapter, I mentioned Carl Rogers in the context of humanistic psychology and, more specifically, client-centered therapy. Rogers suggested that one of the core conditions necessary for effective therapy is *empathy* on the part of the therapist for the client.

Some questions that may be of relevance to coaching:

- What is empathy?
- What outcomes might it assist in coaching?
- How else might these outcomes be achieved?
- What 'costs' might empathy involve?
- What unproductive confusions might exist in regard to empathy?

Simon Baron-Cohen, a Cambridge University professor of Developmental Psychopathology, posits the notion of an 'Empathy Quotient' and suggests that women tend to have, on average, a higher 'E-Q' than men. He also suggests that men, on average, have a higher 'S-Q' score than women. S-Q, 'Systemizing Quotient', he suggests, is the ability to organise variables and extract underlying rules that govern a system. My current analysis of the role of empathy in coaching is an attempt at systemizing.

Although they can be enhanced with practice, both capacities tend to be automatic in nature when they are working at the higher end of effectiveness.

Barron-Cohen suggests that empathizing is the ability to identify another person's emotions and respond to them with care and sensitivity. A person with a high E-Q will have a desire, and an ability, to 'sense' how another person feels and that this ability is an important social capacity. Indeed, given that babies are unable to speak for the first couple of years, a parent's capacity to 'know' how their baby feels and what it wants or needs would presumably make a significant contribution to the parent's ability to nurture the baby.

Baron-Cohen's theory might fit with day-to-day observations of how men and women respond to babies' body language and sounds. In my own experience of parenting, I have seen countless situations where a child's emotional state has changed when a trusted 'other' accurately suggested ways, to the child, of reflecting the feelings and perceptions. The degree to which, in response to an experience of empathy, the child in question has moved towards 'closure' or peace after an emotionally challenging experience has, in these events, been tangibly noticeable and more or less consistent. In addition, I would suggest that the process creates a by-product in the relationship – a strengthening of trust on the part of the empathized – their trust in the person empathizing tends to increase or strengthen.

Baron-Cohen suggests three brain types under the heading of E-S Theory (Empathizing-Systemizing Theory). The first brain type has a higher E-Q than S-Q and he calls this a 'female brain.' The second has a higher S-Q than E-Q and he calls this a 'male brain.' The other type is where E-Q and S-Q are more or less the same and he labels this a 'balanced brain.'

If Simon Barron-Cohen's theory is robust, which type of brain might be best for effective coaching? Which part of my brain do I need to use in order to apply myself *to answering that question?* The empathizing part or the systemizing part - or both?

A term commonly found in coaching, leadership and management literature is 'Emotional Intelligence' – or 'EI'. Prior to EI's relatively recent popularity, its academic older brother 'IQ', standing for Intelligence Quotient, has had widespread application. Indeed EI is often presented as EQ or 'Emotional intelligence Quotient.'

IQ is designed to measure a person's intelligence relative to a statistical average. By definition, the average in a given population is 100. Anything above this is an above average IQ and anything below this is below average. Normally, about 10% of the population fall below an IQ of 80 and about 10% fall above 120. Those with high IQs can join 'societies' such as Mensa (IQ=132+) and other such lofty hangouts for smarties. Much debate has occurred over the decades about how best to measure IQ and even whether it is useful at all to measure it.

The idea of IQ and Simon Baron-Cohen's concept of 'systemizing intelligence' seem to me to be closely related. His concept of 'empathizing intelligence' seems closely related to emotional intelligence.

A name frequently associated with emotional intelligence is that of Daniel Goleman whose 1995 publication on the subject was a best seller. In the most simplified form, Emotional Intelligence is the ability to accurately detect and constructively respond to our emotions and the emotions of others.

Goleman, and many other writers, suggest that EQ is a more accurate predictor of success than IQ and, over the last decade or so, an industry has grown up around the concept. As with E-Q (Baron-Cohen's term), EQ, would appear to be relevant to coaching.

In the last chapter, before I did a fleeting skim of the therapy market, I suggested that a key part of the equation, from the client's perspective, is the degree to which they experience insight as a result of the therapy. I suggested that this was just as relevant in the context of coaching.

I also suggested that there were two types of insight - emotional & cognitive and suggested the ICE Matrix as a relevant graphical representation: Insight, Cognitive and Emotional.

**The 'ICE' Matrix**

Therapy (any modality) or Coaching

| Cognitive Insight | Low Emotional 'Insight' | High Emotional 'Insight' |
|---|---|---|
| **High** | **Cognitive Insight** Useful but incomplete 'Heady' or 'disconnected' | **Cognitive & Emotional Insight** 'Integrative.' |
| **Low** | **Neither Cognitive nor Emotional Insight** Waste of time or abusive. 'Blind leading the blind.' | **Emotional Insight** Useful but incomplete Unreasonable? comfortable discomfort? |

The hypothesis is that personal growth coaching is effective when a client gains insight into how they feel about something and what opportunities and challenges their environment presents in the context of those feelings.

**Empathy and Identification.**

Is there a difference between the concepts of empathy and identification? I would suggest that the two words can be used to describe two different processes. I would further suggest that an effective coach will want to be alert to the difference and be aware of how they both feature in their coaching.

Empathy, I believe, is the capacity to 'pick up' the emotional nuances of another person without necessarily having had any experience of what they are trying to communicate to you – or even absorbing a factual account of the event. You might be able to accurately recount the emotions but not be able to understand or repeat the story.

Identification, on the other hand, is the process whereby we hear a story and equate it with a situation we have found ourselves in, in reality or in our dreams, recall the feelings we had at the time, with or without residual charge, and assume that the narrator feels the same way that we felt when we where in that situation.

Empathy, by its nature, accurately picks up the emotions of the other.

Identification, by its nature, is subjective and can exist without accurately naming the emotions of the narrator. Of course, if I identify with a situation, I may well have felt the same way as the narrator – but I may not have.

Whether I identify with a person, empathize with them, or both, the question is what do I do next? And how will my response effect the rapport? Will it contribute to growth, will it restrict growth, or will it have no effect?

I propose that how a coach responds to emotions, in both themselves and the client, are a key feature of effective coaching. That may or may not include the client feeling 'empathized with'.


**Objectivity.**

Not infrequently, coaches suggest that what they are aiming to be able to do is to offer themselves to their clients as mirrors. The idea behind this is that the coach aims to reflect back to the client what they are presenting as themselves and their world. The concept is based on the notion that clients, and coaches are also clients to their own coaches, have a selective perception of what is going on around them and inside of them. It holds that a less selective reflection of this will challenge the client to align themselves more truly to the reality of their humanity. The client, being human, will have a perception of things that will support their current needs. Not seeing this for what it is, is simply another need at work.

In order for a coach to offer a growthful reflection, it is assumed that their reflection won't be laden down with their own selective perceptions. Otherwise, the theory is, the client might simply discard their own selective beliefs in favor of a new set of novel, but just as selective, beliefs and this is only if these new beliefs appear to be attractive enough to adopt.

If this hypothesis is sound, and I believe it is, for better or for worse, a key feature of effective coaching will be the coach's capacity to respond objectively to the client – to act as a mirror, a mirror that is 'unsmudged', if you will, by the coach's own neediness.

This, alas, is probably the single greatest challenge for a personal growth coach and it is the attribute that, when present, makes the difference between a personal growth coach and a coach who is selling themselves based on competencies for example, like being a good listener, or a 'feelgood' factor offered by an adept cheerleader.

So how can a coach be one hundred percent objective with clients – all of the time? Answer – they cannot. In the same way as a space shuttle is constantly checking its position, discovering that it is off course and adjusting its trajectory, a coach, at best, can notice when a dialogue appears to be in a subjective tract and question it at the next suitable moment. Even then, remembering what Bob Woodward tried to convey to General Pace, a coach needs to be 'wonderful' with living in doubt, just as a space shuttle pilot needs to be 'wonderful' with the fact that the shuttle, at any given time, will be off course pending the next correction.

Even with what I have just claimed, the challenge is for the coach to be *as objective as they can* and, most importantly, to be so in a way of which the client can make use. I may be capable of profound objectivity, but if my client is not ready to engage with that objectivity, I will be of little use. In the same way, if I have a good objective handle on the 'reality' of Santa Claus, presenting that reality to a three-year-old child will have little chance of moving the child out of their beliefs if they are not ready. I have to stress that I have never tried to do this to a three-year-old but I have seen older kids try with interesting results. I was once touched by a three-year-old's concern for the wellbeing of a six-year-old when the former took me aside and suggested that the latter had a wild notion that Santa Claus did not exist!

For growthful dialogue to be given a chance, the coach has to be both objective and sensitive to how the client will be able to engage with the objectivity.

If, for example, a client reports that the results of a 360° feedback exercise couldn't be accurate because the people who completed the questionnaires *'didn't know the whole picture',* the coach might easily find themselves wanting to agree with the client. The coach might be identifying with a situation where the client feels misunderstood.

However, let's say that such a feedback exercise is designed to give the recipient accurate information about how others find the client, even if it is not the whole story. The fact that the *others do not seem to have the whole story* is an inherent part of the feedback. In this case, the challenge is for the client to accept the reality that the exercise suggests – that people experience them a certain way. The coach does not have to experience them the same as the feedback respondents – they just have to remain objective in their engagement and sensitive to the challenge that it presents to the client.

This is an example of where a coach can be, potentially anyhow, completely objective. The facts are simple: a 360° exercise has been completed, the results are available, all evidence appears to suggest that the methodology was robust, and the client is wrestling with the implications. The coach does not need to have an opinion on why the respondents said what they said, how the responses might be different in different circumstances or how unfair the results seemed to be in the light of what they know about this client – a person they might admire for example.

Let's say the client is in some way emotionally devastated by the aggregate findings of the exercise and that the feedback was totally at odds with their perceptions of themselves in that environment. Let's say that they were then left with choices in how to deal with this new uncomfortable reality. In these circumstances, a coach's response, and their very presence, will help or hinder the client's negotiation with this new reality as it offers opportunity for growth.

So how does a coach develop their own objectivity? Do we not all have our realities and is it not a case that these are valid in themselves. The key here is to look at the needs and thinking that might underlie our reality.

I knew, when dealing with the three-year-old, that Santa does not exist – at least in a way that would allow them to order toys for themselves into their teens and twenties. This is an example of objective reality in the same way as oxygen and gravity are features of objective reality. Admittedly, they are simple and easy elements. I accept that accompanying a governmental decision-maker as they come to see that simply jailing more citizens, without stopping to see how policies designed and implemented without enough 'ethical' maturity will generate more and more crime in the future, may represent a greater leap of faith than that required to accept the non-existence of Santa for a three-year-old.

However, the emotional challenge for a forty-three-old to open their minds to the possibility that their perception of how crime is generated, and how it should be dealt with, has actually been a self-serving selective perception is easily as great, if not considerably greater than the emotional challenge a young child has to face when considering the possibility that Santa does not exist.

In fact, I would suggest that it is generally easier to come to terms with the fact that we have been a victim of an injustice than to come to terms with the fact that we have been the perpetrator of an injustice. Interestingly, sometimes people can do the latter if they can see that they were also in the former group.

It is in this very arena that a coach will need to have as clean a mirror as possible. The one pervasive block to our seeing new layers of ourselves is fear. Unmastered fear or judgementalism in the person of the coach will be sure to smudge the mirror and leave the client with little in the line of compelling new perceptual territory capable of providing reliable footholds in the climb towards self-actualization.

In conclusion of the subject of objectivity, let me suggest one more matrix.

## The 'GROUSE' Matrix

Response Effectiveness

|  | Ungrowthful | Growthful |
|---|---|---|
| **Objective** | **Objective Ungrowthful**<br>'You're one of the bad guys - learn to live with it now!' (When client not ready). | **Objective Growthful**<br>'How would it be if you discovered you had a blind spot?' |
| **Subjective** | **Subjective Ungrowthful**<br>'We are the good guys. They must be the baddies.' | **Subjective Growthful**<br>E.g. 'I know how you feel.' (Lesser of two evils). |

**G**rowthful **R**esponses **O**bjective **U**ngrowthful **S**ubjective **E**ffectiveness

The LRQ represents a response that, whilst not particularly objective, can challenge the client to consider one step towards objectivity. A man may need to temporarily see himself as *'at least not as bad as those others'* before he feels safe enough to face his own ethical cul-de-sacs. Later, he may then be able to face the next layer of his dependences - remember PAUSE. The subjective response may be conscious or unconscious on the part of the coach. In fact, I believe that some coaches have an unconscious competence in this area. With experience, they get to see this as a conscious competence and, after an initial awkwardness in their new awareness, can then hone their skill to greater precision.

I am hoping that the other three quadrants of the GROUSE matrix are self-explanatory. If not, the next chapters may offer some elucidation.

**Chapter Bullets:**

- Coaching can be about moving to 'abnormal functioning.'
- Coaching is a market offering.
- The Prime Competence is about a conversation.
- An effective coach needs to be clear about effectiveness.
- There are different ways of defining coaching effectiveness.
- Coaching embraces both 'results' and 'delivery'.
- Coaching 'aims' to deliver.
- There are 'achievement goals' and 'personal growth' goals.
- Whatever the goals, personal growth is part of the context.
- Coaching embraces both 'content' and 'context.'
- There is a 'macro-context' and a 'micro-context.'
- Coaching embraces a stated contract and a psychological contract.
- Effective coaching 'works' both contracts.
- People play 'games'.
- All that is called 'coaching' is not the same.
- The RARE and RUGED matrices can help surface expectations.
- Freud offered his version of a topography of the unconscious.
- Dialogue is CAUSED.
- 'The Parallel Effect' is a feature of personal growth coaching.
- Attitude effects coaching.
- Optimism is a resource – if grounded.
- Oxygen is an example of reality.
- The House on the Hill.
- Beliefs can allow us to avoid feelings.
- 'It is too early to assess the French Revolution.'
- General Peter Pace has many medals.

## Aiming for the Pinnacle

- Moving to humility takes courage.
- OAR is about realistic optimism.
- The 'Abundant Universe' can be a house of cards.
- The 'Abundant Universe' can be a tested reality.
- Empathy has a role in coaching.
- ICE is about two different types of insight.
- Empathy and Identification can be confused.
- GROUSE is about objectivity.

# Chapter 6
# Self-Worth.
*Crucial Milestone.*

**Self-Esteem and Self-Worth.**

Another aid, which I believe offers opportunity for understanding and precision, in an exploration of personal growth coaching, is an appreciation of the difference between self-esteem and self-worth. For the more semantically precise amongst us, I invite you to at least consider the value of using the terms separately.

On occasion, I have seen the terms self-worth and self-esteem used interchangeably – at least it seemed that way from the context. However, I suggest that there are two significantly different concepts within the arena of personal growth and self-actualization and that these two terms are worthy labels for those two concepts.

Self-worth is a term I use to refer to a condition wherein a person sees themselves as intrinsically of value *without reference to anyone else and this perception of themselves stands up to ongoing scrutiny.*

Self-esteem is something we rely on pending the arrival of our self-worth.

Some questions relating to self-worth:

1. What value is self-worth to me?
2. How do I know if I have it?
3. How do I obtain it?
4. How do I maintain it?
5. What value is knowing if someone else has self-worth?
6. How do I know they have it?
7. How can I help someone move to their own self-worth?
8. What can I do with someone who has self-worth that I cannot do with someone who has not?

## 1. What Value is Self-worth to Me?

By 'me' I mean whoever asks the question.

Maslow suggests that we have a hierarchy of needs which can be represented as a triangle or pyramid. At the top of the triangle, is 'self-actualization' – meaning 'becoming all I can be.' Just below this top section lies another set of needs which center around 'self-esteem'. If Maslow's hierarchy is valid, then, in order for me to become 'all that I can be', I need self-esteem. I personally want to become all I can be; therefore, attaining self-esteem is of value to me.

However, I suggest that between self-esteem and self-actualization, there lies another layer which is represented by self-worth. And again, if I want to aim for the pinnacle, I need to embrace this need.

Maslow aside, is there a way of understanding the value of self-worth without reference to any psychological academic model? Is it not true that the term itself implies that it is of value? 'Worth' is 'of worth'. I suggest that experiencing ourselves as 'self-worthy' is of value in and of itself in a way that is at least as valuable as any other experience and, in my opinion, of far greater value than most. I would also suggest that, when a person encounters real self-worth in themselves, whether it is something that they have just developed or something that was with them all along but they just realized it, they inevitably see how valuable it is in its own right.

Breaking into what I suggest is the penultimate section of the pyramid, i.e. self-worth, brings with it emotions of a particular quality that tend to leave the experiencer with a compelling sense that this new way of being is the way things are meant to be. It brings with it, particularly for the novice, a new sense of solidity and humble confidence that previous 'breakthroughs' simply did not offer. This includes a sense of how they had previously had a '*shortage*' of self-worth. It might be described as suddenly having something that I would have needed to have, in order to see that I needed it! And yet somehow, it seems to have fallen into my lap. Furthermore, when the dust settles, the new owner of self-worth will often, on reflection, have a sense that previous situations, obstacles and opportunities, now seem, retrospectively, somehow to have been part of a kind of conspiracy to getting them to a point of self-worth. This then can be interpreted in different ways by different people. A common one in my culture is to see it as simply that I was unconsciously getting in my own way in order to get me to wake up to something – this self-worth thing. Another way of describing it might be that *'I now can see'* having deduced that *'I once was blind.'*

A feature of self-worth is, I believe, an acceptance that it doesn't hugely matter how it came about. The feeling of humility, that comes as part of the package, is sufficient to convince us that, even if we did conjure up an explanation of how it came about, we may well have it wrong and it doesn't really matter! This is because self-worth carries with it a worth of its own that leaves philosophical debates about where it comes from in the shade. I would even propose that a compelling interest in how I attained self-worth could suggest that I am not yet operating from a place of genuine self-worth!

## 2. How do I Know if I Have Self-worth?

One of the tricky parts of working with self-worth is that it is often confused with self-esteem. In fact, I would say that, more often than not, what is thought of as self-worth is actually self-esteem. As I suggested earlier, self-esteem is something we rely on pending the arrival of our self-worth. Self-esteem is what we get, whether we notice it or not, when others claim we are of worth in a way that works for us but that, in the absence of those claims, we would have a very different experience of ourselves – a far less confident and able version of ourselves.

Self-esteem is therefore reliant on the perceptions, desires and actions of others. It is also generally reliant on our actions – simply because we get it as a result of our actions – those which feed the satisfactions of others. Maslow suggests that self-esteem is a need we need to have fulfilled before we can move up the pyramid to the next stage. I appreciate that I am taking a deliberately narrow interpretation of Maslow here, but I believe that the essence of it applies. However, whilst *some* self-esteem may help a person move in the direction of self-actualization, I suggest that any more than that *some* can inhibit a person's development towards self-actualization. I appreciate that this is a rather radical view on self-esteem.

## Aiming for the Pinnacle

I find it useful to look at self-esteem and self-worth in terms of treading water versus standing on solid ground. If I thread water in order to keep my head above water, I use ongoing energy. If I get tired, I may be tempted to hang onto the next person who, in turn, might be tempted to hang on to the next person. Each person is managing to keep their head above water and congratulate themselves, and others, for their achievement.

However, at the edges of the group of people in the water are people who are also getting tired but have no-one else to grab onto! They either become exhausted and drown, or break away from the group to take their chances alone. They may even be thrown a life-line from some unforeseen source. Self-worth is about getting our feet on solid ground. We need little energy to stand on that solid ground and very little to lie down and re-charge. Self-esteem has to be continually fed. Self-worth does not. It might need to be minded but not fed in the same way as self-esteem needs to be. If this is true, and it is possible to grow out of a need for self-esteem, can I reach my fullest level of effectiveness without outgrowing my need for self-esteem?

The need for self-esteem has, I believe, a finite shelf-life and is at its most growthful when met in conjunction with the meeting of other needs including security, social and 'stretching' needs. By stretching, I mean situations that challenge us to look at alternatives to feeding ourselves on self-esteem. I believe that a great number of people go to their grave without really encountering their own self-worth. Still more of us touch a sense of it, in the Autumn of our life, having felt a pang for what life might have been had we known this earlier.

I know I have self-worth when my *illusions about my self-worth* have been dismantled or pulverized so well, so consistently, that what I have left is standing on solid ground. That means that, when I try for something, and fail, and feel 'bad' about myself – insecure, shameful, fearful, whatever – that this experience tells me that I am not yet at a point of full self-worth. I may relieve these feelings with claims from others about how wonderful I am, bolstering my self-esteem, but it is at that moment of deprivation that I can get an insight into my level of self-worth. I am not saying that, at that moment, I necessarily feel of worth but I will get an insight into the degree to which I have genuinely reached a point of self-worth.

I will later explore how I believe emotional experiences offer insights and opportunities in our journey towards self-worth and self-actualization. At this point, I would just like to say that, in one's path towards self-actualization, self-esteem is a common bottleneck. Feeling good about myself is not an indication of self-worth. Sensing myself as a tiny speck in the scheme of things may be a more reliable indicator of my self-worth being within arms reach. Pride can offer us a very positive sense of ourselves – so can cocaine seemingly.

Humility, however, can strip away positive perceptions of ourselves and offers us the only true solid ground on which to see built our genuine self-worth. No matter how confident you think I might sound as you read these words, you have no way of truly knowing my level of self-worth – the level to which I genuinely believe myself to be of worth, *without reference to anyone else's worth or opinion of me.* Even if you could estimate my level of self-worth, how would you measure it?

I suggest that I am the only one who can reliably determine the degree to which *I* have self-worth. It does not matter how much you believe that I have intrinsic worth as a human-being or that I have inalienable human rights, I am the only one who can decide whether or not I have self-worth. By definition, self-worth demands this – if I cannot do it, then I probably do not have self-worth. Beware however, if I do claim to have it, it does not necessarily mean I have self-worth – remember PHOR.

I can fool myself into believing that I have self-worth – when I need to believe that I have reached that point. This is not an uncommon need amongst those drawn to coaching and psycho-therapy. It is a double-edged sword. Whilst it can be a subtle and seductive cul-de-sac to tell ourselves we have self-worth before we have reached that point in our own growth, the desire to reach it can be a very positive direction seeker – in the right environment. That environment can, in turn, include the services of a coach. However, if the coach is deceiving themselves about their own self-worth, with all the trappings that can go with well-marketed coaching, they are less likely to venture outside the tried and tested comfort zones of self-esteem.

The environment in which I walk can help or hinder me on my journey towards self-worth. This environment will be largely a function of the degree to which the people in it have gotten to a place of self-worth. However, I still need to 'connect' with something inside of myself that tells me, unequivocally, that I have no choice but to be humble and that, in that, I am 'fine' and things are okay. This applies irrespective of whether anyone or everyone around me thinks I am arrogant or weak or incapable. It also applies irrespective of whether they think I am fantastic.

How do you know you have self-worth? You will know it when you get there. One of the ways you will know you are not there is when you have a need to prove to yourself, or others, that you have gotten there!

Looking at how we might know if someone else has self-worth – not to be confused with if someone else has *worth*, a completely different question – will aim to throw more light on how we identify it in ourselves.

## 3. How do I Obtain Self-worth?

The simplest answer I can suggest to this is that I let go of all that is *not* me. This involves a rigorous interrogation of my beliefs and an increasingly ruthless pruning and purging of perceptions, assumptions and beliefs that serve only to enable me to thread water without seeking a path towards solid ground. It means mastering a simple but profoundly challenging art – *letting go!*

We have very *very* convincing beliefs that we cling to on a daily basis. Jonathon Glover in his book 'Humanity – a Moral History of the Twentieth Century', suggests that our belief systems can be looked at as 'load bearing walls'. We simply cannot contemplate that they might be erroneous or flawed unless we have recourse to some sort of support structure, in the form of a different set of beliefs, acting as a replacement steel girder that allows us to begin dismantling the wall and re-modeling our perceptions. Letting go of those beliefs is an emotionally challenging process. Accepting the fact that our view of reality is a selective, self-serving view of reality can present us with an emotional abyss. This abyss is generated by ourselves through the accumulation of self-serving dependences that have served to bolster our opinion of ourselves – our self-esteem. These dependences started out with statements such as 'well done – your crayon drawing of mummy is sooo great!', in the early days, to, in latter times, 'you have increased the sales figure by 23% in real terms – you're brilliant!'

In order to move towards self-worth, we need to look at our need for self-esteem. We need to take a hard look at our motivations for what we have been doing. We then need to identify the specific ways, in which we have built our self-esteem, that suggest that we deserve more than someone else – in a world of limited resources. We need to apply the principle of 'universality' to our behavior. The principle of universality is the principle of 'sauce for the goose' – what I believe is my right must also be the right of others.

Those who genuinely subject themselves to this interrogation will discover that an inevitable and humbling part of our humanity is the discovery that we have been treading water and hanging on for dear life to the next person – without them even knowing it. We have been feeding our self-esteem in a way that took us past the toddler hunger for acknowledgment, through the rocky terrain of teenager validation, over the stumbling blocks of early adulthood acceptance, into the trail of settled achievement and up to the solid oak gates of meaningful self-actualization. We then peer in through the gaps between the gate-planks. At first we wonder and, gradually, perhaps after a few more tastes of the momentarily preferred fruit of achievement and distraction, we more than wonder – we begin to reach out. But the spaces between the planks seem too narrow – we can't seem to fit through. Self-actualization seems like an un-attainable fantasy. What I cannot yet see is that, in the journey thus far, I have over-fed my need for self-esteem and I have accumulated the accompanying obesity. In my efforts at personal growth, I have rendered myself psychologically, emotionally, spiritually (whatever word works) unfit for the job at hand – the job of reaching my full potential. I peer through those planks and wish the gates would just open and let me through in my current state. However, if I am lucky, I get to see that I am not pushing against a closed gate but, rather, I am being excluded by a membrane – a filter that offers a chance to let go of all that I am not and simply be who I am.

Identifying what is not me (i.e. not the me than can move towards self-actualization) is at the root of the move to self-worth. There are no easy answers to this challenge, even if the suggestion seems simple. I would stress again, however, that the process is primarily an emotional one. A decision to let go of all that is not my worthy self (my self-worth) can help, but making the decision is only the first step. The process will involve opening myself to seeing myself anew. This new seeing can only be 'surfaced' through the radar of my own personal growth. In a sense, I have to feel my way around my own unique life – I have to touch the boundaries of my own version of existence, as I look for my own self-worth. But, at the early stages, I can only do so without the advantage of the vision, the sight, that comes with actually having self-worth!

A client once described this process, retrospectively, as 'rummaging in a dark room to find both a door to open and the right key to turn the lock.' She described a recurring process of opening a series of what she thought were liberating doors only to discover new dark rooms the other side. It even took a while to realize that the room was dark. Wishful thinking can be a powerful thing – she had *had* to believe that she was happy – to be any other way was too scary. There were moments of disappointment and despair and then, almost as if she were no longer living off the hope of change, something shifted. Another door opened. This time, however, a chink of light appeared – this was different.

So how do I obtain my own self-worth? – In summary, I would suggest engaging in a patient interrogation of who I think I am and a courageous letting go of all that is not worthy of that higher me. An effective personal growth coach can help – to be effective they will have been opening their own doors.

### 4. How do I Maintain my Self-worth?

A related question here is 'is my self-worth perishable?' I would suggest that self-worth is perishable – to a degree. However, paradoxically, self-worth, by definition is also self-perpetuating. Self-worth, when built to a certain critical mass, brings with it a knowing of what it needs to sustain itself. If we move from a reliance on self-esteem to a foundation of self-worth it is like a child moving from a tricycle to a bicycle or from a bike with stabilizer wheels to cycling with no stabilizers. The child will be slow and uncertain at first. They may fall over or even crash into something. Having someone run alongside them can help – even if the co-runner doesn't need to touch them.

In time, the cyclist becomes more stable. They know how to avoid potholes, to look ahead for no-go areas, to work around broken glass, even to stop, get off the bike and put it on their shoulder for a time. However, a cyclist gets to cover new terrain and more terrain. She gets to feel the wind in her hair and a tantalizing horizon seems reachable. She could even hold hands with another cyclist for some of the journey – if she is stable and understands the terrain.

How do I maintain my self-worth? In summary, remember to keep my balance, learn to identify pot-holes, service the machinery and be prepared to get off and walk when required. Self-worth is of value in and of itself. If we neglect ourselves, other then in extreme emergencies, we are probably not operating out of self-worth.

## 5. What Value is Knowing if Someone Else has Self-worth?

Engaging with someone with self-worth is a different experience to engaging with someone short of self-worth. I suggest that, in the same way that self-worth is worthy in and of itself, engaging with people with self-worth is of value in and of itself. This is not to say that engaging with someone short of self-worth is not of value in itself – it presents different challenges and opportunities however. Two people with ample and solid self-worth will meet each other in a different way to two people wrestling with a need to feed their self-esteem – even if they are not aware of this wrestling or of the true source of it.

If I am walking with my self-worth as my solid ground and I encounter another human being who is also on that solid ground, we are already free of a need to prove ourselves to each other or to latch on to each other in order to tread water in life. We may 'check each other out' to see what ground this other person is standing on and, in the interim, we may keep them at arms length. However, two people with solid self-worth and a modicum of communication skills have the potential to co-create something more than the sum of their parts without using each other to bolster their self-esteem at either the expense of that person or at the expense of a third party or group.

In meeting someone for the first time, and accurately discerning that they are living from a base of their true self-worth, I will not need to protect myself from becoming part of their buoyancy aid system of life. I will not need to continually watch out for the selective reasoning of someone who has not yet faced who they really are. I will not need to constantly listen to the intuitive niggling inside of me that there is something missing even if what I am hearing externally sounds logical or reasonable. I will not need to expend energy trying to turn their head to see the elephant in the room – the big bright elephant with 'Self-Deception to Avoid Fear' silk-bannered across its flank.

Instead, I will be able to sit in peace with someone even when we argue a point. We will have identified our shared discovered country and be able to help each other see more of the dusty corners still remaining in our psyches and waiting to offer us a top-up to our humility. We will be able to plan, to set shared or individual goals without a need to convert the other to wanting what we want them to want. I may present a persuasive argument for a course of action but the other person, with their self-worth alive and well, will decide for themselves where they are going to go. Agreeing with me will not just be because of the persuasiveness of my arguments but because they listened to the arguments, decided on a course of action and brought themselves on the journey, taking full responsibility with each step – no blame, no hedging of bets.

With the freedom from the need to feed our once ravenous self-esteem need, we can settle down to the job at hand – the community outreach centre, the building of businesses, the caring for a loved one, the mountain climbing trek, the making of love. Whatever the reasons for our successes or failures, it won't be our self-centered need to bend reality to fit us rather than change ourselves to meet reality. We will have taken the adult sized psychological pacifier out of our mouth and packed it away with the other mementos of a previous stage – along with letters from Santa Claus and the poster-paint hand-prints entitled 'Johnny – aged two.'

## 6. How do I Know Someone has Self-worth?

I have, on more than a few occasions, had a conversation with clients around the notion of 'substance.' It is usually early in the relationship, most likely in the initial negotiation discussion. The client might suggest that they want to come across to their audience – their media audience, their voters, their staff, whoever – as solid, of substance. I then ask them if they want to *be* solid, of substance, as well as coming across as so. Those that care little about who they are, and a lot about how they come across, tend not to have allowed our relationship get this far – more likely seeking the services of a 'spin-doctor' rather than a personal growth coach – what I sometimes refer to as an aspiring 'substance doctor'.

The paradox of self-worth, and I find this to be wholly consistent with Maslow's and the humanistic approach to human potential, is that a person with genuine self-worth tends to be less selfish than someone without genuine self-worth. Don't get me wrong, I am not suggesting that only the Mother Theresa's of this world have self-worth. In fact, I have no idea what level of self-worth Mother Theresa was working from. My guess is that she was well into that realm – probably far more than many labeled by history as 'great'. No, a person who is operating from self-worth will still need to eat, they may even have a nice enough house, they may well drive a car. They might be grumpy, they might be unsociable. However, if you were to do an audit of this person's life, you would find certain patterns. You would find that they are free of a need to prove themselves. They are free of a need to control you, unless, in very rare circumstances, they genuinely and humbly felt it was good for you and, even then, they would be looking for an opportunity to liberate both themselves, and you, from that control.

Have you ever told someone something that was the truth but they were disappointed when they heard it. "I don't like that shirt/dress." "I don't love you", "I'm afraid the job has been given to someone else." Having self-worth won't mean that you never hear disappointing news. However, how I deal with disappointing news can give me clues as to the degree to which I carry myself with self-worth.

Of course there will be those who will do everything they can to give the impression that they operate from the solid ground of self-worth, but this can so easily be an illusion. In fact, I would say that it can be far easier for a person to pretend that they have self-worth than to attain it. Talk to any human resources manager – they will likely tell you that the person they interviewed for a job is very often not the person that, a few months later, they discover they have employed. How often are voters disappointed by the behaviour of the politicians admired on the shiny colorful posters?

There is an old saying – "If you want to know me – live with me!" I believe that building our own self-worth can help us see the degree to which another person is operating from their's. However, we are human and one pervasive feature of the history of humanity is that people deceive each other – sometimes knowingly, sometimes blindly, sometimes with nominal consequences, sometimes with catastrophic consequences.

I believe that people with high self-worth will have a desire to be accountable. They will have a desire to engage with others justly and have the humility to know that, at a moment of weakness or carelessness or ignorance, they may well betray those very values. In engaging with others, a person with self-worth will not want the upper hand and will not want another to have the upper hand. They will aim for 'win-win' relationships. How a person *contracts* can give us some insight as to where they are on the continuum of self-actualization.

*Kevin wants to earn a living. He has chosen a career in a strongly unionized industry. He knows that it will be very difficult for him to be fired – even if he produces little or no value to customers (internal or external). Kevin has a strong desire to stay in this job and get whatever pay rises his union can extract out of his employers. He plans to go to pension with it. Kevin feels good when his favorite football team does well and is irritable when they don't. Kevin operates from a base of self-esteem – when he can get it.*

*Keren wants to earn a living. She wants to stand on her own two feet and also does not want to be taken advantage of. She has identified her passion and found that, whilst there is quite a high degree of competition in her industry, she is prepared to deliver value to her clients. She is prepared to take the risk that the industry dynamics might change in five years time and, in such an event, she will be challenged to re-invent herself. Keren operates from a base of self-worth – even if she has the odd blue day.*

How do I know a person has self worth? One way is to observe how they contract in relationships. Do they seem to be seeking more security than the delivery of value to clients would automatically offer? Can they work on contract with clearly defined ethical deliverables – or do they want to work in a culture where power is the currency – power over others – the staff, by banning union representation for example, or through the use of mis-information, or by holding the employers to ransom for more privileges without any regard for accountability to clients, tax-payers or other stakeholders? Do they want to profit from investments without any regard for ethical or social consequences?

Alternatively, do they pro-actively seek to include clauses to a contract that protect the other party – do they acknowledge the inter-dependence and the privilege of being able to work together, in a business or a marriage, as a public servant or as a parent? What do they do when they realize they have let down their side of the contract? – even the unsaid clauses like the provision of courtesy?

It is through the pro-active, continuous, consistent engagement of a person's relationships, the transactions in those relationships, that we get clues as to the degree to which they are capable of working from the threaded water of insatiable self-esteem or the solid but humble ground of self-worth – where on the NICE curve we might seem to fit.

## 7. How Can I Help Someone Move to their Own Self-worth?

If what I have said so far about the relative merits of self-esteem and self-worth is a robust interpretation of the nature of personal growth and self-actualization, it would seem sensible to consider how one could nurture that shift in someone else towards their self-worth.

One might be tempted to argue that, for me to try to bring about such a shift in someone else, this suggests a type of arrogance on my part. *'Who am I to decide that someone should be moving in that direction?'* One might well ask.

I offer a threefold answer:

The first piece is that consideration of such a course of action surely suggests that another course of action is to do nothing that would promote such a shift. Even choosing to do nothing in a relationship – and I would suggest that is impossible to nothing in a relationship –

implies an opinion that something should not change. If this is so, is it not also subject to the same criticism of arrogance? Who am I to say that someone should be staying the same as they are? Even if you accept that it is impossible to do nothing in a relationship – and to be in a relationship is to imply surely that one is, or two are, relating – I suggest that it is impossible not to have some effect on the other person. This is even if we believe that they are having a 'bigger' effect on us than we on them. Perhaps we choose to label them as 'leader' in the relationship.

My second justification for promoting such growth in others is that, if we are inevitably going to have an effect on anyone with whom we are in relationship, surely it is wise, and less arrogant, to put some conscious thought into it and at least aim 'to do no harm'.

My third claim, to the value of this course of action, is that self-worth is, by definition, of value to the person who experiences it. If they do not value it, then it is not self-worth. Rightly or wrongly, I claim that, when I act in a way that promotes self-worth in another person, they will be glad I did so when they experience that self-worth and see the connection between my actions and that experience. They may not like my actions in the short term. There may well be a time-lag between my action and their experience of self-worth. But when they get there, they will value it – even if they had hitherto considered me to be arrogant in my actions. Having experienced that breakthrough, they will most likely be challenged to re-consider their perception of my arrogance and perhaps see it is a type of consistent and benevolent challenge.

So having presented arguments for the justification for, the value of, and even the potential moral imperative of, behaving in a way that is designed to promote the move, in someone else, towards their own self-worth, what might serve as such growth promoting actions?

Two things worth remembering when considering this question:

1. There is a difference between self-esteem and self-worth (as I am choosing to use the terms in this discussion).

2. I move towards my own self-worth by letting go of what is not worthy of me.

Promoting growth towards self-worth is not about telling someone how wonderful they are or how much you love them. That does not mean there is not value in saying such things but I would suggest that being mindful of the context is useful. One way of looking at this is in terms of love – specifically experiencing ourselves as loved. There is pretty broad evidence that a child who feels loved, on average, has a different experience of life to a child who doesn't. I am convinced also that simply telling a child that you love them, in and of itself, does not mean they will automatically feel loved. I have worked with many adults who remember their parents telling them regularly that they loved them but grew up feeling unloved. I also know people who say that their parents rarely, if ever, told them that they loved them but who showed all the hallmarks of someone who grew up feeling loved with all the core security that comes with such feelings.

Is it too simplistic to state that love is more than words? That words cannot replace love? That love can thrive in the absence of words?

Maslow suggested that lower order needs, such as love for example, are required in order for higher order needs to kick in and then be met. So, if a coach is interested in the process of moving towards self-actualization, both in themselves and their clients, and they wish to embrace Maslow's precepts, surely there will be value in contemplating the notion of love – what it is, what are the results of its presence, what are the results of its deprivation, and how does one best work with such results in the quest towards self-actualization?

The question of how to relate to someone, in a way that promotes their growth towards their own self-worth and self-actualization, has to be a core concern of a committed personal growth coach – unless of course their understanding is significantly contrary to the model of understanding presented here.


If a coach is claiming, in his or her promotional efforts, that they aim to assist clients to reach their full potential, does that coach not need to have thought out what those words mean? The answer to this question on the subject of self-worth is at the very core of this book. Every page is presented in the hope that it will promote personal growth, that it will help the reader, and me, to grasp at that often elusive wisdom that serves as a system of markers on the right path – like the shiny pebbles

Hansel and Gretel followed as they found their way out of the forest and back to their father's house.

Acting in such a way as to promote growth in a fellow human being is just as it is in helping ourselves to make that move for ourselves. It is about challenging and supporting them to see what is not worthy of them, by their own reckoning and not by our judgementalism, and letting go of their accumulated restrictive dependences. It is about doing so in a way that allows them to dismantle those load-bearing imprisoning walls and move towards the freedom to be themselves. This takes a broad palette of faculties but I find it useful to shine a light on two: how we work with both accountability and compassion.

I often hear conversations in which parties appear to be presenting two values as if they are mutually exclusive. Examples might be socialist/capitalist or pro-life/pro-choice. I believe that the concepts of accountability and compassion are often, implicitly or explicitly, seen as mutually exclusive. I firmly believe, however, that they are not mutually exclusive and that applying them both to ourselves and to others, with discernment, can be a major contributor to a move towards self-worth in all concerned.

## The 'BLACE' Matrix

Effectiveness.

|  | Brutal | Compassionate |
|---|---|---|
| **Accountable** | **Brutal/Accountable** 'Punish them!' | **Compassionate/Accountable** 'What needs to happen next?' |
| **Laissez-Faire** | **Brutal/Laissez-Faire** 'Let them sort it out themselves!' | **Laissez-Faire/Compassionate** 'They have had a hard life.' |

Responding optimally to a situation, with an effective use of both accountability and compassion, requires a freedom from our own needs to keep camp in a less effective quadrant. Applying ourselves with compassionate accountability requires us not only to see a gap between a desired situation and an accurate assessment of an actual situation, but it also requires us to see, in the moment, where the players in that situation are on the continuum to self-worth and what 'intervention' would best facilitate their move forewords.

A key aspect of personal growth coaching is the identification of gaps between what a client is saying they want and what they are describing as their behavior. After the 'low-hanging fruit' of some goal-setting and self-organization (which could be facilitated by a mentor, consultant or a coach with little or no understanding of personal growth), personal growth coaching will challenge a client to see things they did not see before. More specifically, and relevantly, the client will get value from the coaching to the degree to which they are challenged to see things *about themselves* that they would not see before.

*Anthony suddenly realized that his wife was deceiving him about her golf outings. All along she was seeing another man. Marie, his coach, asked him what he wanted to say to his wife, now that he knew this. Marie was thinking about Anthony confronting his wife.*

Marie is an action-oriented coach. She challenged Anthony to consider what strategy he should follow given this new realization. However, an important opportunity was missed in this coaching. Instead of asking Anthony to think in terms of action, Marie could have challenged Anthony to reflect on how he interpreted his relationship with his wife over the life-time of the relationship. She could focus particularly on what he might have been afraid to loose if he had noticed clues that all was not right.

There are no guarantees, but this line of coaching offers the opportunity for the client to see to what degree he has been true to his stated values. In Anthony's case, this was honesty with his wife. But she was being dishonest with him – she had betrayed him, in his mind. Through skillful exploration it is almost certain, and in my mind hugely valuable, that Anthony could come to see that there was a parallel between the way in which his wife had been betraying him and the way in which he has been betraying himself. I am not suggesting, by the way, that this is a justification for his wife's infidelity. I am deliberately avoiding judging her actions. Such actions will be part of the tapestry of her journey towards her self-actualization. Difficult as it is to get a handle on the motivations of a client to do something, it is far more difficult for a coach to make any real sense of the actions of a person who they have never met. In addition, in investing time and energy considering the rights and wrongs or the psychological explanations for the wife's actions, the coach is most likely allowing themselves to be distracted from the agenda with the client. The remedy to this, of course, is usually for the coach to rummage within their own consciousness and identify any selective perceptions upon which they are dependent. Our judgments tell us more about ourselves that those we judge.

**The Correlation Principle.**

Instead of the coach leading the client to consider confronting the third party, in this case Anthony's wife, they, the coach, could have led the client to rummage within their own consciousness for clues about themselves. Through a skillful dance between compassion, including the use of empathy if appropriate, and accountability (to the client's own stated values), the coach can offer far more leverage than a simple problem-solving approach such as confronting the wife at the first available opportunity. In fact, when such a rummage brings forth a significant personal insight for the client, their circumstances often change *without any apparent pro-action on their part*. This phenomenon is well known to seasoned personal growth coaches. I call it the *Correlation Principle*. In Anthony's case, for example, you might have his wife, out of the blue confessing to the betrayal, seeking forgiveness and suggesting they get help in their relationship. In the movie 'Phone Booth', Stu Shepard, played by Colin Farrell, is a man who – if you don't want me to ruin the story for you, you should skip to the next paragraph – is a man who, through a challenging experience, gained an insight to himself and his relationship with his wife. His new insights seemed to be more conducive to a sustainable and loving relationship.

This type of realization changes everything and I believe, that in deepening our understanding of ourselves, our dependences, our true motivations, we often trigger a similar process in others to whom we are relationally connected. Of course, an alternative, to Anthony's wife coming home and seeking forgiveness, might be that she comes home and reveals that she wants a divorce. Whilst one outcome might seem 'better' than the other, in the realm of personal growth, we simply do not know that. Either way, Anthony will be emotionally challenged, and just as is the case when we try to assess the value of the French Revolution all those years ago, and conclude that 'it is really too early to say', the outcome of the current stage of Anthony's marriage will have ripples and implications far beyond what we could realistically calculate. The connections and reverberations are likely to fall into the realm of the 'Butterfly Effect.' Despite this, whatever the outcomes, Anthony can still ask himself what he wants.

As I have already suggested, this seventh question on self-worth is, I hope, in some partial way, addressed by the whole book.

**Chapter Bullets:**

- There is value in differentiating self-worth from self-esteem.
- Maslow suggests that self-esteem is a need before self-actualization.
- I suggest that self-worth is a need after self-esteem.
- Self-worth, by definition, is 'of worth'.
- Self-worth and self-esteem are often confused.
- There is no such thing as too much self-worth.
- Too much self-esteem can slow our growth.
- Too little self-esteem can slow our growth.
- Many people may die without experiencing true self-worth.
- Feeling good about oneself does not necessarily indicate self-worth.
- Worth and self-worth are not the same.
- Remember PHOR.
- Self-esteem can be a comfort zone.
- Reaching self-worth involves letting go.
- Beliefs are like load-bearing walls.

## Aiming for the Pinnacle

- The step into self-worth is like going through a filter.
- What is 'not me' needs to be let go to allow for self-worth.
- The process is primarily an emotional one.
- Self-worth is perishable – to a degree.
- Self-worth brings with it insights for its own nurturance.
- Two people with self-worth are equipped to co-create.
- Self-worth brings with it reduced dependent selfishness.
- Self-worth brings a desire for accountability.
- Kevin operates from a base of self-esteem.
- Keren operates from a base of self-worth.
- Maintaining the status quo could be seen to be arrogant.
- It is of value to 'first do no harm'.
- If it is not valued by a person, it is not their self-worth - yet.
- Maslow suggests love as a need.
- This book is an attempt at promoting self-worth.
- BLACE is about Compassion and Accountability.
- Anthony realized that his wife was betraying him.
- Marie is an action-oriented coach.
- Our judgments tell us more about ourselves then those we judge.
- The Correlation Principle is a feature of personal growth.

# Chapter 7
# Emotional Ownership.
## *The Earth is Round.*

A term often encountered in the therapy field is 'resistance'. Dating back to Freud, at least, it is normally used to describe when a client is behaving in a way that appears designed to refute an insight being offered by the practitioner or, in the opinion of the practitioner, objectively by reality. Indeed, I have heard therapists explain the fact that a client had ceased availing of their services by reference to the client's resistance – resistance to what was 'coming up' in the therapy.

On occasion, I have challenged therapists on the robustness of such an analysis and encountered what seemed to me to be less than convincing arguments that this is the only explanation that could apply. The notion that the client might just have decided that the therapy was doing them no good and they were running out of cash or, perish the thought, that the therapy was 'messing with their head' in a potentially destructive way, did not seem to be open to consideration. The client had one way of looking at things and the therapist another. The client's not wanting to see things the way the therapist saw things was put down to client 'resistance'. I had another way of looking at things. The therapist not wanting to look at things the way I saw them seemed, to me anyway, to also be resistance – but of course this was just my way of seeing things.

Unless the insight being resisted is one hundred percent congruent with 'the way life works' or 'reality', including the reality that the therapist's true motives and needs can contaminate the situation, evoking resistance, as an explanation, surely runs the risk of taking us into the realm of arrogance and blindness. If I train in a particular model of therapy, or coaching, and in doing so, develop a dependence on my belief that this model is accurate in all circumstances, I run the risk of 'messing' with a client's head. The more vulnerable the client, the more likely they will tell themselves that they are wrong and that I am right. As I mentioned before, people are drawn to others that in some way mirror their dependences. A very vulnerable client can end up working with a practitioner who has a parallel vulnerability. This will not be evident, to some others, including the client, because of the practitioner's dependence on their interpretation of convenient psychological concepts coupled with their ability to talk convincingly about them. The practitioner can literally 'blind them with science' by 'explaining' the client's feelings and experiences in terms of 'issues' in a way that leaves the client believing that they need the practitioner even more than they thought. Thus a cycle of dependence is perpetuated – no doubt assisted by the matching mindset of a supervisor with complementary needs.

If personal growth, as in PAUSE, is about outgrowing dependences that limit our ability to reach the pinnacle of our humanity, resistance is something we will generally encounter in ourselves along the way – particularly when close to replacing one dependence with another. Resistance is both a protector and an inhibitor. As a new level of consciousness is hatched, an old level is clung to for a while – until we consider it safe to step outside and eventually to let go.

If I was to identify one area that offers the greatest acceleration of personal growth, towards self-worth and on towards self-actualization, it is also the area that probably provokes the most resistance.

The area in question is what I term 'Emotional Ownership'. It is a concept that is cognitively easy to describe, at a foundational level, but is supremely challenging to apply at the coal-face of life. It is not for the faint-hearted but will present the embracer with, I believe, an unavoidable route towards reaching their full potential. This is a route, which once embarked on, will take the traveler into ever-liberating realms of personal experience – right into the orchard of self-worth and out onto the pastures of self-actualization. Again I stress, this journey is not for the faint-hearted. However, the good news is that the very process takes us out of the cocoon of our faint-heartedness and provides us with the exercise our heart craves. With a fitter emotional capacity, the next stage of the process beckons – we are stronger and ready for more. Each stage takes us a step along the way, and sometimes surprisingly, the process even offers us rest periods – places at which to catch our breath, emotionally and physically. We can pace ourselves but I do suggest a warning: once a person truly embarks on this journey there is no turning back. The insights are so convincing and the results are so tangible, that even if one has a moment of doubt, it does not last long. The more someone 'gets it', the more they see the limited mindset they had been operating from in the past. It is as though the process is one-way. In many ways, the process of physical birth is a mirror of this growth process. Once a baby travels through the birth canal and out into its new life there is no going back. Reality presents itself with all the wonder and wounds for which it is known and for which it seems unapologetic. The baby could be born in perfect health to a caring and peaceful society or it could be born to a less than ideal environment. In the same way, a person who travels the road of Emotional Ownership will see, retrospectively, that it makes perfect sense and that any resistance to it, or skepticism about it, they may have harbored beforehand, was actually a product of their own selective perception which, in turn, was driven by their desire to survive in the only way they knew.

So what is Emotional Ownership about?
Before I explore this, I would like to present some history...

Nicolaus Copernicus (1473-1543) was a Polish polymath – a man whose learnedness and experience covered areas ranging from military leadership to church ministry, to public administration to medicine. An area, which probably did not represent a substantial part of his career, did become the area for which he became best known – astronomy. In the early 1500s, Copernicus began publishing radical new ideas about the structure of the solar system and the cosmos. He suggested a heliocentric model – that the Sun, not the Earth, was at the centre of our cosmos. Copernicus died without knowing just what a stir he had created.

Galileo (1564-1642) was an Italian Astronomer who, in 1633, was found guilty of heresy by the Catholic Church in Rome and was sentenced to imprisonment – subsequently commuted to house-arrest. His heresy was that he agreed with Copernicus and published arguments to support the theory despite the admonitions of the then Pope. It was not until over one hundred years later that the Church rehabilitated his reputation and permitted the full publishing of his heliocentric studies. Johann Kepler (1571-1630), a contemporary of Galileo, also supported Copernicus' heliocentric hypothesis.

Copernicus, Galileo and Kepler are examples of people who looked at what was accepted as reality within their community and saw something different. Half a millennium later, junior school children learn, with the help of diagrams, and even photos, that the Earth orbits the Sun, and does so in a way no more special than the way the other planets in the solar system orbit the same Sun. However, when the heliocentric model was presented, there were many people who seemed to reject its validity – its reality. Given what we now know and accept, it seems strange that so many people were exercised by the notion that the prevailing belief system, the geocentric system, might actually be flawed. This level of exercise led to oppression of numerous people, and the silencing of many more.

The reactions of the opponents of heliocentrism seem to me to come under the heading of resistance. What dependences were these people protecting, as they refused to face what seemed to be logical arguments for a new and more real way of seeing things? Why did they cling to a certain interpretation of the Bible, presumably, in their own minds, employing logical use of language, whilst at the same time reject grounded mathematical arguments that offered a conflicting view of reality and that also employed logical use of language? Why did people vilify those messengers who dared to express what they thought they saw? Why did the perpetrators of the Spanish inquisition, and other such violent pogroms, justify their actions using interpretations of pieces of their chosen scripture, whilst neglecting other pieces of the same scripture, and other scriptures considered holy elsewhere, that would have prohibited violent behavior? One credible answer to this is that these people had held certain accumulated dependences and that these dependences dictated their holders' difficulty in embracing new insights into reality.

History is littered with examples of where, in certain circumstances, ordinary human beings adopted certain belief systems that were subsequently labeled as 'wrong' or 'sick' or 'evil' or 'tragic' and most importantly, 'to be avoided in future'. When a modern western-educated citizen reflects on the history of slavery, oppression of women, war-atrocities, economic exploitation of vulnerable people or peoples, and other situations seen as representing injustice, he or she is more likely than not to see these as dark aspects of history and ones not to be repeated. No parent will want to see their junior school children in a dysfunctional class-room environment that causes them harm – assuming the parent can see the dysfunctionality.

These 'sub-optimal' situations, to put it euphemistically, are examples of 'flawed paradigms' that act as manacles bound to individuals and societies and that prevent them from reaching the pinnacle of their humanity. Before any one individual, within that mindset, can point themselves in the direction of their full potential as a human being, they need to have seen these manacles for what they are and find the key to their unshackling.

**And Emotional Ownership?**

The concept of emotional ownership presents us with a flawed paradigm - one that acts as a manacle holding people back from moving to the pinnacle of their potential. More accurately, it is the process of emotional non-ownership that serves as a barrier to personal growth.

> The Principle of Emotional Ownership, put simply, states that ***every emotion that occurs within us is of our own making.***

How the last statement is understood and interpreted will be influenced by the reader's needs or the point along the NICE curve on which they currently rest.

Those who are at the right-hand end of the NICE curve, the contributory end, will most likely interpret it from a place of self-worth. They will, I believe, be able to see the validity in the statement and will not need to make any selective additions to the statement that would render it irrational. They may temporarily misinterpret the statement but will have no significant emotional attachment to this interpretation. With clarification, they will refine their interpretation with ease.

Those at the left-hand end of the NICE curve will tend to resist the statement and, often quite vehemently, present 'proof' that the statement is untrue. They might say, for example, that if someone wrongs them, it will be the responsibility of the wrong-doer and they, themselves will not be at fault. If you, the reader, find yourself resisting the validity of the statement, I believe congratulations are probably in order. You may well have happened upon another gateway to more of your own self-worth and self-actualization. As to whether you will consider opening the gate, or even knocking on its solid planks, that will be up to you.

You might put down the book. If you are a reigning pope you might even decide to ban the book and issue a decree for my house-arrest or excommunication! I exhort you, however, to befriend your resistance and join me in an exploration of this 'heliocentric' idea. I believe you can only reap a gain – a net gain that is.

**Emotional Ownership Syndromes.**

The first thing I recommend, when considering the principle of emotional ownership, 'EO', is to look out for our self-generated syndromes or 'add-ons.' These are implications that we tag onto the premise, and thereby contaminate it, but which are not contained in it.

*1. The Condemnation Syndrome.*

The first add-on that can occur, in considering the Principle of Emotional Ownership, is that the principle suggests that there is something wrong with emotions. Nowhere in the statement is this suggested and, as I will explain below, the practical application of Emotional Ownership calls us to take the opposite approach – to welcome emotions in order that we can get a better understanding of them.

To say that we are responsible for the air we exhale in no way suggests that there is anything wrong with exhaling - although if we were inhaling certain substances that had the effect of contaminating our exhalations that might be an issue – but not in normal breathing. In the same way, emotions in and of themselves, are 'normal'.

*2. The Pedestal Syndrome.*

This is where the reader, or listener, assumes that the principle claims that the author or presenter operates from complete Emotional Ownership, sees evidence conflicting with this, and therefore decides that the principle is not credible. The presenter may be seen, erroneously, as laying claim to membership of an elite group who are at the superior end of the spectrum of emotional ownership. Not so – a three-year-old child or a parrot in my local pet-store could be thought to verbally express the Principle of Emotional Ownership and it would make no difference to its inherent truth or non-truth. The words could be scribbled as graffiti on a sub-way wall and their veracity would not be affected. This is just as a child or parrot could be taught to say 'The Earth Is Round'. The statement is true or not true irrespective of where it appears. A separate issue is that the presenter may struggle with the concept.

I once saw a refrigerator magnet which might be relevant here:

> *"I know it's not your fault – I am just blaming you!"*

*3. The Culpability Syndrome.*

I alluded to this add-on already when I referred above to a wrong-doing and the responsibility of the wrong-doer. There is nothing in the principle of Emotional Ownership that suggests that the perpetrator of a wrong is not responsible for the wrong-doing or that the emotional owner is in some way responsible for that wrong-doing. Despite this, when I present the principle to a group, there are often those who respond as if I had said that a wrong-doer was not responsible for their actions. If you introduced this add-on, you are probably in the majority. If you can spot that you have brought this add-on into the equation, without rational explanation, and that the logical thing to do is to remove it again, you may already be equipped to wrestle with the concept in a growthful way.

*4. The Damnation Syndrome.*

This is where the EO principle is interpreted as suggesting that there is something 'wrong' with not owning one's feelings. The principle is not stating this to be the case. As to whether or not it is immoral or unethical not to own one's emotions, i.e. to blame others, or outside events, for them, this is another matter, a matter worth exploring. However, the statement in question does not make this claim.

## 5. Collusion Syndrome.

This is where we look around, see that everyone around us sees things a certain way, the same as we do, and assume, therefore, that this way of seeing things must be correct. In this case, if your friends all disagree with the Principle of Emotional Ownership, you conclude, 'logically', that the principle is not valid. However, when it comes to dependences, we tend to surround ourselves with people of a similar mindset and to re-enforce this mindset as we engage with these people. If we challenge the consensus reality, we may get to see the degree to which the group around us is emotionally dependent on that mindset. In extreme cases, the group may turn on us or exclude us – 'the system' may strive to preserve the mindset – to insist that the cosmos is geocentric.

## **SOBBED.**

Having considered the above syndromes, and inoculated ourselves from them, the next issue to look at in relation to emotions is in the area of awareness. Most approaches to therapy suggest that there are things within our consciousness of which we are not yet aware. They may not all agree on what is under the consciousness radar. The Freudians might suggest that the Oedipal complex represents a conflict buried within our unconscious whilst the Rogerians tend towards client-specific conflicts and are mostly interested in the feelings rather than the analytic hypotheses. However, the idea of burying aspects of our consciousness seems to be more or less accepted.

Even without recourse to any psychological models, most people, I believe, will have had experiences wherein they looked at themselves retrospectively and figured that they had felt strongly about something but did not acknowledge it to themselves at the time – they did not notice it or 'name' it at the time.

A regular feature of personal growth coaching is when a person embraces a certain emotional state, either in the company of the coach, or following engagement with the coach, that leads to them seeing a situation anew. Clients regularly describe this in terms such as *'I now realize how strongly I feel about this – something was blocking me from seeing it so clearly.'*

Combining the aspects of awareness and ownership gives us what I call the SOBBED Matrix. This reflects two key features of human emotion and, I believe, can throw some light on how we might streamline our emotional management.

### The 'SOBBED' Matrix

Emotions.

| | Blamed | Owned |
|---|---|---|
| **Surfaced** | **Surfaced Blamed** 'He took my money and that made me angry...' | **Surfaced Owned** 'He took my money.' (Hmm... That's interesting I feel angry too). |
| **Buried** | **Buried Blamed** 'He took my money and these chest pains are your fault.' | **Buried Owned** 'He took my money.' (Hmm... I must do something about these chest pains.) |

### Surfaced Owned Emotions.

The URQ (Upper Right Quadrant) of the SOBBED matrix represents what I believe to be the optimal management of emotions – the most effective way of dealing with them. In this case, I am aware of the emotions and know that they are an expression of part of me in response to a situation. I accept that those emotions are of my own making and their power, relative to the part of me that observes them as opposed to feeling them, the executive management part of me if you like, is a reflection of my own personal power. The degree to which I am disempowered by the feelings tells me the degree to which I am not operating from a base of self-worth. As I allow myself, over time, to accustom myself to the discomfort of the emotion, say anger for example, I master that emotion until eventually it is no longer experienced as a discomfort but as something different – simply an effortless consciousness of my presence to myself in what would previously have been a difficult situation for me emotionally.

An analogy might be that of water pressure. If reality can be represented as normal water pressure for a given depth, the deeper we go, in the submarine of our consciousness, the greater the pressure outside. As we build up the pressure inside our craft, the *relative* pressure on the hull decreases – the inside and the outside are matched. With emotional awareness and ownership, we have adjusted to the reality of our environment and are empowered to respond optimally – to respond from the pinnacle of our humanity. The uncomfortable emotions we used to feel have guided us to re-assess our perceptions of reality and allow it to be adjusted.

During this process, I may realize, for example, that in some way I have 'stolen' something that is not mine. I don't necessarily mean by reference to a man-made law but more to the essence of natural justice. Perhaps I colluded with some subtle unethical practice years ago and 'blanked it out.' Perhaps this was because, at the time, I was too far on the left of the NICE curve to accept any responsibility or to see past my own needs. I had a mortgage to pay and mouths to feed. So, I 'bent' reality rather than face the ethical conflicts within myself and face the associated challenges.

A new situation, where someone has stolen money from me, can be interpreted as reality attempting to bend itself back. Far from it being a destructive event, it offers the opportunity to reconnect with a piece of my more ethical self – something I may have parked years ago. In this way, I can see a potential loss-evoking event as a personal growth opportunity. I may wrestle with it, I may give out about it, but, with emotional ownership, I don't blame the thief for the discomfort - just for the theft. I may or may not choose to invest resources in trying to get my money back but these efforts will not be contaminated by my own blamed negative emotions.

**Surfaced Blamed Emotions.**

In this case, I am allowing myself to notice the feelings but I am operating on the assumption that it is the event that has caused them. Using the example above, I now have two loss experiences: 1. My money has been taken and 2. He made me feel angry, or bad, or whatever, and I have a right not to have to feel this way. In this scenario, I feel I have been wronged in two ways. I feel angry but, because of the paradigm I am operating from, this experience will not contribute to my personal growth. I may well want to lock up the thief and throw away the key but this, I suggest, is not operating from the pinnacle of my humanity. I may become reactive and aggressive. It is possible that I may discipline myself to hold myself back, out of a moral code for example, and not let my anger effect my decision making. This, however, takes a lot of energy and is very likely to inhibit my effectiveness. In addition, I risk letting my guard down and 'letting loose' – doing something I later regret. I am not operating from the pinnacle of my humanity. Finally, I am missing an opportunity to let the situation change me – to allow it to move me one step along the way on my road to self-actualization. Instead, I will be destined to encounter the difficult emotion again and again in the future mistakenly believing that this is the way things have to be – that the world is flat – how could it be any other way?

I suggest that, if a person believes, erroneously in my opinion, that others are responsible for the difficult or uncomfortable emotions that they, the person, experience within themselves, they can create a kind of psychological cocoon around themselves that makes it easier to allow those emotions come to the surface. This may help them reduce the incidence of health problems that buried feelings can lead to but, I believe, it can make life harder for others around them – or people who are effected by their behavior. This is even if those people are on the other side of the globe. As everyone leans on each other whilst trying to tread water, someone, somewhere will be unjustly pushed to the margins. In the world of personal growth to the pinnacle of our humanity, this is an avoidable injustice.

Again, if I believe that others are responsible for my feelings, it is likely to be easier for me to allow the feelings to surface. I always have an extra internally generated support system in which to feel safe and it usually takes the form of me thinking that I am better than someone because they did something wrong. Have you ever been annoyed with someone and realized that, not only did you not like what they did, but it was illegal/immoral or 'downright wrong' and, with this realization, you suddenly feel angrier or more annoyed and even more justified in contemplating ways in which you could make them suffer! In addition to this feeling of being on the moral high ground, I may also take some comfort from a modern phenomenon – I *feel* like I am on more solid ground because *'I am in touch with my feelings'* – the implication being that *'you are not and therefore I am healthier than you – I rest my case!'*

I believe that allowing children to temporarily believe that their feelings are not 'their fault', allowing them to blame others, can help them away from the temptation to bury their feelings. I do not believe it is the optimal way to help children navigate the terrain of emotional personal growth, and it requires careful management, but pressing upon them the notion that they generate their own feelings can be very counter-productive for those at a tender age. A degree of fluidity, wisdom and discernment can go a long way. In time, coaching the child out of the blame paradigm and into the ownership paradigm will serve them well. They can then begin owning the feelings they have become familiar with and make serious moves towards their adult self-worth.

In adult life, realizing that I have been blaming others for my uncomfortable feelings, and that that has allowed me to wrestle with parts of my emotional self-awareness that I might otherwise have buried, with unhealthy consequences, can be a humbling insight. It can also corner me, if I am open to the opportunity, to being a little more sympathetic to those who I selectively judge as 'not in touch with their feelings' – there may be a lot more going on here that I realize.

**Buried Owned Emotions**

I may have a predisposition to owning my emotions but may not have developed enough to be 'in them'. In this case, I may have either learned to own my emotions through my formative years, by example, or, decided in latter times to adopt the position of ownership – perhaps I am convinced of the robustness of its logic. However, there is another side to it. Part of my development is also about getting the hang of the emotions, getting used to allowing them to be present in me and not 'turn them off'. This process will not always follow logical lines.

A four-year-old child may feel devastated that they cannot go to their friend's birthday party and that of their school mate. Two invitations, to two separate parties, on at exactly the same time. The child can only go to one of them. Say in this situation the child became very upset and cried and cried. Simply telling the child not to be silly and that they can only go to one of the parties may get them to make a decision but may not facilitate the emotional exercise the situation can prompt. A patient parent, who listens and comforts, who is themselves at peace in the presence of powerful emotions, and who reflects back the reality of the situation to the child, in a sensitive and well timed way, can facilitate that child, not only to make a decision for themselves about the party, but to experience 'being in' these powerful emotions in a safe manner.

By the same token, an adult can be totally committed to owning their emotions but, and here is a real challenge, being so committed can make it harder to 'surface' the emotions. A key element of the whole complementary health movement is that treatment is generally designed to work holistically – on the 'body-mind' or the 'body-mind-spirit.' The implication here is that physical illness is often, some would say always, related to our consciousness of ourselves. The corollary of this is that, where we suppress aspects of our consciousness, we adversely affect our health. This is sometimes interpreted in a way that says that *all* physical illness is caused by our not acknowledging something that is trying to make its way to our consciousness – something I doubt.

Also, it is tempting to conclude that, if I don't have a physical illness, I am not suppressing my consciousness. I do not believe this to be the case. I do believe, however, that ailments can be indicators that we are missing something. A healthy life-style, diet, exercise, proper sleep, reflective quiet-time and the use of effective holistic treatments can, I believe, help us to nurture the process by which we grow into new levels of consciousness. They can help us get and keep our real feelings surfaced. At that point, we can then work with those emotions for the sake of our personal growth.

**Buried Blamed Emotions.**

In the SOBBED matrix, the least effective ways of dealing with difficult emotions lie in the LLQ – the lower left quadrant. In this case, not only am I burying important aspects of myself, I am also blaming others for them and may even be blaming others for the fact that I am burying them! Of course, by the nature of it, I am not aware of this. However, as always in the area of personal growth, a large dollop of humility is needed. It can be tempting to be judgmental, remember the BLACE matrix in the last chapter, compassion and accountability, and think that those who fall into this quadrant need 'sorting out'. They may well need help but we may need to sort ourselves out before we can assist them constructively.

In the context of Maslow's hierarchy of needs, there will be those who have basic survival needs more or less looked after. There will also be those who struggle at the bottom of the triangle – the notion of self-actualization would be as obscure to them as the tenets of quantum physics. In terms of moving from the LLQ to the URQ, it will probably require a stint in the Surface Blamed quadrant. As to whether this is a natural process, that will inevitably happen if given enough time, I don't know. I do believe, however, that it can be accelerated through insightful coaching, perhaps supported by suitable therapy and a holistic approach to healthcare and lifestyle.

## SOBBED and Couples.

It has often occurred to me that two people in significant relationship with each other, married or partnered romantically, often display two quadrants of the SOBBED matrix between them – the Surfaced-Blamed and the Buried-Owned. One partner will be quite expressive of negative emotions but will have a tendency to complain to the other that they, the other person, are causing those emotions, the annoyance, the frustration, the disappointment, whatever. Even if they do no overt complaining, they may deny that they are blaming the other but their behavior belies that blame. The other has not yet surfaced some negative emotions themselves but, if and when they do, they will deal with them differently – they will own them and grow as a result of them. I would have to stress here that couples relationships can be very complex and it is wise not to oversimplify their dynamics. However, I believe that it can be worth exploring such a relationship in terms of SOBBED.

If a couple wish to tap into the huge growth potential their relationship offers them, one simple rule of thumb can assist. If I find myself getting irritated with my partner's emotional expressiveness, perhaps I need to look at what I am not surfacing in myself. If I find myself getting irritated with my partner's apparent disconnection with what I think they should be feeling, I could consider that they might be taking longer to access their emotions and that this is because, when they do, they will automatically own them. If this is the case, it can be of value for me to explore to what degree I am not owning my own surfaced, or expressed emotions.

Whilst I am not laying claim to any empirical data on the subject, I will venture to say that, in my experience, women are more likely then men to be in touch with emotions. Men, on the other hand, whilst more inclined to struggle to access feelings, particularly depending on their stage of development and prevailing responsibilities, have a greater tendency to own their emotions when they do surface them. If this is representative of a fundamental gender tendency, as opposed to my own selective perception, or a contemporary cultural norm, it might be worth bearing in mind. Whether we like it or not, we may have built-in hardwiring to serve different functions in our coupledom. At least until we reach the pinnacle of our growth, our self-actualization, or at least our genuine self-worth, we may be inter-dependent in far more ways than we can see. If this is the case, our children are even more dependent on our coupled co-relating than we might have previously considered. How we grow will influence how they grow.

## Well I NEVER!

In examining the hypotheses presented by the different schools of therapy, one theme running through the spectrum is around the nature of difficult emotions. The Freudians may explain them in terms of subconscious conflicts originating from our early childhood. The Jungians might see them in terms of wrestling with collective unconscious archetypes. The humanistic school might see them as simply needing to be expressed. The CBT school might see them as the result of flawed thinking. If we add into the pot something around the role of physiology, we end up with quite a complicated tapestry of theories vying for a place in the credibility hierarchy. But what if they each have something to offer and that, by cherry-picking different aspects, with discernment, we end up with a structured understanding of human nature capable of being practically, and successfully, applied to the business of climbing to the pinnacle of our potential – within one lifetime?

I suggest that the most pervasive block to people achieving their dreams is their encounter with difficult emotions. This can be in terms of avoiding them, being distracted by them, being paralyzed by them or being controlled by them.

Understanding the role of difficult emotions, and how to 'work them', has to be a pre-requisite to anyone moving to their pinnacle. I believe that a starting position for that understanding is what I call the NEVER Model of understanding difficult emotions.

The NEVER model proposes that any difficult emotion can be put into one of two categories labeled as follows:

**N**eurotic **E**motions      **V**ersus      **E**xistential **R**ealizations.

A neurotic emotion is one which is the result of faulty thinking on our part. By examining our thinking around a challenge, identifying the flaws in that thinking, and embracing a more reasonable analysis of the situation, such neurotic emotions can be resolved. For as long as we do not return to the faulty thinking, the negative emotion will not return. This reflects a perspective usually found in the cognitive-behavioral school of psychology.

An existential realization is an experience which is an unavoidable part of the growth path to the pinnacle of our potential. No amount of rummaging for flawed thinking will resolve the challenge of an existential realization. The experience is something we need to embrace and walk through, feel the feeling and keep walking. We look the emotion in the eye and take charge without suppressing it. In doing so, we strip away some of what is not us, we are changed, we grow.

Realizing that life is not always fair to us is an example of an existential realization. Accepting that we are capable of being selfish, in a way that we had always thought of as unacceptable, is an example of an existential realization. So is embracing the reality that a substantial portion of negative emotions, which we have been complaining about thus far in our life, have been self-generated. They have been self-limiting, 'only ourselves to blame' products of our desire to avail of all the freedoms of adulthood without equally enthusiastically embracing the responsibilities that go with it. Knowing, emotionally, that we will die is an example of an existential realization.

Existential realizations are the stuff of personal growth and not unfortunate symptoms of a dysfunction to be avoided or cured. In fact, not seeing the emotional challenges and opportunities of existential realizations for what they are, could be described as the product of flawed thinking. This is the very type of thinking that can create neurotic fears. These then become the subject of avoidance and self-esteem based difficult-to-penetrate fortresses long past their childhood use-by date.

Of course, just as it is possible to bury some pieces of our consciousness and surface others, and it is possible to blame some of our difficult emotions and own others, it is also possible to be challenged with both neurotic emotions and existential realizations at the same time. The main challenge then, I suggest, is to differentiate between the two – a task in itself – and then deal with the two bundles in appropriate ways. In practice, this is an ongoing journey which is often a matter of trial and error, of exploration of possibilities and of timing. We tell ourselves, for example, that the persistent sorrow we find continually shadowing us is merely a product of our silliness, only to discover that we have needed to access deep gut-wrenching grief, the origins of which we may not understand cognitively at first, or ever.

Alternatively, we avail of ongoing 'safe-place' therapy to surface the hidden conflicts with our parents, that we assume we have because we have read so many popular psychology books, only to discover that we have been using the idea to avoid taking responsibility for our life and have perpetuated it with flawed thinking about what was 'wrong with us'. Not only were we avoiding one existential realization, adults have to step into self-responsibility at some point if they are to experience some form of sustainable peace in autonomy, but we generated a smoke screen of neurotic emotions – comfortable discomfort zones – which we told ourselves were existential conflicts we had not had the opportunity, the breaks, to resolve before now.

The last paragraph suggests an example of how convoluted our efforts to avoid stepping into our real power can be. Moving into the path to our self-actualization, pointing ourselves toward the pinnacle of our humanity, is the greatest gift we can give ourselves and ultimately to our fellow man. Yet, we creatively, and industrially, work around this opportunity. Such is the fate of man, and woman, until touched by the seemingly random hand of personal breakthrough - of life-changing epiphany. This is an existential reality.

**The GAINER Model**

I firmly believe that it is impossible for a person to move to their self-actualization without understanding how they are perceiving the world and their place in it and *how they are perceiving their perceiving of the world.*

Below is the first piece of what I call the GAINER Model:

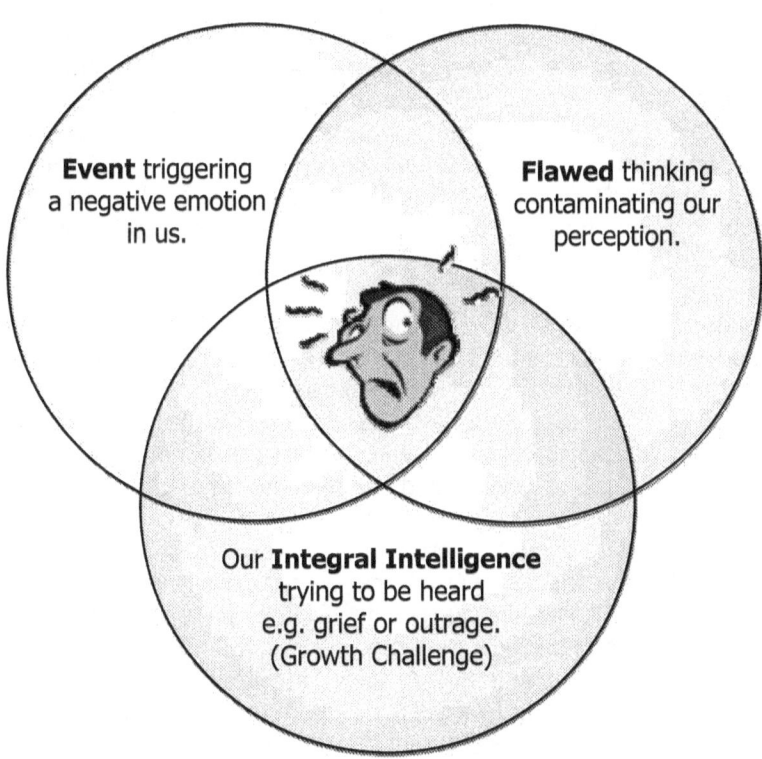

The GAINER model presents three interacting components. The first component is an event. It might be an event that is the result of something we did or a seemingly random event.

The second component is our current bank of flawed thinking – those thought processes which we have accumulated over time, that worked in the short term for us, but have yet to be flushed out and replaced with more robust thinking. The interaction between the event and our flawed thinking creates our neurotic emotions which, in turn, become 'an event' which we then interpret, at least partially, with our flawed thinking – and so the cycle continues.

The third component in the GAINER model is what I call our 'Integral Intelligence'. This is the part of us that we both *need to access* if we are to travel the path to our self-actualization and we inevitably *get more access to* as we travel that path.

If the currency of our flawed thinking is fear, fear of letting go of unproductive dependences, the currency of our integral intelligence is wisdom – including the wisdom to know how, where and when to be courageous. Our integral intelligence is the part of our consciousness that enables us to see an opening into the next stage of our growth. It sees the event and assesses it. It also observes our own flawed thinking, the fears that underlie them, and identifies the door through which we must go, in a specific situation, in order to move one step towards the pinnacle of our humanity.

If, as we grow up, we spend a lot of time in survival mode, we are not likely to have easy access to our integral intelligence or, at least, to have had the time to learn to recognize it and listen to it. If we have been connecting to it, we may then have found ourselves struggling with the symptoms of a conflict between what it is trying to tell us, what 'the world' is trying to tell us, and getting our basic needs met.

If we were fortunate enough to grow up in a growthful safe environment characterized by respect and nurturance, we probably have some access to our integral intelligence but we still need to integrate it with the reality of our adult environment. We may not be beset with neurotic fears but we might still carry an amount of unrefined idealism or untested naïveté – innocent but impractical in a less than perfect world. We may get a good start but this is no guarantee that we will freewheel to our full potential. We will be tested. The journey may well entail an apprenticeship involving walking with the fallen – if nothing else to cure us of our complacency.

Taking the GAINER model a step further can offer more insight – specifically looking at the points of contact between the components.

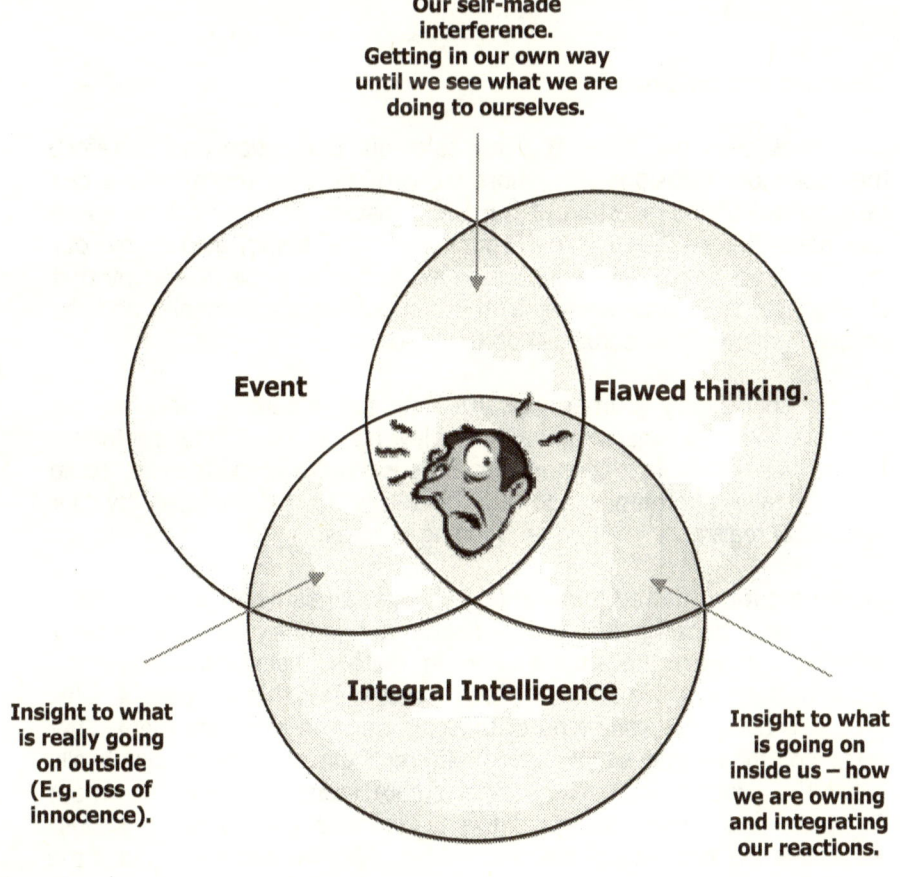

**GAINER** Model:
**G**rowth **A**nd **I**ntegrity **N**egative **E**motions **R**elationships.

I once heard an Irish politician, Pat Rabbitte, describe another politician, Michael McDowell, who was from a different party of course, as having been *"wrestling with his conscience"* on what Rabbitte considered to be an ethical issue. Rabbitte added *"Unfortunately, it seems Michael McDowell won!"* Perhaps the GAINER model might be relevant to this situation. Perhaps McDowell had been the subject of a negotiation process between his fears, of losing political clout, and his integral intelligence. Or, of course, perhaps not. Perhaps it was one set of fears wrestling with another set of fears.

**Cleaning the Software.**

Our needs color our thinking. They color our perception and therefore they color our decisions. The more we can see this, the more we can take control of the direction of our lives. Instead of being controlled by our need-driven selective perception, we are being guided by our integral intelligence. The more we allow ourselves to be guided by that intelligence, the closer we get to the pinnacle of our humanity and the unique version of self-actualization that is ours.

In the challenging journey towards our full potential, cleaning the software could be considered relatively 'low hanging fruit.' Moving from a life of unsustainable dependences to sustainable dependences could actually take a lifetime. Allowing ourselves to be changed by our existential realizations will be an ongoing process.

Cleaning out our flawed thinking is, I believe, a relatively finite process – at least as a backlog clear-out. A period of rigorously interrogating our thinking can turn the ship around in quite a substantial way. The problem is how do we do this? Albert Einstein said that we cannot solve problems using the same kind of thinking we used to create them. That does not mean that simply using different thinking will automatically solve the problem – it might even create more problems. The path forward, I suggest, needs different *more hygienic* thinking, less subjective thinking, more objective thinking. We need to check out if the world is flat or round, is orbited *by* the Sun or is it *orbiting* the Sun. We need to check out, for example, if trust in our relationships enhances our lives and those of our children or hinders them. We need to check is our version of reality actually reality or a self-serving version. We need to discover the wonderfulness, as Bob Woodward might put it, of not being certain – of being open to the possibility that the only reason that our horizons seem narrow, is that we carry blinkers with us. We need to discover, if the wonderful horizons in front of us are grounded in the reality of our humanity, at its pinnacle, or if they are the fantasies of wishful thinking, the product of 'an unexamined life,' our dose of the "*das Opium des Volkes*", as Karl Marx might have put it – "*the opium of the masses.*"

So how do we get that 'hygienic thinking'? I hope that reading a book like this might help. Writing, teaching and coaching I believe have helped me. Transforming my life will have been both a cause and an effect – probably a far greater contributor than anything else. Making a decision almost twenty years ago to go 'the road less traveled' – even if I hadn't yet heard that phrase at the time, was probably a significant milestone. It might sound like a noble decision but the hygienic thinker in me knows that life had cornered me into it.

On the one hand, we might walk with unhygienic thinking alongside others in our community, in our society, in our culture – both local and global. We, in groups, cannot see the elephants in the different rooms, that some of the emperors are going '*Au Natural*' down the street. On the other hand, we have our own unique blind spots – that we are one of the good guys, for example, and that *they* are the bad guys. We refuse to see the shackles of our own self-limiting selfishness. We tell ourselves that our selfishness is the healthy kind of selfishness under the banner of 'our rights' without disciplining ourselves to see the corresponding 'our responsibilities.'

Thinking that other people are the reason for our difficult emotions is an example of flawed thinking. There may be a correlation but that does not mean there is causality or, most importantly, no free-will. Understanding the subtleties, the challenges and the opportunities of emotional ownership will go a long way to harvesting the liberty that free-will offers us. With hygienic thinking, we will see that freewill is a reality – we have no choice but to accept it! In fact, we do have a choice to accept or reject freewill. We can choose to open ourselves to the possibility or not. I believe that the degree to which we distance ourselves from our freewill is a measure of the distance to our self-actualization. As we look from the foothills of our consciousness to the pinnacle of our humanity, we see obstacles and barriers, We see no pathways. Contemplating the trek, however, is the first step. Allowing ourselves to play with the vision of what we could be, even for a moment, can nudge us to look again even if not straight away. Ruminating on the possibility that there might be more to life, that it might just be possible for 'little old me' to break from the herd and venture into new terrain, can sow the seeds that next year can present the shoots of inspiration, the saplings of discovery.

**Projection.**

Another concept, dating back at least to Freud, as a 'professional' term, and I believe of constructive use to the growing man or woman on the street, is that of 'projection'.

Projection, in a psychological context, is the process with which we attribute something to another, or others – motivations, emotions, traits or impulses – that are more accurately, or more relevantly, residing within us but which we do not accept as part of us. Being open to the possibility that we are projecting onto others can be significantly beneficial to raising our awareness of ourselves. I would even go so far as to suggest that learning to ignore what we think are other people's motives or feelings, or at least park them, is an extremely useful competence for anyone interested in their own personal growth. It can help us to inoculate ourselves from our own projections.

There are two potential exceptions here – (1) When we need to predict the likely behavior of someone and (2) When we want to give someone something. Outside of these two exceptions, I believe that the vast majority of interpretations run the risk of serving as distractions from what is really going on inside of ourselves. In normal day-to-day relating, there is no need to bog ourselves down with the analysis of why people are doing what. It might be interesting, but it is not necessarily effective. It can also present many a wasteful cul-de-sac off the road of personal growth.

Projection is one of the ways in which bend reality to fit our version of it. If we discover we are projecting, we unearth a clue as to the gap between how we currently see the world and how our integral intelligence would have us see it – that is, how we would see it if we operating from closer to self-actualization. Addressing the flawed thinking around our projection, brings us out of those ungrowthful cul-de-sacs and challenges us to wrestle with the existential realizations offered to us on the road – the revelations of our true potential.

In the case of projection, we see not what is happening but a version of it that is contaminated by what we don't want to see in ourselves.

**What we see.**

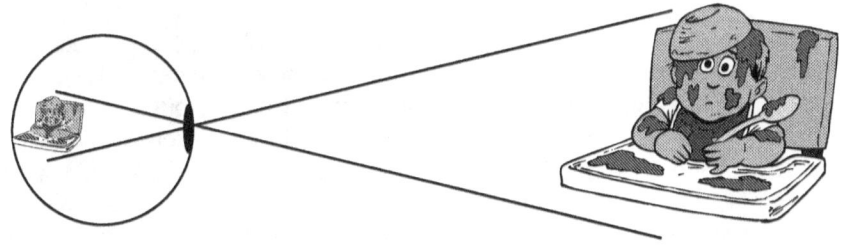

**What is actually happening**

In this case, sure the child is playing with his food. But if I, as the parent observing this, disown something about myself that is in some way about being 'messy' – perhaps I need to sort out my finances, for example, and I am in denial about it – I may add to the situation. To be more Freudian about it, if I never integrated the feelings of guilt, fear, shame, that have been hiding in the shadows of my consciousness since I was in the high chair, all those years ago, I may contaminate the situation. This, of course, run the risk of leaving the child with the job of carrying the same load.

By committing to one hundred percent emotional ownership, I can limit the possibility of my pushing my 'baggage' onto others. I can operate from a code of behavior more loyal to the pinnacle of my humanity. I can cut through the brambles and overgrowth on the path to my self-worth. I can ultimately claim as much of my self-actualization that my remaining years will allow. It's never too late to start.

**Bucking the System.**

The moment we begin to own our emotions – not to be confused with 'naming' our emotions, which is the process of identifying feelings and giving them a name – we begin a challenge, not only to ourselves, but to those around us. There are a few fairly predictable outcomes that tend to come with this territory. 'Fore-warned is fore-armed' as the saying goes. Just as a robust understanding of personal growth can give a coach the peace of mind to work elegantly with their clients, it also offers all of us a degree of comfort as we meet the range of reactions that can be encountered with a more 'heliocentric' approach to our existential reality.

*Insecurity.*

Things just aren't what they used to be! If we have been relying on a belief or set of beliefs and we outgrowth them, we often go through a period of insecurity as we move from the old paradigm into the new. What acted as crutches before, and we tend mostly to only see this retrospectively, is no longer available and the new territory seems unfamiliar. Returning to the treading water analogy, when we have to stay afloat, without the subtle ways in which we ungrowthfully lean on others, many of whom, in turn, lean on others still, we can feel a little nervous. *'How will I stay afloat?'* is the sentiment or *'How will I swim ashore?'* Taking it a stage further, when I do manage to swim ashore and move on to terra firma, I find I have to use muscles that I haven't been needing to use – either ever or in a long time. These muscles are weak and out of condition. It's a little like when astronauts return to earth after a long spell in a space-station. Their bodies need time to adapt to gravity after re-entry.

Of course, I am using the term 'muscles' figuratively here. The challenge is actually emotional. We are challenged to face some of our fears, own them, and allow them to change us. Remember, it is the existential emotions that will change us. Fear that is generated neurotically will just have us going around in circles and avoiding what we need to face. We stay in our 'comfortable discomfort' zones as distinct from our real discomfort zones and, as the saying goes, 'life begins at the edge of our comfort zone.' A big part of personal growth coaching is clarifying which emotions are neurotic and which are existential and therefore how they need to be handled.

The insecurity that comes with emotional ownership will pass with real growth. We may find we encounter a new layer of insecurity later but that will bring with it new opportunities and this too will pass. As each layer is 'processed', we gain in strength – even if it feels like the opposite at times. As we give up a redundant dependence for a more productive and sustainable one, we momentarily step into unfamiliar territory. At times, this insecurity can seem almost unbearable. It can seem grossly euphemistic to call it insecurity – 'panic' might seem like it better fits the bill. Sometimes we step into such challenging space for a short while and pull back. We consider that job change, we play with the idea of getting closer to our lover, we picture making that dream trip around the world, we contemplate the notion that we have been overly controlling in our relationships and tentatively poke our potential vulnerability if we were to change.

But even that momentary venture into the insecurity of a growthful step forward can help us make a more permanent move later. This is especially if we understand what is happening to us and can reflect on the valuable trade-offs – temporary discomfort for a permanent move towards our pinnacle?


*Abandonment.*

Part of the challenge of personal growth is that, as we grow, we become less and less tolerant of certain interpersonal dynamics. The more you genuinely move into 'the driver's seat of your life', – genuinely, as opposed to wishfully thinking it to be the case – the more you will see the degree to which people around you are not in the driver's seat of their lives. Whilst this is not a huge problem in itself, you can find that some people 'pull back' from relationship with you. The theory is that if they are not ready to make a similar jump in their growth, they will experience a degree of discomfort as they try to relate to you in the way they always did. They may not even notice the discomfort and, for this reason alone, I would recommend that you do not try to tell someone that they are 'threatened' by *your* growth – tempting and all as this might be. And, there is always the possibility that you are imagining it all! In general, I suggest that we do not shop-front our growth but be mindful of it to ourselves and observe both ourselves and others' responses. Real growth brings with it natural results that make sense. Trying to convince others, or ourselves, that we are growing, or have just grown, is usually a dependence in itself – an attempt to cling to the illusion of being part of a group of 'better' people or even 'acceptable' people. Alas, it doesn't work that way. Remember, I am suggesting that self-worth is a necessary stage on the way to self-actualization and self-worth is, by definition, not reliant on a comparison with anyone else – including 'who I used to be'.

If I have been living at the left-hand end of the NICE curve, and I start to move towards the right, I may challenge others around me to move similarly – without them knowing anything about the NICE curve or personal growth. However, in time, you might hear them comment on how *they* used to be different without any reference to the fact that *you* started the ball rolling!

It is also possible that some may loose interest in the relationship. Say, for example, that you and your peers are dependent on seeing yourselves as 'holier' than another group. Say you are a group of hard working union members who feel that the oppressive capitalists are the embodiment or evil, or you are a group of hard-working entrepreneurs who feel that the 'staff' are the epitome of irresponsible lazy freeloading. You might be a member of a group of women who see all men as users and losers, or you might be a group of men who see all women as manipulative sluts. And say you begin to transcend these unproductive stereotypes, bringing in a little more discernment and a little less judgementalism. When you do, there will be those who will be remaining in the prevailing mindset of that group. There is no guarantee that they will share your new insights. In extreme circumstances, you might be seen as a 'turncoat' or as betraying the cause – of 'the worker', 'free-enterprise', 'the sisterhood', 'the club' or whatever. In even more extreme circumstances, your life might be at stake – perhaps you have family connections with crime, violence or political corruption and the vested interests take exception to your lack of loyalty. Not only are you abandoned but you are being 'taken out'!


*Resistance.*

When abandonment occurs, following personal growth, it is usually quite passive. You notice that the person doesn't call anymore or that, when you do meet, there is little in the way of rapport. When you do try to bring the conversation to something more meaningful, meaningful to you, your erstwhile friend seems unengaged. Your gentle assertions that you do not wish to engage in the usual gossip about 'them', whoever 'they' are, are, for all intents and purposes, ignored.

However, your gentle assertions might not be ignored. Your friend might react more energetically and, subtly or otherwise, try to tell you that there is something wrong with you. They might suggest that you are 'touchy'. They might accuse you of being 'holier than thou' or 'superior.' Don't forget that pre-self-worth stages of development have a tendency to see things in terms of comparisons. In the self-worth stage and onwards, such comparisons are irrelevant. Your friend might intimate that *'that coaching business'* is tying you up in chains. *'Gossip is harmless'* they might assert. *'Don't be such a kill-joy'.* They may even recruit another peer to convert you back to the good old days.

These circumstances, while inconvenient, actually offer us opportunities to interrogate our analysis and conclusions about our new mindset. As we assert our fresh values and meet with resistance, we get to deepen our understanding of just what these relationships are about – currently and historically. We also get to encounter more than a few emotional reactions in ourselves as our friends effectively try to shame us back into place. Applying emotional ownership to these feelings moves us further up the line. Our old response might have been: *'How could you be so hurtful to say such a thing!'* as we effectively try to shame them into something. It is worth bearing in mind that old habits die hard. Instead, we choose to note to ourselves that we feel shame in response to their words. We reflect on it in the moment and afterwards. *'Interesting, I was generating a wave of shame there – another insight to that gap between my self-image and my self-worth.'* Instead of rejecting the emotion and looking for an external cause – *'It couldn't be me, it must be your fault for saying that!'* – we accept it as part of ourselves and allow our integral intelligence to 'integrate' the experience. We allow it to be part of us in the same way that we allow an upset child to cry in the safety of an accepting family. We don't look for a culprit – *'who said that?'* If necessary, we deal with the 'culprit' later, having dealt with our own emotional reactions – but this is a different challenge.

*Persecution.*

There is safety in being one of the herd - keeping the head down and not rocking any boats. However, your growth, particularly in the area of emotional ownership, can bring with it huge growth challenges for the herd and the herd may or may not be equipped to rise to those challenges. If the mindset of the herd is that the majority version of the truth rules, this is further compounded. At the left-hand end of the NICE curve, you will find groups that are very dependent on flawed but self-serving thinking. If you present an alternative mindset, one that is more in alignment with natural justice and that threatens to show up a weakness in the group's thinking, you stand the risk of becoming a lighting rod for other people's negativity and projection. The mob will be unsettled and will look for a scapegoat. You might well be chosen to fill that rôle.

Perhaps the most challenging aspect of personal growth is dealing with persecution. It is important, I hasten to add, not to confuse persecution with 'a persecution complex.' The latter, a persecution complex, is where we imagine we are being persecuted, whilst the former is where we are actually being persecuted. Being told, in response to growthful, self-defensive assertions, that *'Ah, it's only your persecution complex!'* can be part of a system of persecution. It is not likely to be seen as such by the persecutors – *'they know not what they do'* – but the result will be just as challenging to the persecuted.

## Aiming for the Pinnacle

Just as Copernicus, Galileo, and others throughout history, were seen as anything from inconvenient, or irritating, to 'the devil-incarnate', anyone in a group, that puts their head above the parapêt, can draw the fire of the collective denial of the group. This does not have to be an overt confrontation of issues – it can just as easily catch the 'black-sheep' unawares. An innocent child skips and jumps into the new class-room with a carefree outlook and is perplexed by the mean acts of those less free within the cohort. A recently graduated idealist is puzzled by the awkward silence that ensues when she highlights potential ethics conflicts in her new place of employment. A psycho-therapy trainee is thrown by the tension in the room when the trainer is challenged on a point of logic. A teenager is labeled 'the problem child' as they begin to question the family's long held political dogma. The experienced coach, at the seminar, is surprised by the 'looks' received from some of those they expected would be their fellow self-actualizers when a sacred cow is challenged.

The common thread, in these situations, will be the way in which those at the right-hand end of the NICE curve will throw those at the other end into discomfort. How those people interpret that discomfort will determine what they do about it. If they see corresponding behaviour in others, with similar dependences, they may well fall into the trap of blaming the 'free-spirit' for too 'something.' That something will tend to be seen with negative vocabulary by those who are impotent, even if they do not feel impotent, – vocabulary such as 'aggressive', 'opinionated', 'insensitive', but with positive language by those at the right end –'assertive', 'out-spoken', 'challenging'. Two worlds collide.

As you begin to take ownership of your emotions, you may well become a lighting rod for other people's projections. Of course, when someone is projecting, they tend not to know they are projecting. They may even be unaware of what projecting means in this context. Telling them that they are projecting could be like trying to teach a cat to dance – it doesn't work and it annoys the cat!

Part of the challenge of this aspect of personal growth is to do three things:

1. Not to take things personally – whilst remaining humble to nuggets of insight about yourself.

2. To protect yourself from the effects of blind groupthink – including 'getting out while you can'.

3. If possible, to model 'a better way' – to take a leadership approach.
*Healing.*

One of the positive outcomes of emotional ownership is a sense of healing of old wounds. It is very difficult to hang on to emotional baggage, associated with a past perceived injustice, when you fully own your emotions. The related event may well have been a gross infringement of natural justice but that is a separate issue. If I accept that the emotion I am complaining about is of my own making, I can no longer continue blaming the perpetrator. Once I resolve the hurt, I no longer consume energy, and attention, by dwelling on this issue – I am free of it. I may decide to lobby for legislation to prevent it happening to someone else in the future but my motivation in doing this is positively generated, a 'towards' motivation and not driven by my hurt, a negative, 'away from' motivation. To the outsider, this might not look that different but the effectiveness of the lobbyist will be greater. There is also the released emotional energy available for other activities, like playing with children and toasting, with loved ones, to what life has given us!

Again, in letting go of old wounds, we can find ourselves in unfamiliar territory. Good personal growth coaching can provide some support and direction as we navigate this territory. It is useful to remember however, that we need to do our own growing. No-one else can do this for us.

*Forgiveness.*

One feature of emotional ownership, and personal growth in general, is that we begin to see that the world is not quite the way we thought it was. We see things a little less subjectively and a little more objectively – step by step. We may even discover, 'Oh the shame!', that we have been one of those 'low-lifes' who indulge in projection, or persecution or some other despicable, immature, blind, needy, *unforgivable* acts of ungrowthful degradation!

Two things:

# Aiming for the Pinnacle

1. Welcome to the human race, more specifically what Karl Jung – remember Freud's recalcitrant breakaway disciple – called 'the shadow', and,

2. Forgiveness is at the heart of personal growth – especially forgiving ourselves. Again, stepping into the space of awareness of this capacity within ourselves can bring with it the discomfort and insecurity of unfamiliarity. I am referring here to real forgiveness of course. This is a gift to the 'forgiver' not necessarily to the 'forgiven' who could even be dead. To forgive is a gift to ourselves even though we sometimes interpret it as 'letting them off the hook'. Holding someone accountable is another matter and over which we may or may not have control.

Emotional ownership is a reliable way of generating real organic forgiveness that releases the injured party in a way that does not rely on the actions of the perpetrator. This is true personal growth at its most powerful and its most empowering. Again, it is not for the faint-hearted but definitely a must for those aiming for the pinnacle of their humanity.

*Empathy.*

With the gradual dilution of our subjectivity, and the advancement of our objectivity, comes another very valuable by-product – empathy. Rather than locking ourselves into a polarized *'I am right and they are wrong'* mentality, we tend to move to a *'I think I'm right and I think they are wrong but let's see the world from their perspective'* mentality.

When we take this approach we open ourselves to being changed by a new reality. That might mean that we change our perspective on an issue and agree with our contender, or we might retain our perspective but see it in the context of the perspective of the other person. We might see the world through their eyes and get a better insight into their dependences. If so, we may see a route forward to having them see the wisdom of our perspective – a growth path if you like. Or, we might see that we are wasting our time. We might conclude that reason will not sway them no matter how much of it we have on our side.

I suggest that empathy works in different ways depending on where on the NICE curve the object of the empathy lies.

## The 'NAME' Matrix

Subject is empathizing...

|  | Left — NICE Curve — Right |  |
|---|---|---|
| **Aware** | **Aware Needy.** Possible emotional catharsis/self-insight. Hope of breakthrough. | **Aware Mature.** Meeting of minds |
| **Unaware** | **Unaware Needy.** Damage limitation. I see their world but I cannot reach them. | **Unaware Mature.** Non-critical. 'Taken as given' Move to URQ if necessary. |

Object (of empathy)

**N**eedy **A**ware **M**ature **E**mpathy matrix.

The NAME matrix shows empathy applied in four different situations. The LLQ is where the empathizer accurately feels the situation from the other person's perspective but cannot reach them emotionally. In this case, the 'object' of the empathy is too needy and unaware. There might be a gap but it is unlikely that there will be an opening now.

*Jim's wife left him seven years ago. Stephen has a good sense of what this was like for Jim, both practically and emotionally, and can express it to Jim, but Jim is locked so deeply into a victim rôle that Stephen's empathy has little effect. Without any knowledge of what Stephen has been through in his life, Jim stills has a 'You have no idea what it has been like for me' mindset and does not seem close to breaking out of it. Jim sees this and responds peacefully and patiently.*

The ULQ is different. In this case, even though the person being empathized with is at the needy end of the NICE curve they are being reached with empathy. This is likely to be a product of the empathizer's empathy, the trust in the relationship, and the empathized's readiness to take that emotional step.

*Janet feels almost ready to take the leap and set up her own business. She suddenly senses that Jennifer, her coach, knows what this feels like and is quite at peace in it. Janet suddenly lets out a deep breath and feels more connected to her fears about the move. This helps her tweak a few parts of her strategy and she decides to 'feel the fear and do it anyway' – more confident but also more grounded. Steady as she goes.*

The LRQ suggests a situation where one person sees, and feels, the others person's perspective but it is no big deal for either. It acts as a natural lubricant to the relationship and not much energy or time is required for both parties to keep singing off the same hymn sheet.

*Joe presents his strategy to Maggie, his boss. Maggie is able to see the issue through Joe's eyes and is happy enough with what she sees. Joe is oblivious to Maggie's empathy and ploughs ahead. After a while, he realizes that Maggie 'gets it' from his perspective and, after a little negotiation, they agree some tweaks to the plan. The empathy moved up to the URQ.*

Of course, in the last case, it might well be that Joe also has empathy for Maggie's position as boss and this too aids their co-operation. In fact, the more responsibility a person takes for themselves, as in emotional ownership, the more they get to discern the way in which people in authority actually take responsibility. This can be a double edged sword – we can become more empathic of those who carry the responsibility with maturity and less tolerant of those who carry the rôle from a position of neediness. Either way, we get a better understanding of other people's worlds – even if we wish they were different!


*Connection.*

A key outcome of the growth resulting from emotional ownership is our capacity to meet someone else in a deep, meaningful and healthy way. To connect with someone when we are needy gives a momentary rush, a brief and seductive taste of something we are missing. However, as time passes, this rush dissipates and we are left with the real me and the real you – two diamonds in the rough with expectations of more from each other and the inevitable disappointment of faded novelty.
However, at the right-hand end of the curve things are different. Two people, each with a critical mass of their own self-worth, will engage

with each other in a different way to two people at the needy end. With the substance of their own self-worth, there is a meeting of two people without the potential black-hole of their combined emotional neediness. There is also the emotional resilience to open up to each other and witness the treasures each one brings to the equation. If we think back to Eric Berne's Transactional Analysis, or TA, we can get a glimpse of what might be at play here. Berne, you will remember, suggested that people play 'games' in relationships and that, rather than falling into a parent or child rôle in a relationship, the optimal is an adult-adult relationship.

Taking a typical romantic relationship, there are a number of dynamics that might occur. If both parties are at a sufficient level of self-worth they can be themselves in the relationship and are not overly bending to meet the needs or the approval of the other. This type of relationship offers at least some chance of sustainability and, in fact, has every chance of growing in its beauty and mutual nurturance. In addition, if there are children in the orbit of the relationship they will bathed in a synergy not as likely in a relationship characterized by neediness.

Using TA terminology, and simplistically speaking, we could look at a relationship in terms of four possibilities.....

## The 'PACT' Matrix

Couple in TA Rôles...

|  | Child | Adult |
|---|---|---|
| **Adult** (Party 1) | **Adult-Child** 'You need to do this for yourself dear.' Potential for growth – or difficult to sustain. | **Adult-Adult** Optimal Mutual love allowed – not forced or needed. Healthy interdependence. |
| **Parent** (Party 1) | **Parent-Child** 'You can't manage – let me do it.' Compatible but at a price. | **Adult-Parent** 'Give me space. I can make my own decisions.' Potential for growth – or difficult to sustain. |

Party 2

**P**arent **A**dult **C**hild in **T**A.

## Aiming for the Pinnacle

The move from the LLQ to the URQ, within the PACT matrix, can be a journey of substantial growth. When I look around, I see some couples managing to traverse that route together. It might have taken some time, and there may have been a few wobbly moments, but they seem to have gotten there – at least for the time being. Other couples seem to have split up and found new partners – perhaps partners more innately compatible, who knows? I don't propose doing an analysis here of why some relationships survive and others don't. However, I do believe that, if one attends to one's growth, with copious amounts of humility, that it will evoke whatever needs to happen for that growth to continue. This does not mean that the road will not be rocky, but using a robust understanding of growth as a compass will nudge us up against any limiting child-like co-dependences. If we choose to go there, it will take us on to the path towards our self-actualization. As always, our free-will will be challenged albeit with the compelling sense of a natural order.

Of course, the PACT matrix does not cover parent-parent or child-child relationships.

### Taking the Plunge.

Embracing the GAINER model, and the task of emotional ownership it calls for, is potentially the greatest challenge a person can embrace. In fact, I believe that many noble challenges, embarked on by spirited and inspiring pioneers, might well have been the less scary of two paths. One might be up the side of Everest, or the dizzying heights of the corporate or political ladder, the other into the realms of our true selves and what it would take to scale the rock face of our personal growth and aspire to the pinnacle of our humanity. Either route will present us with boundaries and none more demanding, but ultimately liberating, than the exigencies of the world of ethics – the subject of the next chapter.

### Chapter Bullets:

- 'Resistance' dates back at least to Freud.
- Practitioners can 'Blind them with science' (clients).
- Reality presents itself with all its wonders and wounds.

- Copernicus claimed that the universe was heliocentric.
- History shows many examples of resistance to truth.
- History has what are retrospectively seen as dark moments.
- Emotional non-ownership is presented here as a flawed paradigm.
- Interpretations of EO vary depending on maturity of the interpreter.
- EO can evoke up to at least five 'syndromes'.
- The SOBBED matrix looks at two ways in which we handle emotions.
- Couples can exhibit the 2 sides of the SOBBED matrix between them.
- The NEVER model presents two types of negative emotions.
- The GAINER model offers an understanding of Growth and Integrity.
- McDowell was said to be 'wrestling with his conscience'.
- Our needs color our thinking.
- We need to detect 'das Opium des Volkes' in our thinking.
- Hygienic thinking will show us the challenge of freewill.
- Understanding 'projection' aids personal growth.
- Analyzing others' motives can be a redundant distraction.
- It's never too late to grow!
- Stepping into EO brings a range of challenges.
- The PACT matrix looks at four different relationship pairings.

# Chapter 8
# Ethics.
*Growth on a Plate.*

How we look at and understand ethics will be influenced by our needs, our maturity, our social conditioning and our *current* ethical intelligence.

I believe that for a person to aspire to the pinnacle of their humanity, they will inevitably have to enter the atrium of ethical thinking, or more accurately, ethical knowing. This experience may or may not be associated with the term 'ethics' by the individual but the essence of the experience will be indistinguishable with the essence of 'ethics' as presented here.

For anyone to reach their full potential, they will have to traverse the terrain of their redundant dependences and come out the other side with a lighter load. If growth represents the terrain, 'ethics' is both the compass and part of the reward. Again, as I have alluded to before, personal growth leads to a more ethical life and further accelerated growth, amongst other things. However, personal growth requires us to examine our life through the Petrie dish of our dependences and with the lens of our ethical understanding. The more refined that lens becomes, the more clarity we bring to our examination.

Just as in our gut we carry 'friendly' bacteria and 'not so friendly' bacteria, the examination of our dependences reveals 'friendly' and 'not so friendly' dependences. The bacteria in our gut can be friendly to the life systems that are attempting to function in the inner world of our digestive tract with all its enzymes, amino acids, membranes and foodstuffs "just passin' through" – they can be pro-biotic. Alternatively, the 'unfriendly' variations restrict, inhibit, corrupt, hi-jack those processes for reasons that are just as self-serving as those of the pro-biotics but misplaced. From the perspective of the host, they are parasitic. Sustaining the natural functioning of our gut requires the nurturance of the life-sustaining and collaborative bacteria in our system and the elimination of those activities that get in the way of that functioning. And so it is with our outer life – moving to our full potential requires us to find and nurture those activities that are life-sustaining and collaborative as well as to detect, eliminate, protect ourselves from, or convert those that are restrictive or parasitic.

So what is the essence of ethics? I suggest it is about a way of living that is *non-parasitic*. This may sound somewhat shocking at first but I suggest that the term parasitic fits quite well. A parasite is something that lives off of another living thing – 'without its permission'. On the other hand, a *symbiotic* is, I suggest, a word that one could use to describe something that lives in a way that is dependent on another living thing but in no way detracts from the health of that other and, in fact, may add to it. For the purposes of this analysis, I also suggest that it does so with the permission of the other party – either explicit or implicit – and in a way that does not take advantage of the other person's inability to understand the interdependence.

## Some questions around ethics...

1. Why look at ethics – i.e. what value ethics?
2. How do I examine ethics to extract value?
3. How do we live ethically?
4. How do we deal with our own ethical shortcomings?
5. How do we deal with others' ethical shortcomings?
6. What about ethics and self-defense?
7. Who are the stakeholders in ethics issues?

## 1. Why Look at Ethics - i.e. What Value Ethics?

A good starting point for anyone considering looking at ethics is to look at their own motivation for doing such an examination. In my experience, these motivations can vary from person to person depending on level of maturity and prevailing needs. Don't forget, I am using the term 'maturity' in the context of personal growth, self-worth and self-actualization and not by reference to a given cultural set of expectations – as in 'men don't cry'. Having said that, I fully admit that my interpretation of growth, self-worth and self-actualization will be vulnerable to my own cultural conditioning and for this I can offer little defense. However, I will pin my colors to the mast and claim that much, if not all, of what humankind has generated, for the better, has been the result of independent thinking and questioning. I also believe that, by its nature, self-actualization brings with it higher degrees of ex-culturation and objective thinking. As to whether *I* am viewing the issue at hand from an ex-cultural perspective is another matter. I will be doing my best to interrogate the robustness of my thinking. The reader will be wise to do similarly – with both their own thinking and mine. Finally, the road towards self-actualization has a starting point, or a 'next starting point' – this is inevitably a product of our cultural conditioning whatever that culture is.

When one is at the needy end of the NICE curve, the left end when presented as I have done here, one will either not want to look at ethics or will want to look at it from a selective perspective – one influenced by one's needs. I personally take an optimistic viewpoint when it comes to human growth and self-actualization. I assume that, that even if a person is at the extreme left hand end of the curve, they have within them a desire, and a capacity, to understand ethical living from an objective position, from a self-worth perspective, from a contributory and self-actualization perspective, from the perspective of the pinnacle of their humanity. Until they get to the mandatory plateau of their own true self-worth, their interpretation of ethics will be colored by their unmet needs. If they are a dangerous murderer, I would want them under lock and key (my safety needs) but, in the meantime, I assume that, under certain circumstances, they could grow out of their murderousness. Those circumstances may never prevail in their life-time but the potential for growth is there none-the-less.

At the 'Need-dominant' end of the NICE curve, in addition to any altruistic ethical inclinations germinating within my consciousness, I will have other inclinations that will tend to dominate my interpretations.

These more dominant inclinations will include:

*Survival and Safety Needs:*

I want others to behave ethically so that *I will be safe*. My survival needs dominate here. My main concern is that no-one will be a 'parasite' to me. I 'demand' ethical behavior from others so that no-one will take my 'stash' whether small because I am 'a victim' or large because 'I worked for it.'

*Self-Esteem Needs:*

As I move to the right of the curve, my dominant needs change and so too will my relationship to ethics. When my need for self-esteem is alive and well, and I am interested in my own ethical behavior, that interest will tend to be dominated by my need to be seen as one of 'the good guys'. Don't forget that self-worth requires no comparison with any other person (object), including an imaginary version of the person in question (subject) if they were less 'accomplished'. Self-esteem tends to be 'conditional' – in the eyes of the needer that is. Self-esteem transactions normally refer to some achievement or feature of the receiver of that transaction. In this regard, again, ethics will be seen selectively and a degree of comfort may be taken by the presence of others *seen as* less ethical. Remember, on the road to self-actualization, we encounter the need for self-esteem and then self-worth. Without self-worth, a person is very much a 'work-in-progress' and will find that getting their self-esteem need met can feel like a 'shot in the arm.'

At the self-esteem stage there tends to be a need to observe the world in terms of 'goodies and baddies' and the observer will be putting themselves into the 'goodies' camp. They may even be prepared to accept their own ethical 'imperfections' based on the fact that at least they are not 'as bad as' the nominated baddies. In these circumstances, there will be talk about ethical issues, not necessarily using the term ethics. The issue might be couched in words such as 'justice', 'fairness', 'reasonableness', even 'evil' and 'righteousness'. However, the essence will be the same. At this level of consciousness, there will be ethical behavior but it will have a limitation and it will be dictated partially by a person's desire for fairness and partially by what is interpreted as the group mores – what the group says is ethical, fair, just, reasonable.

Ancient Greece had a complex system of laws designed to protect you from the unethical behavior of others – as long as you were not a slave! Modern western society tends to enact quite intricate and thought-out legislation to define what is just and what is unjust in a given jurisdiction. You can be locked up for murder in probably all modern states but the same legislators may not be so careful when is comes to the lives of people in other countries. Indiscriminate bombing, or selective economic policies can result in one country, presumably the more powerful, effectively living parasitically at the expense of another. In addition, individuals in both countries can be living parasitically on others within their respective states. When it exists, this might, for example, be couched in the language of protection from the evil enemy (the baddies) with chillingly Orwellian undertones and the implications for survival.

*And Self-worth.*

I believe that the attainment of self-worth is a significantly more challenging task to an individual than the accumulation of self-esteem. One of the reasons for this is that self-worth demands a more refined understanding of ethical functioning and even more demanding responses to this understanding.

In ancient Greece, a citizen with a critical mass of self-worth will have seen the issue of slavery in a way that was in conflict with the prevailing mores. To confront the system with this perspective, that slaves are equal humans too, would be to risk one's life. To suggest that those in power were in anyway 'the baddies' would rock the self-esteem, the self-image, of those self-same 'powerful people'. This in turn will take them to the edges of their survival needs and will thus have them take up arms. This taking up of arms may well be claimed to be justified on the basis of 'a righteous cause' but closer scrutiny will reveal flawed thinking and selective perception – all designed to meet perceived needs. None of this might be acknowledged or understood at the time and the players may all go to their graves un-enlightened.

By definition, self-worth brings with it a perception that all people are of worth. This is not because to believe this means I get to be accepted by my community as a good guy, but it is an integral part of self-worth, even if I am rejected by my community for rocking the boat. In fact, I believe that this perception of worth is not limited to people but fans out to everything, a reverence for everything, with the associated humility. A person at the right hand end of the NICE curve will tend to have a desire for ethical justice *for its own sake,* and not as a means to have a personal need of their own met. This is not to say that they will not take steps to protect themselves from the unethical actions of others. Far from it, self-worth usually brings with it an automatic tendency to defend one's boundaries – with measure. It might even prompt us to sacrifice something in the support of justice – letting go of a dependence for the benefit of a higher cause. This is also not to imply that those taking an interest in ethics, without having reached a critical mass of self-worth, are not also influenced by their own altruistic desires – they often are. However when it comes to the crunch, when we have to actually do something difficult in order to sustain our integrity, or our stated ethical position, without self-worth we will struggle and we are more likely to flounder. Facing an ethical challenge from a position of self-worth won't necessarily be easy but, without it, the task will be significantly more challenging. That very challenge offers us a way forward.

## 2. How do We Examine Ethics to Extract Value?

In the previous section, I suggested that a person's motivation for their interest in ethics will be influenced by where they rest on the continuum of personal effectiveness – on the NICE curve. Remember of course, that I am referring to effectiveness here and not output – remember DOVE?

However, whilst we can all be at different levels of maturity, and can have very different temperaments, I would like to propose a way of looking at the area of ethics that provides an over-arching and universal motivation – one that 'works' for everyone irrespective of their level of maturity.

I have yet to meet a person who did not want more of something. Someone wants more fun or more peace and quiet. Someone else wants more adventure or more predictability. Another person wants more money or more simplicity in their life. Yet another wants more freedom or more responsibility. What all of these people want is to get something they want. This applies even if they are saying that they don't want something – which means that they want to not have something!

A man who wants a strict routine in his life, without any change wants to have the power to be able to sustain that predictable life. He may even want to be able to do this without the inconvenience of having power! But very often we don't seem to be able to get what we want. The predictable life is thrown into disarray by the job transfer, the new production system, or the redundancy. The ideal globe-trotting job slips through our fingers yet again as the guy with the fancier résumé clinches it ahead of us. The perfect partner turns out to be not so perfect – oh for the glory days of romantic bliss!

The one thing that offers value, to us all, is our personal growth. To move towards our own self-worth and to taste the wholesome fruits of that journey, even in tantalizing nibblets, is by definition, 'worth it'. Even if we make camp on the early plateaus of self-worth and decide to postpone the adventure of the next leg, to our self-actualization, we get something of value.

That path of growth is strewn with challenges to us to come face-to-face with our dependences and spring-clean them with discernment. A commitment to deepening our understanding of ethics, to more refined depths, will provide a series of signposts along the way. Any other system of navigation, unless it incorporates this commitment of ethical refinement, will leave us rudderless, and wandering, and susceptible to being pulled by undercurrents of waywardness, bashed against the jagged rocks of idealism, stranded in the desert of meaninglessness or seduced by the compelling sirens of cultism. By attending to our ethics, and not being distracted, for example, by what we see as others' ethics, or lack of ethics, we open out a scroll and discover a treasure map on which we begin to see the terrain we must travel if we are to get on course to the pinnacle.

By opening ourselves to this way of looking at ethics we begin to see that, rather that living ethically being restrictive and inhibitory, it offers us an opportunity to enter into territory reserved for the ethical. This does not mean the self-righteous or their well-matched reactionaries – but those who choose to pay the price for their own self-worth, who choose to not just look at the map but to go the journey. Most significantly, it is to choose to relinquish all of their dependences that constitute contraband at the border station of their self-actualization.

## 3. How Do We Live Ethically?

It's one thing to decide to live ethically, or in accordance with a personal or group code of ethics. It's another thing, however, to apply ourselves congruently to that code.

One of our tendencies, when we are at the needy end of the NICE curve is to look at ethics as a black and white issue – some people are ethical and some aren't, the goodies and baddies. However, at the contributory end things do not look quite as simple. The first challenge for anyone on the journey through the terrain of ethical living is to see that we are all capable of living ethically – partially. We are also capable of living unethically – partially. It is generally comforting to contemplate the ways in which we *are* ethical – even if, probably especially if, that contemplation is corralled by selective perception. It is generally emotionally *challenging* to contemplate the ways in which we are living *unethically*. How we deal with that emotion will determine how we respond to the insights elicited by that contemplation.

To live unethically offers many options for our behaviour. To live ethically offers fewer. To randomly throw the components of a precision watch or a computer onto a table and expect them to arrange themselves in a way that has them telling the time or processing data is sub-optimal thinking. There are many many ways in which the components might land if randomly thrown on the table – none of which will have either machine reaching its full potential. There is only one way in which the precision watch can be arranged for it to work – the same applies with the computer. It takes effort and know-how to assemble the machines. It takes effort and know-how to point ourselves in the direction of our self-actualization. Once assembled, the watch needs to be wound or have its battery charged. Once pointing to our self-actualization, we need maintenance but the challenge of assembly has been fulfilled. To do an ethical audit, and to nudge the rudder of our life in response, is work, and at times, hard work. This is especially at the early stages of that quest.

Refining our ethical awareness requires more then simply writing and adopting a code of ethics. The real work involves sustained reflection and, for the vast majority of us, a system of objective exploration to tease out those shadowy corners of our awareness that resist elucidation. This may include the support of an effective coach – one little burdened by a simplistic understanding of ethics. That coach may or may not use the label 'coach' but they will offer objectivity and sensitivity and a 'knowing' of our potential to transcend our culturally convenient version of ethics – towards what it is for us to be more. They, in turn, will be turning to a challenging authority for their own ethical hygiene.

To adopt a code of ethics is a useful step towards our growth. However, to do so without a means by which we continually review our relationship with that code, and the ways in which we apply ourselves to it, can be a recipe for denial. Every professional code of ethics I have read has come across to me as noble – on the face of it – some even inspiring. However, the real power of that code is seen when those committed to it are challenged to reconcile it with a live ethical issue. It is at that point that the growth challenge begins – where players take up their positions on the NICE curve.

Ethics codes abound and I do not see value in presenting a new one here. How we engage with a given code will provide more for our growth than the 'feelgood' factor that comes with associating ourselves with that code. The coal-face of ethical engagement will be where we will chisel out the nuggets of growth by seeing past the mist of consensus reality and befriending the elephants in the room. Clarity will offer us a much needed compass.

### 4. How Do We Deal With Our Own Ethical Shortcomings?

It is very difficult to see our own ethical blind-spots if we also carry a belief that we cannot survive without the fruits of those ethical blind-spots. In general, that belief will be sub-terrainian and surfacing it can help in the process of finding the blind-spots, shining some light into them and outgrowing them.

*Derek is a nice guy. He has a nice house, nice wife, nice car, nice career, nice income. He is not happy and doesn't understand why – that's not nice for him. Derek has energetically applied himself to his goals in life and had difficulty understanding why others didn't just 'do it' – less of this 'navel gazing' and 'analyzing things to the $n^{th}$ degree'. Now, in his mid-forties, he is wondering why he is not so enthusiastic about his career, the company, moving on and up. Derek decides to avail of the services of a coach – mainly because he thought it would look nice on his résumé.*

*One of the first questions Mark, Derek's coach, asked of Derek was 'What's important?' Derek's spoke for about a minute.*

*Mark then asked, 'Given what you have said, to what degree do you think I could understand what is important to you?'*

*Derek looked puzzled, 'I would have thought it was obvious' was his reply and repeated a slightly abridged version of what he had already said.*

*'To what degree do you feel you have answered my second question Derek?' Mark then asked.*

*'Oh' said Derek – non-verbally.*

Mark was reasonably clear-headed – no Einstein, but well within the realms of normal in Derek's view of the world. But having asked Derek that simple first question, he began a process within which Derek was to totally review his perception of himself. The essence of the issue was that Derek did not know what was important to him but one thing became clear – it was important to him to see himself as falling into the category of people who know what is important! His need for self-esteem was clouding his capacity to look himself in the eye and acknowledge a gap between what he considered to be ethical behavior, which was actually important to him, and his actual behavior. All the 'economical' tax returns, the 'creative' accounting practices, the 'regulatory short-cuts', the health and safety 'work-arounds', the hi-way speeding, the tucked away bank accounts and the visits to legal brothels at regular industry conferences in Europe, were actually behaviors that were in conflict with Derek's own understanding of ethics. However, his need for accomplishment, financial 'security', and the accolades that come with climbing the corporate ladder, at least the way he climbed the corporate ladder, all dominated his perspectives. His internal need to grow was beginning to niggle him – and *'that wasn't nice.'*

Derek began to do an ethical audit on himself and, with the steadfast consistency of his grounded coach, he began turning the ship around. This was not an overnight event and Mark only played a part for a little over two years. However, Derek began to reap the rewards of the 'growth on a plate' that a genuine commitment to ethics can offer us. This will not be to prove to anyone else that he is an ethical person and not one of 'them'. It will simply be to surface the selective reasoning that provided Derek with so many creature comforts but also ladened him with a cumbersome and inhibiting ethical overdraft. In discovering that he was one of the *'bad guys'* – by his own values and estimation, not by Mark's – he was free to begin to shed that load. He had a lot of work ahead of him. He would be learning to live by different rules within which to eek out an existence for himself and his now materially very demanding family.

In looking at Derek's story, two things are key:

1. The story was unimportant. How Derek was being unethical was only relevant if it could be used to raise his consciousness. It was his selective perception that was getting in the way of his growth.

2. It was not Mark's assessment of Derek's behavior as unethical or ethical that was important. If Mark was to adopt the role of ethical policeman it would have been counter-productive from a growth perspective – except in extreme circumstances e.g. real and present danger to the coach, client or others. Even in these extreme cases, taking an 'ethical expert' role can be counter-productive or useless. It is usually much better to take a direct approach and to take action to protect those involved than to try to 'teach' someone ethics. The growth can come later.

## 5. How do We Deal with Others' Ethical Shortcomings?

We are often faced with what we believe to be unethical behavior on the part of someone else. It might be about their finding a wallet and keeping the money or it might be about their mobilizing an army to invade another country. I do not propose here to unpack the ethical intricacies within 'finders-keepers' or of international power politics. However, I do believe, if our commitment is to our own self-actualization, that there is value in reflecting on how we respond, both emotionally and behaviorally, to what we see as the unethical actions of others. In fact, our response will usually entail an ethical challenge. If we accept the concept of DOVE, discerning output versus effectiveness, we can establish a grounded starting point. Just because I wouldn't do what he did doesn't mean that *I wouldn't do it if I had the same limited resources and particular circumstances that he had.*

Often our response to an unethical act is driven by our emotions. I believe that unethical acts are generally the product of immaturity on behalf of the actor. I believe, rightly or wrongly, that, embedded with the humanity of everyone, is the capacity for self-worth and its associated maturity. I accept that that capacity seems to be more deeply buried in some than others. I see no merit in rejecting the universality of this capacity and a lot of potential value in embracing it. But likewise, I believe that many people's responses to the unethical acts of others are driven by immaturity. They are reacting emotionally, and may be burying some other emotions. Most importantly, they may be overly certain that their perception of that situation is complete.

*Breda arrived to her coaching session seething. Her face was red and her hands clinched. Dave noticed and was curious, to himself, about her body language but kick-started the session in his usual way, by asking Breda how she would like to use the hour they now had together.*
*'I want to continue with where we left off last week', Breda replied, avoiding eye-contact with Dave.*
*'Which would mean......' Dave responded.*
*'You're the bloody coach and what's the point in taking notes if you can't remember?' She retorted aggressively, this time glaring into Dave's eyes.*
*Dave remained silent – keeping gentle eye contact with Breda.*
*His intuition told him to stay silent at that moment and 'await further instructions'.*
*Breda's face was still red. Her eyes wide, with what appeared to be rage. Her hands clenched the arms of the seat and her lips were pursed.*
*An old inner voice tried to distract Dave suggesting that he had been a bold boy and made Breda upset – although the voice did not suggest how this might have happened. Dave noted the voice, parked it within his consciousness and it soon dissipated – from lack of attention.*
*After a few very long seconds, Dave offered..*
*'What's happening Breda?'*
*Breda looked into the fireplace – two real but decorative logs rested there - unlit.*
*'Cleaner's thorough as ever' Dave thought to himself momentarily and brought his eyes back to Breda.*
*Breda clenched her teeth – she was working hard with whatever was going on.*
*'They should be locked up for life and... and castrated!' She released through clenched teeth.*
*Dave was puzzled.*
*'Who.' He asked what seemed like an obvious question.*
*'Those bastards that killed that little toddler.'*

# Aiming for the Pinnacle

*Dave realized that Breda was talking about a news item that had been fronting the day's bulletins. A two-year-old boy had been seduced away from his mother in a shopping mall, by two ten-year-old boys, and ended up dead on a nearby railway track.*
*Breda was consumed with rage.*
*'If I lived there I would be doing everything I possibly could to make those two scum pay. Hanging them would be too good for them!'*

Dave continued working with Breda in that session and found himself entertaining the notion that, either Breda was going to give up the coaching or that, if this emotion persisted, that Breda might not be coachable and was preparing himself for a sudden but managed termination. As it happened, that session allowed some growth work and led to more being done in subsequent sessions. Breda considered the two ten-year-olds to be 'evil' (for which you might read 'extremely unethical' – parasitically getting their kicks at the expense of another). In addition, she considered that they should be punished severely for their actions, by her own subsequent assessment, to ease her emotional response to the event. Dave also saw the acts as evil but did not consider that they should necessarily be punished – not in the way Breda expressed anyhow. He did consider that there would be a need to protect others from a repeat of such acts. In addition, he saw Breda's planned use of her power - Breda was a public representative - to have the laws designed to protect defendants from wrongful conviction watered down, of questionable ethical integrity. However, he was not setting out to teach her a lesson – at least not in the way she might want to teach certain 'low life' a lesson.

Dave saw his role as helping Breda get clarity as to who she is and what she should be doing with her life – such was the contract. By remaining non-judgmental of Breda, he had a better chance of fulfilling the contract. His own emotional ownership and self-worth, all be they works in progress, also assisted – quite considerably. In time, Breda began to loosen her thinking and perceptions and to develop a measure of empathy for those growing up in disadvantaged communities. By her own words she did find more of who she really was – and that was not a reactionary 'lock-m-up' extremist. Her commitment to public service remained but showed signs of moving towards a more compassionate and wise version of the same woman – more in the direction of the pinnacle of her humanity. Dave wondered would she outgrow her political community – or could she take them with her.

The essential points here again are around increasing self-awareness and allowing a natural process to unfold. I have had more than enough experience of this natural process occurring to be totally confident that ethical living through raised awareness and humility is immeasurably more productive and meaningful than a rigid adherence to a simplistic list of ethical rules. However, in the absence of that awareness and maturity, a simplistic and proscriptive 'ten commandments' might be an excellent precaution. Adding on an eleventh along the lines of 'thou shalt not use this code to justify a rigid mindset' might be a growthful add-on!

## 6. What About Ethics and Self-defense?

In the Breda and Dave case above, I presented an example of one type of ethical issue. Breda eventually came to the conclusion that she was capable of gross ethical violations in order to get her way in the political system in which she had some influence. However, Dave had little control over her behavior and, though he regularly thought about the type of society his kids might end up growing into, Breda's actions were several steps removed from his life.

However, what if Breda had a habit of not turning up for sessions and doing so without any warning? Dave used to consider this behavior as unethical. He quickly learned to adjust his contract terms so that, even if he was sitting on his own at an arranged appointment, his clients would still be liable for fees.

But what if Breda owed Dave $1,000, terminated the relationship and decided to ignore the debt? What if she did so knowing that Dave would be unlikely to invest more resources in legal proceedings – and that he knew that she was well connected in legal circles? In this case, Dave is left with a decision about how to respond. Whilst he might be sure that his client's actions were unethical, he is challenged to respond to this in a way that is congruent with his own ethics. Sometimes that involves 'taking the hit', sometimes it involves taking action. Every situation will be different. However, approaching any ethical challenge from an understanding of personal growth will provide growth opportunities – tough and all as they might be. I believe that, in essence, self-defense is not contrary to ethical living. *How* we defend ourselves might be unethical however.

## 7. Who Are The Stakeholders in Ethics Issues?

In my experience, people's understanding of ethics issues tend to range from the simple to the complex. A simple understanding might be that you obey the law of the land. A complex one might be that you obey the law of the land unless it would be unethical to do so! A simple one might be that I break the law to support a higher cause - the survival of my company. A complex one might be I adhere to a particular law, even though I passionately disagree with it but, by doing so, I may show up its inherent injustice for the benefit of society. A simple one might be that you never have sex outside of marriage. A complex one might be that there is nothing unethical about having sex outside of marriage in certain circumstances and, in fact, it is unethical to have sex within marriage under certain circumstances. A simple one might be its never unethical to have sex outside of marriage once it is between consenting adults. A complex one might be that, even if they are consenting adults, people engaging in sex outside of a certain type of marriage contract are acting unethically and, even if people are married, not telling their partner the truth about why they do not want sex with their partner is unethical. A simple one is that stealing is wrong and should be punished. A complex one is that stealing is wrong but often people steal because they are in an untenable position created through the unchallenged unethical actions of others with more power and assets than the thief.

In general, I find that the most common difference between simple and complex valid understandings of ethical issues is that they embrace different sets of stake-holders. A simple valid understanding of an ethical issue is correct within limits. A complex valid understanding of ethics tends to broaden out the limits. At the higher end of ethical intelligence is an acceptance that my understanding of an ethical issue is based on my subjective perception of it. This subjective perception might be different tomorrow and, therefore, I may need to respond differently to it. Effectively, a refined approach to ethics dictates that it is unethical to act as if my perception of an issue is objective.

*Bruce feels strongly about violent crime. He wants the death penalty brought back. He is appalled at the horror victims of crime have been subjected to. He believes that building more prisons and generous use of the electric chair would 'make society a better place'. Bruce sees the failure to build enough prisons as a failure of the system.*

*Deirdre feels strongly about violent crime. She feels that many kids and parents are neglected by a greedy and money obsessed society. She believes that more humility and compassion on the part of the 'system' would be 'make society a better place'. Deirdre sees the need to build more prisons as a failure of the system.*

In the case of Bruce and Deirdre, they are both looking at the issue of violent crime from an ethical – or 'moral', or 'justice', perspective but have come to different conclusions. The difference is that Deirdre is seeing more unethical behavior around her and sees the connection between the 'innocent' or 'justified' lying of politicians, for example, and the psychological distress many young people in the society are trying to relieve through drug and alcohol use. Bruce cannot see the complex tapestry of systems that affect all stakeholders. He can only see the crime and the criminal. Whilst in his mind, he is being ethical by protecting people from murderers, in Deirdre's mind people also need protection from Bruce's immaturity. How that can be achieved is another matter and, again, is an ongoing ethical challenge for Deirdre – how do you deal with unethical behavior in others without behaving unethically?

*Another example...*

*Alice is a coach. Mike is her client. Alice's contract with Mike states that all information shared by Mike is confidential. Mike trusts that commitment from Alice. His contract also states that she is an accredited member of a professional coaching organization.*

*Alice is a friend of Rachel. One day, Alice and Rachel had arranged to meet for a coffee and Rachel was a little early. As she approached Alice's practice rooms she recognized a car parked in the small parking area. It was one of her employer's company cars and she knew to whom it was allocated. As Rachel sat in Alice's waiting room, she heard the door of Alice's room open into the adjoining corridor and a male voice saying*

# Aiming for the Pinnacle

'Thanks Alice – see you in two weeks.' She then heard the outside door, at the end of the corridor, open and close with a 'ding'.

Rachel and Alice sat for a chat over coffee, the two friends catching up on everything from their challenging teenage kids at home to the latest episode of 'Lost'. Rachel suddenly changed the subject...
'I saw Mike Valentine's car outside and I heard his voice as he was leaving. He is one of our sales team you know.'
Alice stayed quite as she thought about coach confidentiality and things ethical - not to mention the soundproofing of her practice room!
'You know..' continued Rachel..' and I know you can't talk about clients Alice but...we're thinking of offering him a promotion.'
Alice remained silent... with the best poker face she could conjure up for a long time buddy.
But you know, for his sake, we don't want to offer it to him if he doesn't want it. If he doesn't want it, he might take it out of fear of seeming uncommitted, or he might decline it and feel like he was burning a bridge.'
Alice stayed poker face but was beginning to find it a little challenging. Mike had mentioned to her that he suspected that he might be in the frame for promotion but, for him, the timing was just not right – he hoped they would not offer him the promotion.

Alice spoke eventually...
'You're right...' she said.
'You mean he doesn't want the job?' replied Rachel, wide eyed.
'No – I can't talk about my clients!'
They both chuckled.
'Please don't tell him what I said Alice...' continued Rachel... 'this is really confidential HR stuff...but... if we knew whether he wanted it or not, it would be very useful to him - himself.'

Alice said she could not talk about it but wanted to reflect on the ethics of it. She was due to meet up with her peer group in a couple of days and intended to bring it up. She also intended to bounce it off Sean, who she used regularly as a kind of 'on demand' consultant on things ethical.

After extensive discussions with her peer group, and with Sean, looking at the angles and possible alternative solutions, the general feeling was that it seemed, on balance, to be in Mike's interests to tell Rachel that he did not want the promotion at this time. Alice met up with Rachel a *second time and discreetly conveyed to Rachel that Mike would prefer not to get the promotion.*

*A few days later, Alice met Mike as planned. Mike walked in with the body language of someone who had gotten some good news. Right enough, he had just had a meeting with his manager who explained sensitively that they were not promoting Mike on this occasion and went to great pains to affirm Mike's ongoing performance. Alice breathed a sigh of relief – it was the right decision she thought. She also thought that this fell into the category of refined ethical intelligence – going outside the rules a little to deal with the subtleties of the matter.*

Was Alice's decision 'the right decision' – ethically? Let's try giving it a stress test by looking at it in terms of dependences.

Alice was dependent on Mike, and her other clients, in order to sustain her current material standard of living.

Mike was dependent on Alice for the delivery of her service for the money he paid. Any unhealthy dependences, parasitic dependences? Not on the face of it I suggest. So far so good.

Mike is dependent on Alice to protect him from the negative consequences of any leak of confidentiality. There might be some people out there, if they had access to what he shared with Alice, that might ruin, in an unethical way, his career prospects or even his livelihood, leaving, amongst other things, his chronically ill daughter without her vital healthcare. However, in this case, rightly or wrongly, Alice concluded that this piece of information would do the opposite – would enhance his career plans and his ability to provide for his family – so it would be okay to 'leak' it. Let's give Alice the benefit of the doubt and suggest that her analysis of Mike's career situation is more or less accurate. Let's suggest that, with a ring fence around Alice's and Mike's relationship that neither would ever see that Alice's actions were in any way unethical and, in fact, Mike would be eternally grateful if he knew that Alice had made a contribution to the decision despite their overt contract.

However...

# Aiming for the Pinnacle

*Alice is dependent on the fact that all her clients, and future clients, will be making decisions based on her association with the coaching organization of which she is an accredited member. Betty, a coach who lives two hundred miles West of Alice's town, is also dependent on her association with the organization and strives everyday to keep her part of that pristine. This in turn helps Alice's credibility. As a result of Alice's decision, word had gotten out that she, as a coach, 'can be trusted to do the practical thing'. This rumor is spreading on numerous golf courses and HR manager informal network meetings. Gradually, Alice begins to get more calls from companies seeking her services to coach their staff. Meanwhile, Betty notices a gradual change in the way companies are interviewing her within the tendering process. There seems to be an unsaid expectation of her but she can't quite 'grab' it. It's getting harder to compete for new business – attitudes within the corporate community seen to be changing – subtly.*

*George works for a company two hundred miles south of Alice's town. His employer has bought in the services of an outside coaching company who stress confidentiality as part of the service. The company is thinking of promoting George. Jack, the company's HR manager, brought it up with Penny, George's coach. Penny has stated that she is not in a position to offer any information. Jack has heard stories of coach's 'co-operating' with companies on such things and concludes that she is 'covering herself'. He decides that he can therefore read between the lines. He concludes that George doesn't want the job. George gets the news and is thrown into a tornado of confusion. 'It just doesn't make sense!' He keeps saying to himself. 'I thought I understood how this supposedly transparent promotion system worked...aaaaaagh!'*

When we take off the ring-fence, and factor in a few more inter-dependencies, we see that the criteria we use in the smaller arena, 'everyone is happy with the outcome', may not apply now that there are others involved. These other stake-holders will have been operating on a reasonable interpretation of the ethics code. They will have been working hard to sustain the integrity of the code and they are not happy. Not only that, they do not have enough information to disregard their reasonable assumptions and have no option but to accept the changes that are happening, working harder until such time as the bubble bursts and everyone gets to see what was going on. In the meantime, someone somewhere is benefiting from the situation at the expense of the healthy efforts of others. Some are benefiting parasitically from the conscientious efforts of others – the result of immature ethical intelligence.

The key issue here is that there are more stake-holders that one might be initially inclined to include. Just because some people are happy with the outcome does not make it ethical. In fact, even if everyone is happy with the outcome, it does not necessarily mean the decision is ethical. There is always a bigger picture – ethical reasoning demands humility.

One last thing. Once Alice broke confidentiality she most likely compromised her relationship with Mike – even if only she, only he, or neither of them realized it.

## Is it Really an Ethical Issue?

Over the years, I have often noticed that trainee coaches or recently trained coaches present an issue to their trainer or support coach (sometimes referred to as 'supervisor') under the heading of ethics. However, after some unpacking of the situation, it does not reveal an ethical issue. Instead, it turns out to be more a confidence issue for the coach.

*'I was going to say......., but I was worried that it might be unethical,'* a coach might reveal.

After some analysis, they cannot find any way in which the client, or any other party, might be wronged, either contractually or morally. It often turns out that the new coach is afraid to challenge their client into a discomfort zone and is justifying their reticence by reference to an ethics conflict. In time, they get to see that their dominant need is to stay in their own emotional comfort zone and that a possible ethics issue offers cover. The novice coach is, in my opinion, showing a comforting commitment to ethical practice and the fact that they bring up the issue at all may auger well for their development.

## Ethics – A Big Issue.

The development of ethical intelligence and the application of ethics to life and to professional practice, whether in private practice or in-

## Aiming for the Pinnacle

company, is a 'big' subject. In this chapter, I have made only a brief reference to it. Its importance and complexity warrant a book of its own and I would recommend that any one interested in personal growth coaching makes it their business to marinate themselves in matters ethical on an ongoing basis. It is the stuff of growth and, I believe, a mandatory module in the apprenticeship of our humanity.

**Chapter Bullets:**

- We see ethics through our needs.
- Ethics are ethics by any other name.
- Personal growth takes us to more ethical living.
- Growth requires an examination of our dependences.
- Ethical understanding provides the lens for that examination.
- We have friendly and not-so-friendly dependences.
- Ethical living is non-parasitic.
- Symbiosis is healthy inter-dependence.
- It is of value to examine one's motives for examining ethics.
- Our interpretation of ethics is colored by our own unmet needs.
- The Ancient Greeks discussed ethics – and had slaves.
- Self-worth demands a more refined understanding of ethics.
- Personal growth offers everyone value.
- A commitment to ethics offers signposts to the pinnacle.
- Commitment to ethics is one thing.
- Application to ethics is another.
- Real ethical re-alignment is often emotionally challenging.
- We can transcend our culturally convenient version of ethics.
- Ethics code schedules can come across as noble – even inspiring.
- Derek is a nice guy.

- Derek's needs dominated his perspective of himself.
- His internal need to grow was beginning to niggle him.
- That wasn't 'nice'.
- Derek's ethical audit provided 'growth on a plate'.
- Derek had his creature comforts.
- He also had an ethical overdraft.
- Identifying his selective perception assisted his growth.
- There is growth potential in how we respond to others' ethics.
- Remember DOVE.
- Breda was seething.
- Dave's intuition told him to 'await further instructions.'
- Dave saw his role as helping Breda get clarity about who she was.
- He did not see himself as her ethical policeman.
- Valid ethical understanding can be simple or complex.
- There are stakeholders in ethical issues.
- Alice told Rachel about Mike.
- Betty, George, Penny and others never knew but were effected.
- Is an ethical issue really an ethical issue or something else?
- Ethics is a 'big' issue.

# Chapter 9
# Organizations & Leadership.
*Managers, Visionaries and Prophets.*

A typical dictionary entry for the word 'organization' might suggest 'a group of individuals who work together in a structured way for a common purpose.' An early type of organization might have been a hunting team. A group of men, for example, with weapons, working together in a structured way to find and kill or capture animals for food. Another example, from early stages of human evolution, might be a group of women gathering and preparing food for consumption by all those within their village.

We take for granted the notion that groups of people, organized together, can achieve things that one individual, on their own, cannot achieve, or would take so much time to achieve that it would not be worth their while.

Every time I drive near an airport and a wide-bodied passenger jet-plane floats above me on landing, I marvel at the airborne products of organized human ingenuity. I imagine with awe that the pilot has control over this machine as she trusts this tangible expression of engineering to keep herself and her passengers safe. No matter how many times I behold this sight, it seems surreal to me that these massive lumps of metal can glide majestically fifty yards above me as if connected by strings stretched from above the clouds and held by the hand of some invisible cosmic schoolboy with an interest in highly detailed model aircraft.

The aircraft magically floats to a touch-down on the organized tarmac. It then taxies to the organized terminal for an organized egress in the hands of organized ground staff. Meanwhile, I continue on my drive past the airport and catch the news headlines – which of course, are being broadcast by a group of organized media people. The headlines tell me that a group of people had organized themselves and invaded such and such a country. Almost in surprise to the invading organization, individual 'insurgents' had organized themselves and had started shooting at the invading army. A third group is now organizing themselves to go in to assist the wounded using a motif of a red religious symbol to differentiate themselves from other organizations.

Each of the various organizations has an internally shared purpose: to build a plane, to lay a runway, to write the news script, to invade the country, to repel the invaders, to heal the wounded. Or do they? And even if they do, are there any unshared purposes? If there are unshared purposes, which of these are obvious and to whom? Finally, is the stated or manifest purpose really shared? Or is it just believed by a proportion of the group to be shared by the group with or without available evidence to the contrary?

When humans organize, they can work towards soaringly noble goals and produce immeasurably useful results. All the participants may or may not be inspired by the achievements or nurtured by the success. Some or all may even be dead before the fruits are obvious.

When humans organize they can achieve diabolically destructive outcomes and mind-bogglingly profound abuses of people and resources within and outside of their organization. Such people and resources can include those that belong to future generations. Few, or even none, of the members of the organization need have any idea that this is happening or, if they do, that, seen objectively, using their own terms of reference, they themselves fall into the broad category known as 'the baddies'.

I suggest that an effective coach and, indeed an effective human being, needs to understand the difference between a functional organization and a dysfunctional organization and how each type of organization works, evolves and responds to events in its path. An in-depth and robust understanding of organizations offers us opportunities to collaborate with others towards noble goals and avoid colluding with abusive mindsets – mindsets of varying degrees of transparency – depending on the blinkers of the observer.

I am not suggesting that a coach needs to be an expert organizational psychologist, as perhaps a consultant might be. However, within the context of a personal growth commitment, a coach turning the stones of organizational life, and seeing what lies under, can take themselves through further chapters of their own growth – complete with revelations of their own naïveté and hidden fears and needs. They will question their own relationship with the organizations of which they are a member – including professional bodies who 'talk the talk.'

When a few human beings get together, they pool their belief systems, their needs and their levels of awareness. In some group situations, the result of such pooling will be a raised awareness as the collective insights are pieced together with humility and examined with care and patience by all. In other group situations, there will be a rush of relief as the hatches are battened down, the fortress sealed and the collective potential of the individuals drowned in the seductive rhetoric of 'vision' and the hyperbole of a commodity called 'leadership'. Primal needs prevail and the fate of the group is clan-destined. Their destiny is shackled by their clannish outlook – or lookouts.

No one chooses to join a cult. Some discover they are in one. Others remain the slave of cultish thinking to their grave. Perhaps all of us fall into the category of cult member. Perhaps in five hundred years, the western lifestyle will be examined by insightful historians as the product of yet another historical cult. The twentieth century will be seen as the cult of nationalism with all the bloodshed that goes with it. The twenty first century might be referred to as the era when humanity aspired to higher levels of shopping as devout members filed in a line up the aisle of the mall, with their trolley load of offerings, to surrender themselves to the alter of customer services and avail of the bread and wine of a new age – plastic cards and cappuccinos.

Meanwhile, there will be those irritating deviants who insist on having more. Not happy with economic success, fulfillment, political emancipation, freedom to choose, endless labor-saving devices and fashion accessories, these awkwards want more. From the height of their sun-blessed south-facing decks, as they survey the landscape of spaghetti junctions, financial services office-blocks and construction cranes stretched out beyond the horizon, they will insist on wanting more – they want meaning, the ultimate luxury. Alas, it seems I am one such case. Even without the sun-blessed deck from which to survey the industrious activity of 'progress' I, for one, am lumbered with this particular brand of greediness. I want to see more meaning in that landscape. I want to see stuff that matters. With all our organizational success, will the next generation be handed something of value?

The cumulative effect of individual behavior is the culture prevailing at a given time. Each one of us processes transactions every day that contribute to the consensus reality. Those with access to power, media power, communication power, political power, economic power, military power, sexual power, make a greater contribution, for better or for worse, than those without such access. That contribution will carry with it the footprint of our maturity, or lack of.

Will our footprints be carefully placed amongst the weeds, nettles, flowers, newly sprouting oak saplings and fragile beginnings of fruit bearing new growth? Or will our footprints be the random stompings of hob-nailed boots – perfect to protect us from the world but doing little to protect the world from us? Will our footprint leave a legacy that invites the next generation to do proud the best of humanity? Or will it leave a legacy that burdens our children with the 'sins' of the parents and a society so much to the left of the NICE curve that the very survival of the planet is in question, let alone the luxury of human survival needs, the indulgence of self-esteem or the outright extravagance of self-worth and mutual respect?

## Who Are The Leaders?

Every follower is a leader. As I choose to follow something, or someone, there is someone else watching me and deciding if they will do likewise. In following, I am leading. As I drive along the freeway and count the number of cars passing me at considerably more than the speed limit, knowing that the law enforcement in my state will be unlikely to catch them, I realize that I am challenged to drive slowly and hope that this will lead others to do similarly. This is even though, at the next junction, I will be at the back of the line with all the other leaders of safe driving and behind the queue of lawbreakers who 'need' to put other's lives at risk to save themselves some time. They will get home earlier then I will, to spend a fleeting session of 'quality time' with their loved ones. These ostensible loved ones will tomorrow venture out into the world – making themselves available to the ever-growing list of tragic road death statistics.

The concept of leadership has become a commodity – usually measured by either the number of people following the leader or the financial gain the leader presents to the shareholders in return for his or her thirty pieces of stock-options. We sing the praises of a great 'leader' as he taps into our unresolved needs for protection from pain and loss and seduces us with promises of more 'stuff' and a vision for vision's sake. And yet we are the ones doing the leading. The politician acting on the results of a focus group is the ultimate follower. The public representative that does what he believes the people want him to do is not the leader - even if the media insist on feeding the insatiable elephant in the room and admiring the emperor's oversized new clothes with un-examined language and lazy thinking – all to meet deadlines – dead lines indeed.

I believe that what we often call leaders are not leaders at all – they are managers. What we often call visionaries are often just very good fiction writers who have found a formula for a stirring speech that taps into as yet unexpressed emotions for long enough to get a vote and more funding for focus groups and opinion polls. Tony Benn, the retired British politician suggests that we can be one of two types of people. We can be a weather-vane or a signpost. A weather-vane will turn with the wind. A signpost will resist the elements and remember something in a variety of circumstances. It will not change reality just because the clan changed its mind when offered 20% off.

## The Unfolding Future....

A personal growth coach sits with a client, listens and engages. In that moment, that coach makes another few footprints. His steps will be informed by his needs, his passions and his awareness. No amount of fancy tools, personality profile systems, acronyms or even competencies will influence the shape and configuration of those footprints more then the coaches awareness, his awareness of who he is and where he is pointed, his 'values-in-action' rather than his 'values-espoused'.

In developing his, or her, awareness, a coach needs to peel off the layers of illusion to which the human race has been prone since time immemorial and the shapes of which are re-invented with every generation. The coach does not need to be a manager – except to manage her practice, which, to a large degree, can be subcontracted. She does not have to be a visionary – enough of her clients will have their ladders up against the wrong wall from allowing themselves to be moved by others' visions.

A coach will, however, need to be solidly confident in the process of growth and where it will take us. They need to have a personal understanding of their own growth, accumulated through experience, and at least a glimpse of what can be.

In short, a personal growth coach needs to find the prophet in herself and allow it to guide her through the brambles and thickets of the human condition. In doing so, she will carve a path to her unique destiny, to the pinnacle of her humanity, and shake hands with those who made it up the other faces of the mountain. Then they can set to work.

**Chapter bullets:**

- To thine own self be true.

www.ingramcontent.com/pod-product-compliance
Lightning Source LLC
Chambersburg PA
CBHW030339240426
43661CB00052B/1686